BAGHDAD MU[...]

In the twentieth century, a Je[...]
MESOPOT[...]

Ivy Rabee

In Tune Publications

First published in Great Britain by
In Tune Publications Ltd
England
2008

ISBN 978-0-9561020-0-3

Ivy Rabee(Vernon) has asserted her right under the Copyright, Design and Patents Act, 1988 to be identified as the author of this work.
Website::www.baghdadmemories.co,uk
Printed in Great Britain by Newsstand, RMS LLP.

I cherished you from the moment that I met you,
And you still remain dear to me,
Even more so now that I have left you

From 'Baghdad' a poem by 'Nazar Qabbani'

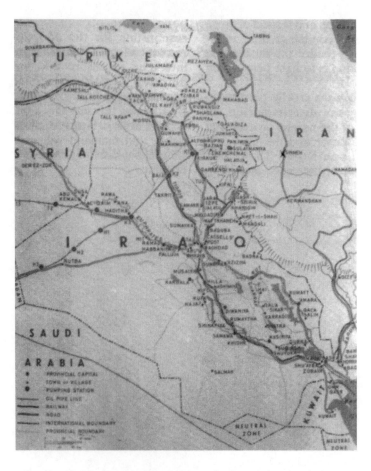

Iraq, neighbours, towns, cities, desert, lakes and rivers

Preface to the second edition

It is a fact that no work of literature is perfect, and it might be that the book's first edition contained errors too. I have sought to rectify this in the second edition with the help of constructive criticism from various friends, re writing episodes in the process! I hope sincerely these efforts will translate into yet more enjoyment of my tale.

A BRIDGE TO A DISTANT PAST

Ever since I left Baghdad, I have tried to cold shoulder its Arabic inheritance; what other option had I but to let it recede into past tense? No one can navigate cosily between two totally opposing regimes like East and West: in every way they are those distant globes! A more vibrant tempo exists in the West, and a different reality challenges its inhabitants nearly every day! Be it the economy, the job market, newspaper scandals, political issues, technology advances, new rules and regulations – they all have to be taken on board.

The natives, lucky for them, have learned intuitively to accept them, but the poor immigrant still requires a lifetime of trial and error! A lifetime of letting go of the old values and embracing the foreign ones! Another lifetime to be convinced that the strange ones are the right ones! These lifetimes represent the wilderness years.

During the wilderness years, I used to envy pensioners who did not have to take on life's new realities nor needed to find a job, likewise people who knew that they would be going to their old home after the wars ... Not being in either of these categories, there was no alternative but to adapt and seek adoption. Till the day that I became convinced that the wilderness was my real home...

Which proved to be wishful thinking the moment that the reality of Saddam's fall followed us right here into the West. What a shock that was! The year was 2003 and the most dramatic moment came when his very concrete statue was toppled by a booing crowd of men. After a lot of kicking to dislodge it, they had to call on an enterprising man with a crane, and when the strong black figure fell they kicked it a lot more! For anyone under the force of his regime, past and present, it was an anticlimax of revenge.

As images of a very modern Baghdad flickered on the screen by courtesy of the hundreds of reporters who descended upon it, I held my breath! The city had expanded and become different but was beautiful nonetheless. Much renovated, it has rejoined the 21st Century while my back was turned, acquiring state of the art buildings and at least a dozen more bridges. Even some of the people in the West who sadly and eternally thought of the country as a backwater in the middle of nowhere were expressing their admiration for its attractive landmarks.

Stateless with no country to boast of till then, I found myself changing positions, becoming as a virtual tour guide, pinpointing scenery to friends and relatives on the television screen. For quite a few years to come, Baghdad continued to join us in nearly every news bulletin, while its people and their lifestyles, its markets and their produce were brought alive by the most advanced of digital cameras.

Not only that but a proliferation of satellite channels ensured that we were getting news and views directly from the mouths of such as "*Abu el Jassem el Wared*" or even "*Jabbar Abu el Sharbat*" the drinks seller", via many free agents like Al Baghdadiya, Al Irakiya, Al Fayha, Al Jazeera, to quote but a few. Sanctions did not exist anymore and there was a surplus of new ideas –these communicated most welcome news. The Iraqis have at long last gained their democracy and free thinking. They were already voting for a constitution and even better they were asking the exiles to vote. Inconceivable! So some of my friends went to a polling station tongue in cheek. Maybe a miracle had happened, and we could come forward and admit to a long lost kinship?

What can I say? After the good news came the not so good news, of people blowig themselves, of killings in the markets, of maiming of patients in hospitals - while at funerals even the dead in their coffins were being targeted with rockets! Hot on the heels of these tragedies, a rapid deterioration in security and public amenities, even a lack of food! How can that be, we asked unconvinced. Baghdad has always been a city overflowing with riches and plenty, surrounded by two generous rivers to provide for its every need- industrial, agricultural and environmental. The Iraqis are well endowed in terms of petrol and natural resources; they were sincerely trying to restore their country's fortunes after a long period of suffering. How has it come to this, the killings and the desolation? I could not equate the easy going Iraq that I grew up in with the scenes of despair on television. It must be that if I share my memoirs, people will realise how very different it all used to be, how the earth has moved many many times since then....

The lost identity

PROLOGUE

It seems to me that at certain points of this autobiography, I take on the mantra of Daphne Du Maurier's heroine 'Rebecca', especially at the end when the heroine went back in a dream and confronted the evil destruction of the palace and the gilded life. I too have been striving to do the same thing! It is left for that rarer breed of brave woman to cross those tracks in a more physical sense. As for me, I will never go back to the country of my birth: too fearful of the changes that have taken place, too vulnerable at my age but to be treated with tender loving care. It is best to cling to my stable existence and eye the past through rose tinted glasses: that is when the happier times will crystallise, and I can concentrate on them to tell my fascinating story on how fate made the Jewish people descend into Mesopotamia the land of the two rivers - dwelling there as natives for thousands of years. While this not so brave new world is obliterating and eroding their memory without grace, I owe it to everyone, my parents, grandparents as well as their parents before them to track their footsteps and sing their praise. Bitterness and lament true, they are there still, along with utter bewilderment, but they will not disminish from a worthy tale.

Once upon a time this same Jewish community settled in Iraq; and since then, our Fathers and their Fathers both cleaved their being to it as befits their only home. For 2500 years they shared the good times as well as the bad times with the rest of the natives - in the meantime managing to contribute phenomenally to the country's well being and progress. A very workable partnership with their fellow Arabs developed whereas everyone pulled the boat deftly forwards merging their different perspectives in thinking of the country as a whole.

It was of course the Big Powers' politics and the way they governed and divided the region that succeeded in souring this relationship, and gave us an enemy status entirely against our wish. My generation tried to maintain it, not admitting to a connection with that common enemy in the Middle East, Israel. It was not a familiar body; on the contrary Israel was always portrayed in Iraq's media as that totally criminal, immoral nation. During our growing years, it was only ever mentioned as a capitalistic hideaway, its politicians as one eyed gangsters carrying the omnipresent gun. They were always referred to as *al issabbat el sehyoniya*, (the Zionist gangsters). As Moshe Dayan had a patch so all its people had a patch; as Golda Meir and David ben Gurion were old and wrinkly, the caricaturists had a hayday with depicting everyone in that land as ugly and decrepit too.

What's more it was impossible to go beneath the surface to understand where the real issues lay as that country was only ever mentioned in expletive terms and heated tones. In addition, the term Zionist became associated with swearing nuances and even worse profanities. This led to an irrational fear of a *faux pas* on my part so I never dared to ask a question about Israel or even pronounce its name; consequently my ignorance was never assuaged. I couldn't imagine how Israel looked like, but came to conclude that its people fought in the streets as a permanent occupation. I think my parents felt apprehensive about mentioning the subject in case our knowledge might get us into trouble with the authorities. However, something definitely smelled fishy here: while there did not exist any borders between Iraq and Israel and no contact between Israel and all the Arab countries, the Iraqis still blamed everything foul that happened in Iraq and the Arab world on a Zionist conspiracy; whether it was connected to a failed revolution, an economic deal that did not materialise or infighting amongst the Arabs themselves and their leaders. That exonerated everyone automatically and we all went back to leading our life again as normal.

I expect these days people can find out the true facts with the advent of the Internet. In our days, the local radio and television were the usual sources and they were both government run. To know what went on behind the scenes, the only way was to rely on rumours from someone who knew someone with a relative in the government.

Never mind all the above rhetoric, my generation identified with our nationality and were integrated sufficiently to believe that the way forward was in helping to build a more prosperous Iraq. This was why the realisation only dawned very tentatively through a slow and painful process after the 1967 war: that our place was elsewhere, that the die was cast. We became an object of hate while keeping to the same spot; the very same people who were looked up to and respected were relocated to the bottom of the pile. The cause was murky enough, but we suspected again that big poker game between the powers which we had never had the wherewithal to confront or to solve.

Ever more gradually, we came to embrace the writing on the wall that said "you do not belong here anymore, it is time to leave, leave with your lives, all the rest is denied".

I suppose that is why some of those memories are fond memories; they conjure up other times and climes when there was an *entente cordiale* between the citizens no matter their various sectors, and life flowed seamlessly to the delight of all.

In this context I must clarify my frequent use of the pronoun we, instead of the regal 'I' as in most other autobiographical texts. The explanation lies in the physical closeness of the community who lived and worked within the same neighbourhood, and also their close blood ties because of constant intermarriage over thousands of years. The grandparents all had Ottoman passports with shoddy birthday dates: rumour had it that it was either due to fear of conscription or burnt records, or maybe one led to the other. All lost most of their relatives through a hiccup in 1950 called the *"Tassqueet"* (mass emigration). More similarities existed between us, for example everyone was glued together during the summer heat with no trips abroad, ending up in the same swimming pools when our school broke off. Truly we lived, acted and thought in an identical manner, so that a bird's eye view revealed a line of pomegranate seeds squeezed together in a vacuum, tight.

As the children went to the same primary and secondary schools, so the Mothers met to gossip in the mornings and compare notes on the homework they had helped with the night before; later on they returned home and competed to have the neatest house in the neighbourhood, as well as cooking in the best Iraqi way. As per tradition, the husbands worried less about work and more about their daughters' dowries. Then in the summer we all met again either walking on the Tigris Corniche at night to take in the air or on the Tigris shores in the morning for galvanising swimming action.

Come the autumn and there were more greetings in the street on our way to the Synagogue. There in addition to praying, we took the opportunity to continue gossiping about the very same people who were now sitting next to us.

Everyone drew on the services of the same Jewish butcher and his stout Moslem mate for the supply of meat and chicken, as well as the one Mohel who became very adept at sweetening the painful ceremony with a few drops of wine.

Likewise the white haired matchmaker who tried to accommodate all from the limited stock as above.

Of course if anything went wrong everyone instinctively joined ranks to criticise the one and only perennial Rabbi. When this did not help and the blows kept coming, we sought to escape to the greener hills of the beyond.

This autobiography was begun to track happy childhood recollections in Baghdad which I feared might be lost forever. A hitch developed when I realised that, while busily growing up, I had ignored the background to these events both politically and historically. It was not easy to admit that I sailed through my life there without asking pertinent questions about the hows and the whys. While successive governments destroyed their enemy's ideologies, there remained no books or textbooks to read about the particular epoch that we were living in or the ones that we inherited: an indescribable state of constant flux. Nobody alluded to what went on before I was born and opined how that history shaped the present history and the future too. No one spoke of the insignificance of my generation compared to the vitality of the one which had left the country, and that we were a mere remainder of a much more glorious past. Catching up on all this, I broadened the scope and thrust of this book by researching zealously. My conclusion is that it is good to know, the proviso being that after such a long time, some memories might have dimmed and some may have acquired even better hues. One truism to contend with in Iraq is that most facts could never be set in stone, but depended very much on the sort of contacts and inroads to authority that your "milieu" had. If you come upon any such variances dear reader, please forgive.

The Gardens of Babylon of yore

DEDICATION

To a future generation who may look back on colossal happenings. This book will help them to undertstand.

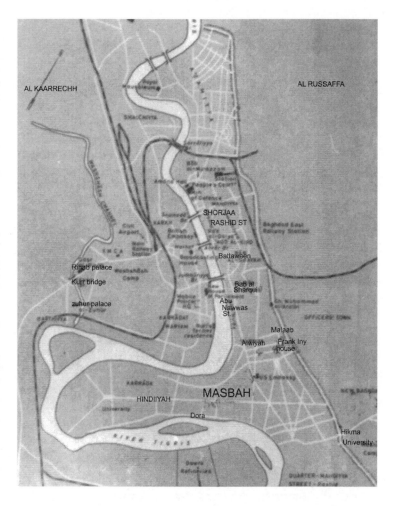

Baghdad bisected by the River Tigris into the Russafa and the
Karkh

GOING BACK TO BIBLE STORIES

This tale is intertwined with the story of a community with very deep roots in the land, roots that go back to the beginning of the world as we know it. Religion and legend have it that our Patriarch Abraham was born in Ur just south of Babylon and Baghdad. He was advised by God to leave it in 1800 BC to seek Monotheism, which I am sure we all agree is a much better way of worship.

He instructed Abraham to go to Canaan (Israel). Even though Abraham made himself a new life among other people and countries, he still ordered his son Isaac to go back to Iraq and marry a girl from there. Thus Rebecca is from Mesopotamia and later Rachel, Jacob's wife, hailed from the old country as well. In fact, eleven out of Jacob's twelve sons were born there.

And then history did an about turn, and the Jews came back to Iraq by force of their conquerors the Babylonians. They were led by Nebuchadnezzar in his two ambushes on Jerusalem in 598 and then again in 587 BC. He plundered the Holy City and destroyed the First Temple taking 18,000 men in the first invasion, skilled craftsmen all. He used them to build Babylonia into a beautiful city to vie with Assyria, Hamurabee's city. In his second invasion, he razed Jerusalem further to the ground, taking 100,000 able bodied Jewish men to dredge the silting irrigation canals of Babylonia.

Thus the song made famous much later by "Bony M":
"By the rivers of Babylon, yeah we sat down
Hanged our harps and wept, when we remembered Zion"

However, the prophet Jeremiah from Israel, set the aggrieved slaves a dependable common sense charter by which to conduct their lives and thrive in exile: "These are the words of the God of Israel to all the exiles whom I have carried off from Jerusalem to Babylon. Build houses and live in them; plant gardens and eat their produce; marry and beget sons and daughters, and never stop seeking the welfare of the city to which I have carried you off and pray to the Lord for it, for in its peace you will have peace." We did dear Jeremy, we did.

Only fifty years later, the Persian King, Cyrus the Great, recaptured Jerusalem from the Babylonians. In an unprecedented and unique gesture he proved very magnanimous towards the enslaved Jews in his territory because it was unheard of in those days to think of slaves as humans. Not only did he liberate them from that atrocious mantle but kinder still, allowed them to practise their religious beliefs. To top it all, he proffered money from his own coffers to facilitate their resettlement in Israel and the rebuilding of the Temple. An inscription containing these same instructions was found in the ancient city of Ur. That is why the Bible confers on Cyrus the title of Moshiah, the Saviour.

Here comes the rub: most of our ancestors chose not to go back. Only 40,000 returned to Israel – the remaining 80,000 stayed on, to become at one with the populace and prosper and to make their adoptive country prosper too.

That must be because they had re-discovered their connection to the land, right from their roots at the time of Abraham and it proved surprisingly easy to establish an affinity with the locals too. After all they were as cousins with the same blood, running all the way back from Isaac and Ishmael, sons of the distinguished ancestor. View its gentle climate, its luscious produce, they found Mesopotamia a most natural place to settle down in, growing to love the simplicity of its life and that of its people; later on they were allowed to become landowners and in the ripeness of time, achieving a native stature too.

Maybe we can hear the lament transformed into a song:
"By the rivers of Babylon, we decided to stay
"We still cried, but then found the most optimum way".

For a thousand years, there ruled a King of the Jews in exile, the Exilarch, who descended from the House of King David; he set his own laws, organized his own courts and managed the community's affairs autonomously. In 485 BC Queen Esther married King Achashverosh, King of Kings of the Persian Empire. Much later on, the Caliph Al Mansur, established his capital near the Jewish settlement in Iraq, and greatly honoured the Exilarch's authority at his Royal Court.

Babylonia flourished amid the Arab world, it also became the cultural and spiritual centre of world Judaism; thanks to its prophets and its giants in learning, the "Gaonim" who established the avant-garde Jewish academies of Nahardeah, Sura and Pumbedita. They were copied by the West and renamed universities in the twelfth century. The *Talmud* took 300 years to compile by those same academies and its value has proved eternal. At one time Babylonian Jewry numbered a million in the country. Unfortunately successive waves of Mongols and Tartars decimated Iraq and its people and caused the rivers to run with blood; this spelled total regression for all the inhabitants in the land of the two rivers for a very long time.

As befits people with a reputation for financial acumen, the Treasury of Iraq was in Jewish hands for centuries; this important position was called the "*Sarraf Bashi*" of the country. People from Alqosh (an enclave in northernmost Iraq) as well as Mosul still talk of the past and happy presence of the Jews in those towns. A traveller to Basrah at the turn of the last century wrote that Jewish factories were packing dates to export to all corners of the world while the influential merchants shipped horses of impeccable breed to China and India upon the orders of their grand Rajahs.

Before the 19th Century, the only studies that the community sent their boys to were the private *Staths* (one teacher schools for boys) that taught the Torah and the Hebrew language to the very religious communities. Then there were changes in Iraq that led to the establishment of large public educational institutions in Baghdad; Hebrew newspapers brought in from abroad facilitated renewed contact with fellow Jews elsewhere. As a result, two Talmud Torah schools were built in the very late nineteenth century, which gave free meals to the students, and great Rabbis like Yosef Hayyim arrived on the scene. His eminence was such that everyone crowded in the Great Synagogue while he gave three hour sermons. The community opened its first modern school in 1864 (the Laura Kaddourie school for girls) and asked the Alliance Universelle in Paris to send a principal to run it.

So it was that the new curriculum made gigantic paces and vied with the best of European learning. However, a controversy of sorts followed. The leaders of the Jewish community insisted on Arabic as the main language and also on keeping in within the local customs, while the French principals insisted on placing more stress on the "superior" French language and French traditions. There followed differences of opinion and real power struggles. Rich philanthropists then started to bequeath to the community its own schools to be managed by them entirely with teachers flown from Israel, Syria and Europe; generally, the schools started out by being single sex schools but incorporated the girls as well nearer the end of the last century.

Arabic, English and French languages were taught to a very high standard; this enabled the students to land lucrative administrative jobs when the British conquered Iraq during the First World War. For example the Ministry of Finance was given to Sasson Heskel and the Railways had a heavy input of

21

Jewish employees. Another offshoot from the study of languages was the superior ability of the Alliance pupils to conduct their own commercial businesses in import and export with India and Britain. It is worthy of note here that a former Moslem student in those schools,Tawfiq Al Sewaidy, later landed the top job of Prime Minister of the country in the forties, while distinguished Moslems competed to get a place for their children there as the schools' standing soared.

In my grandparents' Kasser, being initiated into handwriting skills by a young aunt, with the Tigris and Russafa as a backdrop - 1950

A "Jewish" culture thrived: as a consequence: four clubs built in a luxurious style became renowned in the twenties and in the forties to provide the focus for social family get togethers: the Laura Kaddourie club, the Zawra Club, the Rafidayn Club and the Rashid Club. As usual the money was donated by various philanthropists among them Sir Elly Kaddourie.

MY PARENTS

I was born in Baghdad in Iraq, a town like a very big village where two rivers come very close to meeting. My grandFather had a Turkish passport because Iraq used to belong to the Ottoman Empire, and he, along with all his family were born there. The story goes that my grandFather was the Mayor of a locality in Baghdad where all birth records were kept; a big fire once flared up which engulfed all the records, and everyone's birthdates disappeared in flames. So it was that in later years, my uncles, my aunts and even my Father, never knew the exact date of their birth! When settled abroad and confronted by red tape as well as the need for identity cards and passports, they resorted to conjuring birthdates out of a hat. To facilitate matters they picked on an easily memorable date: my Father's became Christmas Day; his brother borrowed his wife's. Still another with a bit more flamboyance put down Frank Sinatra's.

The only sighting I ever had of my grandFather was in a dog-eared black and white photograph which my Father kept as if a treasure. It depicted an elderly gentleman in a *tarboush* (Ottoman headgear) with a maroon open necked *dashdasha* (robe) which was the typical dress in Ottoman Iraq before independence. He sat on a chair with one leg akimbo, the other leg on the floor with his knitted gaiwas (slippers) and a walking stick by the side; oh and I must not forget the worry beads in his hands. Come to think of it he looked quite worried with a frown instead of a smile for the camera. This little nondescript picture had a life of its own and popped up in multiple surroundings: tucked at the corner of shaving mirrors, on dining room tables, inside the linen cupboards, even inside other frames the better to see it with! My poor Father juxtaposed it just about everywhere. It would be his sole connection to his family for nigh on twenty years.

My Father was sent to the Midrash to learn Hebrew, which constituted the earlier form of schooling for boys only; then on to the Alliance schools in Baghdad which opened beginning in the second half of the nineteenth century. The community was lucky to have the young generation access a modern quasi western curriculum with some excellent teachers. It was there that my Father acquired the English which served him well in his career as a businessman. In those days, formal typed letters formed the essence of import businesses, and when he discovered he needed to type to establish a company in the days before he could afford a typewriter, he decided to improvise and teach himself. So he resorted to cutting squares of similar shapes to the keys of a typewriter and placing them in a keyboard format, practising daily to remember their position.

This skill came in handy throughout his life as, without recourse to a secretary, he typed all his correspondence himself using two fingers only. He addressed world class companies from a huge rather rickety black manual typewriter which took pride of place on the centre of his desk. His business consisted of importing foodstuffs from England and selling them both to wholesalers and retailers. He did so well in this field that for a time he was the sole importer of Nestle in Iraq. All his life he continued to sign his letters with some very archaic expressions like 'your very humble servant' and 'with my very best respects' as laid down in a book he once studied. But credit is definitely due him as he built a very successful business. He always remained the active partner with an array of Moslem partners, which law demanded.

If ever we visited him in his room in the upstairs floor of the dark yet sprawling *Khan* (warehouse) off Al Benouk Street, he turned it into a treat for us. He opened some cupboards to reveal sweets, some other cupboards to reveal a homemade sandwich or two, crisps, asking his assistant to bring bottles of frozen coke. Another treat was to let us tap on the huge black metal typewriter. The most excitement happened when he had to send a telegram abroad. Then he would have to book it via the Telegraph Office, type it and have an employee race it there to be on time. In those days a telegram was a gigantic manoeuvre, likewise a call outside Baghdad or abroad; a lot of stress and agitation were involved and it cost much more money than a simple e-mail. Any adult visitors were regaled with sweet Turkish coffee on a tray along with a jug of ice cold water brought in from the nearby snack bar. However, when the social hour stretched, then somebody was sure to order kebabs and a salad, and the men would enjoy eating it in company inside the office.

Still, in Iraq no business is easy or risk free so that whenever a revolution or political turmoil struck, my Father suffered a lot financially and started bemoaning life and fate. Either the new government seized all merchandise in the port or all government offices ceased functioning to be granted a holiday. Nobody could work till the politics and military sides were sorted out in line with the refrain from the multitude: *hatal yom chenna nareeda* (this is the day we were waiting for). In both cases, the imported foodstuffs were left to stagnate in the port under a blistering heat and could easily become unfit for consumption.

My Father shared the dubious honour with my Mother of being the eldest among eight siblings. Thus it was when my grandFather died my Father inherited the title of head of the household and that meant acquiring a huge responsibility at the young age of 17. I would remind you that in those lands the girls grew up with nothing less than the expectation of being married at a tender age and my Father had to straddle that task somehow. Indeed he felt as a man condemned, he told us, until he had seen his three sisters married. The kitty emptied when his own Father became ill and the family bought various medicines and consulted a multiplicity of doctors. These dire circumstances were exacerbated in view of the fact that his Mother was only ever qualified to look after the family and that is why they needed every penny my teenage Father could earn. In those days and even now among communities in Iraq there are so many stigmas on how to conduct your life in a seemly manner. It is best to signal from now that everything one did or wanted to do was either clouded by a stigma, a taboo or a crippling fear of gossip. My Father was required to pull off the impossible in finding three husbands for his sisters who were not allowed by society to be on the lookout for future grooms themselves.

This society was quite unforgiving, especially where single girls were concerned, and that made each girl's reputation very transparent. Any transgression against what is seen as the social dictates had the poor girl branded for life, unfit to be connected to a "good" family; the extent of the damage was rained on her siblings and extended family as well, resulting in the whole tribe suffering from social stigmatisation.

One rule was not to allow married women to work as this reflected poorly on the husband's capabilities. Of course things did change in my time, and the single girl's status graduated so she could work in a respectable office: as long as it was crystal clear that it was a mere gapfiller till the day when good luck brought her the groom. On the other hand, if girls were not married off, then that was also a permanent stigma on the name of the family as they were seen to be lacking or too mean to fund a dowry. This contrasted (not so positively) with the Moslems' opoosite tradition of the boy being required to give the dowry to the girl.

My Father, a product of this society, was very conscious that everyone's happy destiny could only be attained through marriage. When we reached Israel after leaving Iraq he grew very worried, not so much about negotiating the unknown future, not yet anyway, but for the fact that his younger brother remained unmarried. Daoud was fifty one years old when my Father met him again after a gap of twenty years. He accosted him right after clearing customs to berate him for not having a partner and warning him of the awful consequences awaiting him in his old age. In vain my uncle pleaded that he was not the marrying kind, that he was indeed a contented bachelor. My Father was adamant that it was a matter of the utmost importance that he marries. He was as good as his word: by dint of researching and further networking among people whose acquired language he did not yet speak, my amazing Father found him a suitable match. Within two weeks the deed was done! She was a girl in her forties with a good job and a born Iraqi to boot. Both in cachet and status she was truly immaculate. It took a while and a lot of protests for my (ever deferential) uncle to get out of this one!

While a bachelor, my Father (Selim or Shalom) was known by the honorary title of Abu Dawood, as in Arab lore. This is based on the Bible's King Solomon being a precursor of King David. It was quite touching to hear my Father go through his day. Up at 5am to be at the model cotton farm by 6am to supervise the *fellahin* (field workers) growing the seeds according to appropriate modern methods. He then headed from there to his office job as a clerk in Lawee's motorcar showroom till 4pm, to proceed after a siesta at home to another job in the evenings. Well, the girls were married off all before they attained the ripe old age of twenty one! What a challenge it must have been to negotiate and acquire three future husbands in a trice. My Father, considered bright by his own Father, who had painstakingly put money aside over the years for him to study as a lawyer in Beirut. It would have been a feather in the family's hat. Alas it was one more thing that was not meant to be. But with a touch of wistfulness at the cruelty of fate, my Father would tell how all the money reserved for his studies evaporated bit by bit without diagnosing the disease or finding a cure for the much esteemed head of the family.

Never mind there did occur some bright spots to lighten the load. One of them was the pride at receiving a visit from King Faisal I who congratulated him on the quality of the cotton he was helping to grow. Another was how with his assistance, another brother entered Baghdad University and qualified as a pharmacist. Then the other brothers started working as well and he could concentrate on building his own future. This involved finding a wife as a matter of paramount importance *Bint al Halal* (a good girl). He was now doing quite well as a partner to an elderly MP and at thirty-two considered by society to be a very eligible catch indeed.

In those days men were always married at an older age to a girl of a younger age, or even a much younger age. The idea was that the man should make himself and his fortune first, with a house and enough means to run a credible ménage almost immediately - no mortgages to be saddled with for the next ten years! The girl was at her optimum in the later teenage years, the reasoning being that she would be young enough to be moulded to grow up obedient to her husband and future in- laws. Of course she had all the time in the world to bear her husband the maximum number of children and remain young enough to look after him in his old age. In pursuit of this, girls were discouraged by their parents from continuing their studies, which might make them too learned and uppity, and therefore jeopardise their chance of being content with the first groom that fortune sent their way.

My parents' marriage was "arranged" via a mutual family friend who put my Mother's name forward as a very beautiful girl, which she was, although my Father the businessman, as ever was his way, had to check the deal before signing on the dotted line. To this end, he went to the Headmaster at the Alliance School and asked to see my Mother's grades. Luckily for us, she was very bright and passed this last test with flying colours.

In the Alliance, my Mother was initiated into four languages although she was always at her best in French, as was my Grandma before her. My Mother being the eldest embraced the opportunity of helping raise her younger siblings. She would take over from her own Mother in looking after their clothes, cooking as well as assisting with homework! My Grandma never had the time! She was too busy procreating for a long time - almost till my Mother herself was married. That is how it happened that I had a very young uncle and an aunt who were respectively just four and five years older than me.

My Mother did earnestly entreat her parents to let her continue her education after sixteen but in her conservative family that was taboo. It seems the doors in her face shut due to the dangers lurking in the higher classes because they contained boys. Mixing the sexes in the classroom was not quite the done thing for some families, not yet anyway. This is one area my Mother looked back on with a sigh: whenever I complained of the weight of my lessons, she reminded me how lucky I was to be allowed to continue studying along with the more privileged boys.

My Mother's Father had been a money lender and they were quite well off in the growing up years. With the advent of the 1941 troubles and the anarchy that followed, a lot of people tore up their loan certificates and refused flatly to pay up. So my grandFather ended up losing capital, house and career. It was sheer good luck when my Mother's uncle, a bachelor with a big house on the Tigris River invited them to stay there, taking my great grandMother with him to a smaller accommodation.

My Father extolled often on how happy his engagement period was and rightly so! In poetic terms he described how he crossed the river every day to get to his waiting fiancée, quoting the very popular song of Hassan whose fiancée prays to God to protect her loved one from the wind and the waves. In those days, all the houses built on the river were called *kassers* (palaces) and what a welcome awaited him from his new family. As my uncles and aunts were younger than my Mother and still at home, they must have looked upon the promising future groom as their idol. A sumptuous dinner was laid out every day and then the young couple would take another boat back to the *Russaffa* bank and it always meandered round, there was never any rush.

The river in the evening is so still and silent, yet luminous from the myriad of lights scintillating from the nearby banks. Romance on the Tigris!

My Mother, she is a workaholic as befits any Capricornian. Anybody with this sign in their family will understand when I say that my Mother just loves working. I remember her plodding away with her foot on the old"Singer"sewing machine, continuously stitching and mending, and turning old things around. Nothing was ever wasted. She developed such skills in sewing; cloths imported from China and Japan in another one of my Father's earlier ventures were made into coats for myself and my brothers, trousers, dresses and school uniforms. Household items like curtains, pillowcases, aprons: nothing was too difficult or too time consuming. Along the way she acquired some very good taste in clothes and many people phoned to ask her opinion about what to wear and what not to wear. One of these sessions could last hours (she acted like a latter day Style Guru but without charging their exorbitant rates) while the ladies alternated between this or that cut, how to explain things to

A leisurely boat trip – with a chaperone of course

the seamstress, what lining, what belt, which coordinating jewellery: her friends relied totally on her perceptive judgement. In those days, the handbag had to be exactly the colour and the shade of the shoes. We adhered to the proprieties of style much more than the modern icons of today, In our days fashion did not provide as much flexibility nor freedom.

There were only two viable department stores in the whole of Iraq: Orosdi Back and Hesso Achwan, and we were extremely lucky in that they both existed side by side in

Baghdad. Adolf Orosdi, a Hungarian army officer, who had found refuge in the Ottoman Empire, opened this clothing store with the Back family, which also hailed from Jewish Austro-Hungarian stock. Once or twice a year, they renewed their fashion stock importing the smartest of clothes from France and England, and then whoever had inside contacts were tipped off to be the first to come and buy. That was considered an important date in my parents' calendar as my Father insisted on being a part of those very early morning jaunts, even before going to work. His taste input was always valuable, and needed, as was his money. Moreover it was a feather in his hat if his wife upstaged everyone and was the best dressed lady among their acquaintance.

If you could not find your ideal dress in either one of those stores, you went to a seamstress's house, and you searched in her own magazines to select the cut of the dress you wanted. Then she advised you on where best to locate the cloth. There were only two very superior seamstresses and they were called Aghawnee and Shoshaneek, I agree they neither sound Iraqi nor Jewish; invariably those fashion buffs were Armenians. If someone wanted a top dress for a wedding for example, then they sent them to 'Vogue' another small family run business which imported the most elaborate *kalabdoons,* sequinned and silken cloths from Lebanon and France: the English were not really considered to have as elegant a taste in those days.

For ordinary everyday wear we made our way to the Khan Daniel market in pursuit of value for money. In the summer it had to be very early so we could get in and out before the sun's rays became too fierce. We left at seven a.m. hitching a lift with my Father to his warehouse. This was right opposite the city's *Bennook Rd* so from there to the souk, our destination was a very easy five minute stroll. We entered its beginning: dirt strewn unpaved road covered by a colossally high dome. As our eyes became used to the dark, so we breathed a sigh of relief thankful for its relative coolness! But it was not quiet, no quite to the contrary in fact!

Everybody was very busy here already. Imagine the

Khan Daniel Market

scene: barefooted *hammammeel* (porters) carrying loads on their backs or bent double carting boxes either in *zannabbeel* (big straw bags) or *gunneeyat* (jute bags). The coke seller was already uncorking his bottles for thirsty customers; the ice seller's trolley contained a big chunk of ice which he hacked at continuously. A young *Abu qahwa* (coffee seller) banged a mountain of cups in one hand and held a steaming pot of Turkish coffee in the other. If we were really thirsty we caught the eye of the yoghurt seller who stopped instantly to proffer a glass of refreshing *laban* laced with ice. In the background were sitting traders with trays on the floor in front of them shouting for example *shaar banaat* (candy floss) wein *awallee wein abbat*, in a catchy rhythm! The only polite element, the mute donkeys, weighed down with *gweenies* of all sorts tried at least not to bump into people, but under duress sometimes uttered pathetic Hee Has. There were also the odd camels with

33

a decorative carpet on their hump, being led through the souq to better pastures. We interacted with everyone while simultaneously keeping our eyes open in case of treacherous banana peels or chewing gum, to avoid hurtling over a sleeping beggar or getting in the path of a supplicating one; it was paramount as well to skip over the dirt water flowing continuously into the middle rivulet.

Then all of a sudden there appeared a clearing and a big din which heralded *Souk el Saffafir*. Tens of men in traditional dashdashas sat shaping copper into wondrous light and bright things. Fascinating to watch them but the eardrums nearly exploded after a few minutes. As they sat on the edge of the dome, so they were bathed in sunlight; in addition a further glow was reflected on their faces from the copper that they banged. They had the honour of making all the pots and pans that we used for cooking and frying as well as those for dunking clothes in for washing.

Everybody needed their services at some time or another, either to buy the utensils or later on to *bayyethouha*, dipping them in a solution to replace their protective tin coating. This process resembled electro plating but in a more antiquated kind of way

At this point in time we usually took a sharp left into the hidden corridors of the souk, and kept on marching straight. The labyrinths now became much cleaner and lit with electrical bulbs and fluorescents. Furthermore they opened up wider in the form of various neat chambers one on each side! Each chamber was full to overflowing with rolls of cloth piled very high to form a wall on three of its sides, the fourth side open partly to constitute a doorway to do business with the customers. The salesman in his *arakcheen* (Arab headgear) and local costume stood to attention in the middle of this chamber, which could be big or small just like a shop. Spying us as we turned the corner he greeted us with abundant expressions of welcome and invited us to sit down on the comfortable settee formed from the stacked rolls. This welcome extended to shouting for an acquaintance to get some *barreds* on the quick which meant 2 bottles of quasi frozen cokes, without which nobody can start the all

Souk al Saffaffir or the Brass Market

important business proceedings! He asked us what sort of cloth we were after, and by dint of a long stick and a ladder which he climbed very deftly, he reached the rolls in the highest echelons! If either of us found something we liked that suited our purposes in the cloths that he was showing, we declined to let on any enthusiasm but quite to the contrary gave it a very bland reception indeed even went on to ask for the prices of the others so he would not guess where our real interest lay. Then we would start bargaining for the prices of the many other varieties of cloth till coming down to our real preference, we asked him point blank for the best price. If he did not go down to half his original bid, then our last tactic was to leave the shop temporarily. If he shouted to recall us, then it was nil to him and fifteen to us in this cat and mouse game. Otherwise we had to swallow our pride and come back defeated to be accorded an even warmer welcome to make up for losing face. Of course we were readily forgiven: after all it wasn't our fault for being members of the daft sex.

If the negotiations were extensive or the owner thought that there was a chance of further business dealings then we were offered complimentary Turkish coffee, cakes, tea, they all materialised on a tray as if from nowhere! On the other hand, the cotton fabrics had this all permeating smell that made the eyes water and the breathing constricted! This explained why most of these "shops" invested in ceiling fans which luckily meant much pleasanter surroundings

The fashion was the one set by Paris for that year which we tried to ape using whatever Simplicity and Vogue patterns were sold in Orosdi; and as one colour was paramount so we all adhered to it in our new dresses. Sometimes my Mother had to call on her "architectural" skills as well to remedy a pattern that did not offer the latest shape or cut. To do so she clobbered in seams, collars or even a skirt from a different pattern. For example to make a dress out of a blouse pattern or to make it wider, narrower, longer or shorter. Patchworking I believe we can call it, but yet in its primitive stages. In the few times where a dress would not behave and definitely eluded her sewing skills, it was usual for us to go to her aunt's house to parade it and seek a more august opinion. There all of us including my great aunt's two daughters, my third cousins, would sit down on the sofa and have a whole discussion to pinpoint the problem while savouring their Turkish coffee. Back to the surgical procedures required. It could be the hem was not sitting straight! So I was made to stand on a table while they adjusted it laboriously with a ruler and pins. In those days nearly all the dresses had to be lined securely once or even twice which added to the workload no end. My great-aunt's most popular remedy was centred around the darts "*pinssat*" so after demonstrating the bad effect or the pout that the faulty seam has created, either she made further darts to decrease its scope or made the existing ones narrower to let the dress and its owner breathe. It was always beyond me but her elaborate reasonings were considered holy. In view of the tacit assent by my Mother, it didn't take long. Sometimes the neck opening was deemed to be the culprit so my buxom relative fashioned a deeper neckline *hafrah* using her judgment not to make it too daring. Between such professionals, how can any dress fail to measure? Even if the verdict called for undoing most of the dress and starting again, my Mother never flinched. What mattered was producing a perfect work of art. They called her *Ezraeela* (very capable), which is a complimentary title, although it is related to an ignonimous Bible character too.

With such a beavering set of parents, the catalogue of achievements grew fast. My Father's life was peppered with business ventures. Some did quite well, but when they folded he was always ready to move on. Thus it was at the time I was born he had invested money in Al Sa'doun hospital, and staffed it with German and English doctors as well as Iraqi and Armenian nurses. We were put in the hospital's best wing and had a long string of visitors. One of the many doctors on call was Kamal Sammarae'e who became very well known in Iraq, as well as Sister Najeeba who was a foremost nurse. As was the custom, my Mother stayed in bed for forty days during which her only occupation was to rest, eat and drink plenty of black beer to have enough milk for the baby. How Mothers were spoilt in those days! But she did need all that energy to talk to the clusters of visitors who sat round the bed forming a big circle for hours on end, gossiping and exchanging jokes. The baby's welfare was not supposed to come before that of its parents so the poor soul sucked its milk, slept and cried amid the din, the *Hossa* and the crowd. Baby psychology had not been invented then nor did anyone keep a watchful eye on the clock, and thank God for that.

The Mother and her baby were adequately protected nevertheless by the garlands of garlic hung on the bedposts; for further safeguard, gall nuts and blue shells were sewn on the baby's clothes to ward off the evil eye.

Baby's Amulet (Sambuskayi) made of blue shells and ceramics as well as a garlic clove

It goes without saying that my parents were looking forward to the birth of a boy as everyone does in Iraq, since this is the most prestigious of events that can happen to any family. Very unexpectedly they were confronted with a girl! With a boy there was no need to choose a name; it was de rigueur that he should be called after my late grandFather, so this predicament meant they were too stunned to think of an alternative name. The story goes that someone just happened to lend them a name dictionary, and that it just happened to be English, and that it just happened to fall on an i page when they opened it. Is it worth doing any work for the sake of a girl? My name, how to describe all the problems I had with it while growing up and even later? The Moslem teachers made me repeat it several times but invariably wrote it down as eevy, as did the French teachers. The English teachers could never believe that I was born with it because it sounded strange in an Arab country; they quizzed me endlessly about the whys and wherefores, finally understood when I said it was a plant! Oh a poisonous plant you mean? This exposed me to endless ribaldries from friends and colleagues throughout the ages. For my parents it sounded stylish because of its uniqueness among the crowd, and this must have ticked all the boxes.

When I came to the world, I was surrounded by two very large close and loving families: 14 uncles and aunts and 3 grandparents with a rightful licence to spoil their first grandchild. By the time I became aware of my bearings, they had all disappeared. This occurred against a very important backdrop, the mass emigration of Iraqi Jews in 1951 when I was nearly four. A very large chunk (130,000) were issued with a one way ticket, never to return.

The repercussion from this huge exile has stayed with me and my family to this day, a huge void was created, our small family unit was left bereft.

My Mother being expected to give birth any minute to my brother had to tarry behind with my Father so missed that particular boat. In the meantime view the primitive amenities in nascent Israel, my uncle managed to smuggle a letter whereupon he expressed utter shock at the conditions that our people were housed in. A very basic tent on muddy ground to live in instead of that vast house on the river, not even enough to eat! To compound it all, not only were matters so atrocious, but the Arab Jews coming from third world countries were also seen to be completely lacking in culture and education and treated accordingly. Thus they were sprayed with insecticide when they landed from the aeroplanes, put in dirty transient accommodation, and given a very second-rate class status. This happened because the European Jews were the original founders of the State and definitely superior in job skills as well as learning certificates. In their countries they had had to contend with a much harsher environment and a much more demanding work ethos. Russian existence bears no comparison to the Iraqi way of life, to eke out a living was much harder and the climate crueller. In Iraq, the ambience is so much more relaxed and laidback with a siesta to break the day and *baksheesh* (tips) to oil most cogs! Life was accommodating and life was yielding. And this is why the Orientals in this equation had to lose out. To compound it all, the Arab Jews were looked upon suspiciously by the Israelis as they had all the qualities of their arch enemies the Arabs: they talked like Arabs, looked like Arabs and even tried to continue to live like the Arabs.

I cannot but indulge in a bit of cynicism at this junction. When we left Iraq, we were rejected as its citizens, so how amazing that we ended up representing the Mother country in front of the big wide world? Our nationality preceded us to the forefront of every introduction, every job interview! Everywhere we went, people wanted to know where we came from, so we had no choice but to take on board any prejudices against the Mother country and there were a lot of them thirty years ago. Iraq's violent reputation was very much in the limelight then, so that people everywhere treated us with suspicion and worse; meanwhile that same country had abandoned us like so many black sheep.

Anyway, with a new born baby, my parents decided that the safest option was to stay put! It must have been a triple whammy for my Mother as due to yet another social stigma her own Mother was not allowed to visit her for forty days after giving birth, so my grandMother decamped with nary a glance at her newly born grandson.

That was a very dark period indeed as I suspect my Father's business had also collapsed! From this period I can remember making long journeys on buses at night round a Baghdad bereft of the familiar faces which we used to visit; my Father regularly egged me on to walk the last kilometre of the forlorn journey to our rented house in the Battaween with the promise of *baad shweiyyah lil -cha'eb* (just a little bit more to the end). Apparently I became hysterical when my younger relatives aka my playing companions were wiped out in one coup along with our playing ground. This consisted of the big house with its open courtyard in the middle and a terrace overlooking the river. My Mother was distressed even more I expect but tried never to show us the strain.

A FASCINATING CHILDHOOD

Among my earliest memories was being taken by my Father to help stack the banks of the flooding Tigris with sand bags to shore it up. Baghdad came very near drowning in 1954, and our house was only separated from the river by a promontory at the end of the road. There were hundreds of people doing the same thing including the army. My Mother took a small two eyed burner upstairs to do the cooking with as the downstairs kitchen was under threat of flooding. Another, happier memory this time was sitting at the back of the A*rrabanna* (horse drawn carriage) on a very low stool, having fought with my brother for this privilege and reprimanded by the young maid. Maybe she did not tell my parents of this illegal outing as the district of El Aathamiyah was quite far from our house and we were on our own if anything were to happen? Waking up on a freezing morning to the sound of two cows being led into the garden before I left for school. A farm boy brought them in and proceeded to milk one of them, presenting us with the milk in a big metal jug. We boiled the milk, skimmed the frothy top and had it for breakfast growing taller with each glass: at least that is what the parents promised! We sipped the hot tasteless liquid all the while keeping an eye on the entertaining vista of the cows peacefully munching away at the lawn. Once digging a hole in the garden, I must have disturbed a scorpion which bit me promptly. The old gardener took my wrist and sucked the bad blood off and spit it away. My parents were not home at the time; he probably saved my life

I also used to be sent by my Mother onto strange errands. A frequent one was to the men's only *chaykhanna* very near our house, to buy cooked *bajellahs* (broad beans) in a huge paper bundle shaped like a cone. The big trolley had as its

42

belly a big pot of boiling water. I held up the overflowing cone and the seller rained green *butnaj (an herb)* on the lot! These cafes spilled out onto the streets and the men smoking their *narghillahs* (water based tobacco pipes) leaning back on the wooden benches and counting their worry beads, gave the appearance of sitting on the pavement! My Mother's friend was pregnant and she felt a craving for these spicy broad beans but ladies were not allowed near those establishments. On the other hand it was acceptable for a young girl of seven to waylay the social code. Apart from this, there existed this unwritten law that a pregnant woman must be humoured in whatever food she desired, so that even if it was the middle of the night, the husband was expected to get out of bed and obtain that food ASAP. Otherwise a likeness of that food be it a chestnut or a strawberry will be reciprocated on the baby's skin for life. My friends and I used to try to fathom out what sort of food the lady had felt like when we saw anybody with a birthmark on the face or the leg, in tune with resolving an entertaining puzzle.

More memories, this time of the cultural kind. Hopping back home from primary school in the early afternoon to the sound of French singing wafting throughout the house; my Mother had just bought new records (45 rpm)from Orosdi Back and they came contained within a book of rhymes, pictures of angelic boys and girls, dainty men and women, powdered and dripping in lace and diamonds. My Mother used to have French teachers in the Alliance and she felt at one with the songs. On and on we played them, they were popular ballads, and I still remember some:

> *Sur le pont d'Avignon, on y danse, on y danse*
> *Sur le pont d'Avignon, on y danse tout en rond*
> *Les beaux messieurs font: comme ca*
> *Les belles demoiselles font comme ca*

(On the bridge fashionable ladies and gentlemen dance and bow to each other)

My parents also bought the records of Yves Montand and Edith Piaf popular at the time. By dint of playing around with the needle on the huge black gramophone, and making the record go very slow I tried to decipher the words one by one, write the song down and learn it by heart. After a while the whole record became a zigzag of indented lines. No matter; it was fun to guide the needle out of the groove again whenever it "stuck" and kept repeating its lines. There was a book that taught western dances like the Waltz, Samba and Tango and my parents tried to practise diligently. It was yet another way of keeping up with the Joneses.

For a long time the school concentrated on an in depth French tuition, so that the English was relegated to third place in language priority. Later on as the GCE's were deemed more important so the system switched sides again and brought the English language to the forefront.

On the other hand: "Arabic was always to be our first language while its literature have penetrated our very bloodstream" quoting Dr Salman Darwish. The grammar, very complicated, required years of dissecting the sentence into its primary components. Of course I have to tip my hat off to Arabic as the richest language I know. Having said so, it is more difficult to write Arabic than other languages because it involves translating in your mind the words that you use every day, to the Arabic *al Fassih* (literary) which is confined to the realm of reading and writing. The Jews talked in still another dialect bordering on the Aramaic and very like the Assyrians in the North, the Talkeifs, who are mostly Christians, although it can easily be turned round to be at one with the Moslem way of speaking !

Arabic words are made up of a three letter root, which can be metamorphosed without limits into subjects, objects,

44

verbs, or adjectives by a judicious addition of a few more letters and vowels i.e. fathas, thammas and other (more difficult) convolutions. Any of those can also be made to denote feminine masculine or plural gender by adding one letter only: one more complication being that each letter face presents itself in three different connotations at least depending upon its position in the word!

For example this automatically makes English far easier to type in as it has fewer characters.

My parents bent backwards to shield us children from any sad or ominous events. There must have been many clouds in the firmament past and present but I remained blissfully unaware of them all. So that, hand on heart, I can look back on a happy and carefree childhood. As much as possible, they organised trips and days out with their friends in the weekends For example, taking us for a day out to Habbaniya Lake to swim, Malwiyyah Minaret to climb its

Malwiyyah-going right to the top was such fun

several twisting floors, or to visit the old Ishtar gate in Babylon which was rebuilt by Saddam and whose new bricks

45

are engraved in his name. Then there was the very well aspected Tharthar dam with its fresh clean waters, trips on trains to the North, Mosul Salah el Din, Sarsank and Ba'quba. We made fun of this latter town, calling it Aqquba which means a scorpion. And on to the South: Basrah, Hillah. We saw at first hand one good side of Iraq and that is the generosity and good nature of the Bedouins. They plied us with *khubuz* (brownish flat and round bread), *qeimmer* (crème made from buffalo milk) and drinking yoghurt every time the train stopped at a village - and we literally had to beg them to accept payment.

Some trips were more educational than others as when we went to the North with a guide! He toured us round the many lovely places there and we acquired many new experiences while looking down at some incredible vistas. But very rarely did there exist a hotel or facilities for tourists! So along with the rest of the population, we used to bemoan such an omission blaming it always on the government of the day. The guide once took us to a place being dug up with huge machinery. As we dismounted we saw gas escaping freely from the ground at a great momentum. As it came out it started burning from the combustion with the air and remained burning brightly day and night: it was too strong for anyone to put out! Iraq is that rich in natural resources. On another trip we hit a sandstorm and all of a sudden there were thousands and thousands of fat locusts attacking the car. We closed the windows very tight, but they still went into the engine from underneath and when the engine was full of them, the car spluttered to a halt. The driver covered himself and his face and went out to clear the engine from thousands of dead locusts, but as he opened the door he let hundreds of them in! Some more got sucked in through the air vents and we had to pick them up one by one and put them in bags so as not to open the windows. These locusts descended on a green field

46

by the hundreds, and after an hour the field turned brown when they finished eating up the greenery. Thank God it was only a once in a lifetime encounter.

Most people in Baghdad had maids in those days! They came predominantly from Allquosh, a village in the North of Iraq. The maids welcomed the opportunity to work in Baghdad and send the money back to their families in the villages. They also acted as nannies and cooks and as they boarded with us so they eventually became part of the household. Their names were invariably Meriam and they all addressed the housewife as "Madame". Their heads were always covered with a scarf of many colours and they had on a long floaty dress of even more colours as well as other shiny bits and pieces. They wore heavy gold bangles on their wrists and one tiny one in their nose, and owned assorted gold teeth and tattoos. Everything was decent, except for the top of the dress which was supported by a flimsy popper; this latter's task was sometimes too onerous, so most of the time it was all left to hang loose underneath.

On Friday they washed and plaited their long hair for hours. Devout, they murmured their prayers day and night in a silent recitation, holding on to a tiny cross, and that is how we were introduced to the church. We picked up quite a few stories from our maids about *Yassou' el Massih and Mariam al Athra* (Jesus and the Virgin Mary) and the miracles He wrought. The poor maid must have tried everything to make us go to sleep. There were also romantic stories which all ended in marriage and a happy ever after. They contained angels to help with much needed magic as well as witches and devils, good people going to heaven and bad people finishing up in a horrible way. Often the plots turned multi tortuous and us siblings slept peacefully long before the end beckoned.

My parents never read us bedtime stories as for some reason it was not the done thing. I am positive that we could

47

have benefited from them telling us about the history of our community or even something about our religion, but maybe those rather sombre stories would not have led us to sleep peacefully like Meriam's. Anyway, the good maids stayed with us for years, and once a year there would be a sort of a "money" promotion of one or two pounds. This came in the aftermath of quite a bit of haggling and earnest discussions with her while her friends and relatives from the North interceded on her behalf. It took hours, and we all listened intently gathered in a circle to the toeing and fro-ing of the arguments, while roped in translators explained the vernacular's finer points.

Our maids went to Allquosh often to see their families! On these occasions my friend and I would beg them to bring us things from the North like *summaq wa za'ter*; these were very sour things that we were simply addicted to. We gave them an oral list as they couldn't read, and this had to take into account our pretty limited budgets. They would bring them back in very thin paper cones and the damage to our pocket at half a penny each was much less than the damage they inflicted on our stomachs. You see we doused them thoroughly with salt for more impact on the taste buds.

I remember when my Mother started taking driving lessons and then passed and very soon after that my Father did as well. First time both, and I will let you into the secret: it was just dead easy. The test terrain consisted of a big figure eight and the learner driver had to negotiate this figure on the ground twice, once forwards and once backwards. In addition there were also harder technical questions: my Mother was asked what to do if she had a puncture? And she answered promptly: "I will stop the first man I see and ask for his help!" That was the correct answer and the certificate was stamped with alacrity.

My parents had become members of a jet set of sorts, people who threw huge dinner parties and played cards. It is so easy in a moderate climate like Iraq's to have people out in the garden till late at night, helping themselves to dinner al fresco from centre tables buffet style. But the preparations were enormous: In Iraqi lore, it is not done to provide according to what the guests will eat: no, you have to provide much more with an eye to beat all the competition, so that the tables are heaving with many more dishes than the guests could possibly eat. The kitchen would be turned upside down, big deep cauldrons were laid on the floor and various glorious foods cooked during the two days preceding the party! On the night, they were warmed again on special *fteel* (burners) then laid in front of the visitors on makeshift tables in the garden. *Tabeet, Pacha, qouzi, dolmas, saloona, kubbat halab, kubbat shawander, kubbat burgul kubbas ad infinitum.* In case any men of the cloth are reading I must apologise here for the shorter interval between meat and dairy consumption but after about half an hour, dessert plates were brought out thus: *baklawa, zangoula, white halva and red halva, machbouz, malfouf, luzina, semesmiyah madqouqa.* All this, and I never heard complaints of tummy aches or any other western type illnesses such as high cholesterol or nut allergies! I imagine Iraqi food is very good for you as it does not contain a lot of meat or chicken; instead, wheat, semolina, rice, potatoes are stuffed with bits of meat or chicken and an abundance of vegetables especially parsley. In addition natural ingredients like date syrup, tamarind, beetroots and lemons are used instead of added sugar, salt or today's sauces which contain e colours. All adorned with heavenly smelling spices which are ground by each housewife (or her maid rather) in a heavy copper pestle and mortar set. To further satisfy the palate, the housewife makes a lot of pickles storing them in jars. Of course she was a full time housewife; of course she was worth her weight in gold! Lucky the man who can still find her. Alas, they don't do them in these modern times, sorry!

In those days, there were no big supermarkets in the whole of Baghdad, and as it was not done for a woman to carry heavy things, we had wholesale deliveries only. These came mostly in *gweenis* (big jute sacks). Thus one *gunneyi* basmati rice, *gunneitein* (two)of flour, more gweeni sugar and salt, cokes in dozen crates, big oil containers, some DelMonte cans, and big chunks of halloumi like cheese. These were stored in a dark room lower than the ground level so as to stay cooler, in the shade. We did not need any more victuals as my Mother made the cakes and biscuits herself and there were no breakfast cereals in those days.

My Father used to take us in the car a few times a week after work to buy fruit and vegetables from the greengrocer, if he was not too tired that is. These big stalls all stayed open well into the night! My Mother remained seated conservatively in the car, ladies should not be seen in greengrocers, it was yet another taboo. She wound down the window to tell him what we needed, and his would be the responsibility of merchandising with the shop owner! Bargaining is an art form which is very requisite in Iraq but is carried out with a lot of goodwill and who gives a damn about all the time lost? This little drama will unfold like this:

Selim: "Good evening are these good oranges"?
           (Fingering same)

Shpkr   "Of course! They are the best in all of
           Baghdad, look how glossy, *hulwa shaqar*
           (sweet as sugar), here I will peel one for
           you"

Selim   "Not bad" – but taking care not to be too

50

(eating)   complimentary, "how much do you want
                  for them"?

Shpkr   For you, *Ammi(*Sir*)*, a special price only a
                  dinar a kilo

Selim: Acting a bit taken aback "Wallahee, I
                  bought bigger ones for far less 2 days ago in
                  this same street, you take us for millionaires!
                  I will give you 500fils a kilo, this is definitely
                  my limit"

SHPKR   "But,I swear they cost much more to buy.
                  Just smell their scent, aah! Ask Ummel
                  Jahal   (the   Mother)   she   looks
                  keen"

Selim: "As your best customer, *Walak ya einny
                  (*dearie*)* give me a better deal"

Shpkr: *"Tadallal ya Effendi* 750 fils"

Selim   "No, no. I will go to the other shop *ma'a el
                  salama*" (byebye)". He pretends to be
                  crossing the street in earnest

Shpkr   "Wait, come back, I swear to you
                  tomorrow I will be forced to sell my house
                  and all my family will be in the streets;
                  550fils. Just don't mention this price to
                  anyone else".

Similar altercations for the individual vegetables, watermelons, dates, figs, followed. The negotiating of it was a science; the winning was a joy, and the fifty per cent discount? Lip smacking good.

My Father was also the one to handle any medical ailments and take us to the doctor. He also had the task of meeting the Headmaster if any of us put in a poor performance at school. In those days, it was not seemly for

Abu el Raqqi had a knife at the ready Alal Sacheen
To prove the redness of the watermelon to the client

women to discuss serious issues with men or voice their opinions or argue; they contented themselves with sitting on the back benches: dainty, polite, deferential. I cannot remember my Mother ever setting foot at school although she was the one to give us lifts in the car in an emergency when we were late waking up for example, or if it was raining. The rain brought all sorts of muddy conditions and obstacles that we were not used to negotiate: the whole street abutting the school started to look like a vast mud lake in the space of half an hour and was considered dangerous. Nobody had boots or umbrellas because we very rarely needed them, so usually ended up missing school and staying at home.

On the other hand my Father failed badly whenever a mechanical agenda presented itself, for example our car never ignited in the morning, especially on cold days. What a predicament view the fact that my Father had to be in the office early. A friend in the know told him the engine should be warmed up. To this end, the whole household including the maid was recruited to go out first thing to start pushing the car or even shaking it to ignite a spark. We usually jumped out of bed and straight to the task in the cold mornings. At times we pushed it just outside of the driveway, and something connected and miraculously it sprang to life. At other times we were not so lucky, and as it was not seemly for women to push a car outside the house, my Father would recruit any men walking in the street to the cause. To give those men their due, they always rallied in an enthusiastic manner so that we women could go inside. They struggled till the end of the road and maybe beyond till it "took". This was a recurrent nightmare with all of my Father's cars as he never knew what constituted the workings of them, and never learnt, only lamented their idiosyncrasies. No, my Father was not technical minded at all and I don't think he even knew how to change the fuses. He left all these skills to his wife who had no choice but to learn how to diy them.

The nursery school that I went to acted as a feeder school to the larger FrankIny. As its Headmistress it had a Syrian Christian lady and her name was Miss Kanawatee. She was a very buxom, blonde lady who lectured us a lot about morals and how to treat each other. Her endearing contribution lay in the fact that she made a fuss of us around Christmas, hosting each individual class in her study, where she instructed us how to play little games together. Of course the best part lay in the bag of sweets that she rewarded us with at the end. In those days my life revolved round the numbers of silver stars and angels that the English teacher, Miss Pass, gave me to glue into the textbook. She by contrast was a tiny lady and reminded me of a sparrow. We were made to practise different writings in English and French. The French writing alternated between pressing hard for the dark bits and not so hard for the light bits. I had a lot of trouble as drawing was never a strong point but some pupils laboriously produced veritable works of art.

As I mentioned before, my parents rented a house in the Battaween district, which was convenient for the above Menachem Daniel feeder school in the Senak. This house was built along peculiar architectural lines. It resulted in us sharing a long entrance drive as well as the main outside gate with an Armenian family. Pogroms made them flee and they were frustrated that they did not have a country. It was only natural that their children and I became bosom friends. Shagheek and Facheek spoke with me in their native language so that I became fluent in the Armenian language in no time at all. We acquired some of their culinary talents like hanging *Bassturma* (sausages full of garlic) from the ceiling for weeks to dry, a taste for *tabbouleh* (parsley salad) which has accompanied us always. They also taught me to dance, made me up in their native dress fineries. Between us, and yet some more neighbours' children whose houses abutted onto one another's, we owned several "*Nabeq*" trees in our gardens. We used to climb up the easiest one to sit on its wide branches for long leisurely conferences as well as to eat meals. The fruits of the nabeq are smallish yellowish and have a pit to be thrown out into the garden yet again. We gathered the *nabeqs* in season by grabbing hold of the trunk or the branch and shaking it violently. Whatever fell was gathered in rush baskets, counted carefully and then divided into little paper bags. Further culling were made to separate the ripe ones from the not so ripe green ones. Everyone ended up with a fair balance. The good ones emitted a lovely aroma that I can smell still. We also ate a lot of apricot paste layered in sheets *Qamareldeen* which came from Syria, very dark and dry; we doused them in salt and water. There were also a few lime trees that grew in the garden and we loved to squeeze and drink their juice with either salt or sugar each according to their taste. Loofahs hidden inside big green bushes protruded from yet another fence; they were for scrubbing the body vigorously clean. We secretly pinched big sunflowers from yet another neighbour picked the seeds one by one and ate them. The sun accompanied us everywhere, and made enjoying childhood a breeze!

Looking back, I must have treated the Armenians' house as an extension of ours, spending whole days there and even shared in their sleeping arrangements during siesta times. Lunchtimes used to be so hot that all the children lay on makeshift mattressesses under the cooling *Agoule* at the window; this dry hay was continually watered by the garden hose from outside. Their living room felt like bliss! As they had an icebox with a daily delivery of large chunks of ice, we also stored some of our more perishable foods in this wooden box till the advent of the fridge / freezer.

I cannot remember a ban on sneaking out into the alleyways round the house and so we went frequently outside into the small streets nearby. We bought iced lollies in all the colours of the rainbow from a little icebox in a pram like trolley pushed by a local boy who shouted his guts out "luckeeeeee stick", and were allowed to peer by another peddler inside a magic box for incredible 3D pictures. *Sandooq el wellayyat* (the box of many countries) allowed us lovely glimpses into far away lands and cultures. And the outlay? A very affordable *fils* or two.

Looking good and dressing very smartly was always paramount in our upbringing and especially as we grew older. It was indoctrinated by our parents as well as expected by society at large! In doing so we aped the Western mode of dress as the prettiest and most stylish. (Old) English and French magazines, Vogue and Simplicity patterns formed our whole encyclopaedia. There was an unfortunate dearth in catwalk shows while ready made clothes just did not exist. On the other hand, if you failed to present yourself as society decreed, you were hung out with the washing the very next day by ladies who believed it was good to talk. It seemed that there was no worse calamity than not having any taste in clothes. Even at school the teacher complimented the girls who put on a nicer shirt with their uniforms, or had their hair styled in a novel way! People who did not put themselves together smartly were very much looked down upon…conversely, if you received your clothes from England or France, you were looked up to no end!

In those days, my parents were very keen on us children taking up every skill or discipline that was seen to be modern or forward. Especially if it could also be used simultaneously for boasting among their friends in high society, the catch phrase being that they never had those opportunities when they were our age.

In furtherance of this, the Headmaster once convinced them to send us to the American Institute in the summer holidays. Of course all the pupils were up in arms against it, but the parents predictably said the Headmaster knew best and anything that gave a whiff of books was good for our future! So off we used to troop to the Institute at 8:30 on a scorching morning with our swimsuits underneath the formal yet summery clothes. We could not wait to get into the cooling waters of the swimming pool at the YMCA! The only thing that ever stuck in my mind from these lessons by virtue of the teacher repeating it ad infinatum, was the difference between the way the English say "how are you" with the emphasis on the *are* and the way the Americans say "how are you": emphasis on the *you*. The man who tried to teach us this had just qualified as an MA in efficiency time keeping. How could he, an Iraqi, teach differences between English and American accents to other Iraqis, and shouldn't he have known better with his diploma in saving precious time, than to waste ours?

For us girls there was also ballet for aesthetic body development. Some would go to a class nearby run by Mme Leena in her house; she looked very elegant and sounded French, although we later found out she was only Greek. She shouted at us to do the pas de deux in a bare room with a

at the YMCA pool

from left: Daoud Doury, Kamal Sawdayee, Rachel Elia, Vera Dallal,Suad Kateb, Ivy Rabee, David Gabbay and Lisette Shashoua

big mirror and the eternal wooden handrail. One long awaited day after years of practice, she pronounced me fit to put on real ballet shoes! So after transferring the monies and the measurements abroad, my Father asked a business acquaintance to purchase the nicest pair of ballet shoes available from Beirut. They were incredible when they arrived: light pink, satin and gleaming. But the pointed toe proved unbearably painful, I could only stand two minutes at a time let alone move. My parents, both serious achievers, kept insisting that I should apply myself harder. In the meantime Mme Leena closed shop. There was a rumour that her influential lover had abandoned her to go to greener climes, and it was he who was financing both school and house. How heart wrenching though about the expensive pumps.

Ramaddan is when the Moslems fast for a whole month. We envied them because they could eat twice a day (4 am and sunset) while our fast was much more of a torture. The shops were heaped with foods and stacks of desserts for the *Fittur* (the festive meal), while the *Muezzin* (cantor) intoned rhythmically from the various minarets all day long ! We did not mind at all and went about our own business the meantime. The local boys and girls went round knocking at the houses every night of the feast with a rather charming refrain:

"Geena ya ma geena, Hulloul el cheess wanteend"
(Now that we are here undo the bag and give us some sweets.)

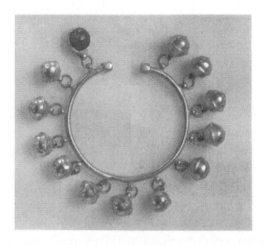

a child's gold anklet with bells designed to tinkle

An idyllic summer's day spent at the neighbours'

A SCHOOL CALLED FRANK INY

I stayed at my school for 11 years, a lifetime. I grew to be defined by it in later life, even all of my life. It was that constant string that I hung on to as all around things metamorphosed at a dizzying speed. I continue to draw my friends from its wider circle i.e. brothers and sisters of the people in my class, who have undergone a sea change. They have now surfaced to become the husbands and wives, aunts and uncles or even grandparents of a new generation. Add a ditto for the kids in my two brothers' classes! With the result that even though the school is no more, I have built up a whole edifice of acquaintances from former students whom I knew or even from the ones whom I did not know in my youth. Indeed, everyone in that school has drawn that same edifice and now exiled all, we turn gratefully to it as the only connection left from that dreamlike life in Baghdad.

This genealogical map allows everyone to be "categorized" in a trice. Confusing? Here is an intelligent example: let us say I hear of the nuptials of Sammy in Holland, he married a Rachel from Canada and I wonder aloud: who are they? Someone will pipe up with their coordinates very quickly "do you remember there was a tallish boy in our class, he was brilliant in Maths? Well, this Sammy is his nephew; you must have seen his grandMother in a red *dashdasha* sitting on the balcony gossiping about everyone who went past". Done it. What about Rachel from Canada? Of course you know her! That pretty girl who was in our class in the 4th secondary and her parents married her off at sixteen to a very rich man 17 years her senior as she could not cope with her studies? Well, this girl is her niece!"

Any more of the same? Of course, we are related, my great grandMother from my Mother's side (a Bashi) well, this millionaire in the paper is her great grand nephew, who has become a Sir. His great grandMother married very well because she was blonde with blue eyes; my great grandMother couldn't because she only had brown hair and brown eyes! My Mother is third cousin with this entrepreneur; do you remember his aunt Layla who used to win the Arab essay competitions? She didn't even bother with a dictionary.

Gossip always came instinctively to us and now it seems there are even more people to gossip about, be it that they are scattered round the four corners of the globe. Jetsetting has become a must and a lifeline both, and when a wedding invitation from the second generation drops through the letter post, it is yet another excuse for our permanent "young at hearts" to reassert their allegiance to the glorious past.

To make an instant connection with people you have lost touch with, there is this need to pigeonhole them by identifying a social cadre from the past! Only then can the present be fully taken on board! Only then can such a huge distance be straddled. And the verdict on the rapid passing of the years? *Qui sera sera,* what will be, will be.

This historical familiarity must carry a sting in its tail as none of the details of anyone's personal life can remain private if they are known to all and sundry. For example, not long ago at a social gathering, somebody asked me my age. I know I am getting on a bit, but do not like to admit to the full catastrophe. I thought it the most natural thing in the world to try to cheat a little. With makeup and a good hairdo I promise I look *"passable"* err nice enough. So I felt like saying fifty six, trying to get away with a mere three years! Suddenly all the women within earshot whether eating or chatting or gossiping stopped in their tracks to give me this incredulous look, and the nearest one pipes up "*Ashlon*"? "I remember in the Tassqueet, your uncle was our neighbour, and he used to bring you to visit us. You looked like you were two then, and that makes you 58!" Good shot Auntie. Another woman with less grey hair but even better maths (maybe the Headmaster was her teacher), pipes up in her turn "I know, you were in the same class as my brother in the 4th secondary, but you were repeating a class then so you must be a bit older than him, and as he was born in 1950, so you must be 59"! Thank you for reminding me of this Auntie. While the best Shakentala of them all proved to be the most annoying as well! "I know, you were born in the winter when my Mother suffered from a bad cold; we sent for Dr Sammara'ee who said he had just delivered your Mother. Of course, you were born in 1948". Games set and match. By now my face reflected all the colours of the rainbow! For goodness sake, have a bit of mercy women, can't you leave me even a few months in credit. Am I on trial?

Maybe it is time to take you on a virtual tour of this very important school so all pieces fall into place. At a very young age, I started attending the downstairs classes, one by one till I completed them. I graduated through the upstairs ones a bit slower as I failed one year and had to sit in the same class for two years. How very embarrassing to have to admit this, but anyway not many people suspect it so keep it hush. Let's proceed nevertheless. I can certainly claim to close encounters with every single brick and elevation, but after such a long separation, bear with me when I say I am a bit hazy about the school's true dimensions; a building which has nursed me from an insignificant weakling to a confident adult can only ever be measured in infinite terms. At each turn that I make, I am overwhelmed by the good karma clinging to its many flowers, trees and shrubs! The sound of the bell, rushing feet on the stairs, the smell of the chalk- its dust saturating our clothes and nostrils even as we wiped the blackboard energetically with the eternal sponge.

The iron gates were very high true but they were always open to anyone who wished to enter. A big marble courtyard led to the main hall with its huge sprawling staircase. This staircase belonged more to the classical Hollywood films, as it very generously branched out left and right to the upstairs classrooms. There was a balcony running alongside the classes on both floors which made for a light and airy feel. A really large well stocked library with musty dictionaries, but also some very good classics from the older era when it was still worth it for the school management to buy stock. To read them I first had to wipe off the dust. I once discovered some lovely magazines underneath an ancient desk that had remained unlisted! After exhausting its Arabic stock, I raided the French stock, and then my Father took away my card as he did not like me "wasting" my time, so I promptly turned to the English books. Our generation was like a skeleton to what it used to be so we had to be satisfied with the stock from the Alliance schools which were closed down after the 1948 war.

Near the library, a laboratory for dissecting animals and doing some chemical experiments, forbidding events both. The only animal we ever dissected was a tiny horrible frog that sprouted a lot of blood; the boys didn't mind and gripped it by its tail, wickedly chasing the screaming girls with it - while an ancient bench collapsed in the middle of a chemical experiment. Well, it taught the teacher never to do any more experiments so we learnt the theories henceforth bird fashion without understanding. Downstairs was the large teachers' *salon* which we avoided like a disease: if they beckoned us in, it was doubtless for a dressing down. In an area of its own there existed a much loved snack bar where an old Moslem man used to make you an instant sandwich and the choice was half a pitta with mango pickle and egg or half a pitta with crisps, take away. You washed it down with coca cola each time and that was lunch for generations of children. Nearby, there was a walled garden with its own courtyard where all the secondary classes whiled away the time between the breaks. The enclosed sun was incredible in the winter. Some architectural spots within afforded these older classes limited nooks and crannies to conduct romantic overtures. I will call a halt here before your imagination takes you too far though! The risk of gossip had to be taken into account and continues to be, so I will keep schtum, otherwise these same players will call me to task - by e-mail this time.

Large gardens and courtyards formed a perimeter round the school grounds, while right in the middle of the school, was an oblong garden full of roses. It was special in that yet another decree said we were not allowed to walk in it but only round it. In the good old days they used this garden to hold big prize days. Then, it would be filled with hundreds of rows of garden chairs for the parents to sit in, and the front rows were reserved for the ministers and dignitaries. The very young children in their best clothes acted as honorary guides and they led everyone to their numbered seats. Such a buzz when a car alighted with security personnel which signalled the importance of the individual. There were speeches of welcome especially to those brave government ministers. The Chief Rabbi climbed the stairs to the podium very gingerly, looking the part in his turban. The pupils came in a row with the little ones at the front and then aligned themselves as per plan on the stage. The Rabbi then proceeded to ceremoniously shake hands with the proud children, and give each child a book bought from the Naqqar prize fund. Both the Rabbi and the very excited student gave a smile of sorts, and the photographer clicked his camera amid thunderous applause. Ah, those were the days.

Of course there had been a lot of preparations behind the scenes to get the ceremony picture perfect: Sitt Semha gave the children the money six months in advance to buy the presents and return them to the school to wrap. Then the Mothers took over and provided the clothes and generally supervised a very smart appearance on the day - as the pictures show. A pretty girl with some flair both in dress and person stood by, solely to hand the Rabbi the book before His Holiness majestically presented it to the clever student.

The Pupils who will receive a prize

After the demise of Abdul Karim Kassem though, the community decided to keep a very low profile, so no more huge ceremonies. No more rose gardens either. Bleaker still, access to the enclosure was cordoned off as we were not deemed to be worth it. We looked at this lost world from the upstairs classes, and regrets, there were a few!

Back on board then, we continue the tour downstairs: on the right hand side of the entrance door was a huge rather dark assembly room where prizes were given out once the ceremony retrenched inside! It had its own impressive stage. It is the same room where we used to queue up, squirming, for regular injections of typhoid and small pox, as well as "*Kanza wanza*" or flu jabs whenever there was an epidemic in the winter. Then we formed vertical queues for the efficient Dr Gourgi Rabie who "finished" the whole school in one day and a half. Sitt Semha proved even more efficient in not allowing any of the pupils to "escape" the jabs by pretending to be sick. The Sitt had all the files in her hand and everyone had to be ticked as processed or else! And here in the same place were conducted all of the end of term exams. I have attended two weddings there as well where an iron edifice decorated with net curtains and flowers became a makeshift chuppah. In the better times that I keep referring to, they used to put on bona fide plays with real costumes, sashaying about for hours in genuine imitation of the classics. I only made it to see the last one: Moliere's *Le Bourgeois Gentilhomme* which was acted out very well in perfect French. The girls had tons of very bright makeup on, while laces, ribbons and long skirts abounded. Both the Indian slaves and the Mahrajas rubbed something very dark on their skins; it was truly superb.

The school was an icebox in the winter and a hothouse in the summer. There were neither curtains to cover the drafty windows nor any rugs on the floor. No heaters either but for one in the nursery and one in the teacher's parlour; no air coolers either. That is why the school's holidays began early June when the heat became oppressive. The walls of bare grey were empty of any picture. In spite of all this, a real buzz came from its resident occupiers who were fresh faced and hopeful. They worked diligently year after year, truly accepting the word of their parents and Headmaster - that hard work will open doors in the future, even doors that have slammed shut because of discrimination.

When I was at school, my Father was the sole importer of "Nestle" products and they were of the tasty kind: chocolates, coffee (Nescafe), sweet tinned milk (Milkmaid), dry milk (Nespray) savoury biscuits and Nestum, this in the days when Iraq had no factories to process the needs of the population.   Nestle, both in England and Switzerland, sent my Father all kinds of promotional material and freebies to distribute amongst the shops to cultivate for it a sympathetic image across Iraq. One of them I remember well; they were the excellent December calendars. These contained pictures of twelve very cute healthy and bouncy babies, gurgling and cooing most fetchingly, one for each month of the year.

We established this tradition that every season I would carry some to school to give to the teachers: a respectful gift to a respected teacher. In those days all of our teachers were very revered and feared even more. I would get my Mother's help to wrap them neatly and once at school put them behind a desk with the support of my mates. As the lesson began and the teacher's back was turned, I did a quick rescue job, and hastened to the middle of the classroom. Once there to present it to the teacher with a flourish and the blessing of the cast sitting behind me at their desks. The teacher, taken unaware, would, for once, lose his everyday ill-tempered persona, turn charming even, while ooh'ing and aah'ing over the babies. We looked forward to this pleasant respite from the tedious lesson all of 15 minutes, with luck. Some teachers even looked out for me in the breaks to ask for one more calendar; for example if a relative wanted to conceive or was already pregnant. These constituted some of the very rare instances when I had a friendly chat with a teacher!

Another freebie that came with a lot of fun attached, were the false chocolate pieces; these looked like the real thing but contained white chalk. Definitely not for the teachers, but we marketed them to friends on the first of April as a big joke! The ones who popped things into their mouths without looking or checking were worse off; all of a sudden they were biting into…building material?

First of April was a no hold barred sort of day. The most common joke was to tell a student that he / she was wanted by the Headmaster! That was enough to drain the blood away from a body! They would tiptoe downstairs their hearts in their mouth and very timidly knock at the door of the secretary! She in turn went into the inner sanctum only to come out a bit puzzled! No, the Headmaster has no time to see you. Thank God! And then as realisation dawned: wait till I get hold of the *jahesh* (donkey) I will teach him to send me to the Headmaster.

There used to be a very tall English teacher called Mr Nicholson who was a bit more on our level and we liked him; but for some reason he bought this very tiny two seater car that could barely take his frame even when folded in two. To add to the joke, its windows were made of transparent plastic sheeting! How tight-fisted can you get! To teach him a lesson, the boys used to go and peel these sheets away every time:

they even lifted the car sometimes and changed its parking place, it was that light! He never tried to prosecute or impose any punishment, so would continue driving for long periods without any cover on the windows! So much for English phlegm!

As for Mlle Vignol, our French teacher, we once gave her a *nabqa* from our stock of *nabeqs*; instead of eating the pith and throwing the stone away, she peeled the pith and threw it in the rubbish bin, swallowing the stone and even thanking us! The whole school was sniggering at her after that, she never lived it down! Mlle Vignol was famous for putting on the latest fashion, high heels and short skirts: the boys were always making out they dropped things on the floor!

My Father, along with everyone else, put his faith entirely in the school system and more importantly in its Head teacher. Abdullah Obadia had a reputation of being very conscientious, so he was allowed to run the gauntlet with the kids. In earlier times he had taught many future ministers in his capacity of university professor. The school was considered among the top two in the whole of the country which is an incredible achievement for a small minority. But it was a military discipline with no let off from academic studies: sport, art or craft, cooking, sewing and musical instruments were all banished as wasteful luxuries! While history, geography, chemistry, physics, algebra, geometry and maths were rotated in three languages relentlessly throughout the years! It was a struggle grade wise to keep our heads above the water even without counting the six days a week rigid discipline! One thing that did help was the shortage of programmes on TV (not much beyond the same Chalgi with a few singers and Lassie and Fury thrown in once a week); another plus was the lack of entertainment venues –apart from the movies there was absolutely nowhere to go; yet another was the absence of holidays abroad (the government liked us too much to let go). In addition there were neither shopping malls nor school trips (no clear reason this, only the Deputy Head kept repeating it was dangerous)! There was nothing to it but try to make it or break it by the limited parameters on offer.

The teachers in that era were the opposite of today's in that they resented giving us any days off. They'd much rather we did not miss out on any lessons! For example Xmas was only half an afternoon off, and only because of the unavoidable absence of the Christian staff. They were licensed to condemn us for souching, untidy hair and nails or even unfashionable dress. There were never any hurt feelings in those days, there was just obedience! Serge grey school uniforms were decreed for us as teenagers, and along with short white socks, were targeted to play down any assets. Istath Is-haaq if ever he saw a hint of makeup on a girl would put her down and embarrass her till she removed it there and then. The lady Deputy Head was very mindful of the length of the hemlines and instituted weekly measuring sessions. We tried to waylay her by pulling the waist down when we saw her approaching and ended up hotly contesting inches and even half inches to avoid the penalty of going home. But I must testify to her superior fashion sense: thin as a rail, all the clothes sat excellently on her, and she put on only of the best. Imagine, working a whole day with dainty heels and the tightest of skirts, with a thin jacket over the shoulders, all the while going up and down the huge stairs monitoring kids and cunning teenagers mostly by shouting at them; her voice had turned hoarse: our fault of course. She had one good eye and one not so good and inasmuch as we never knew for sure where the bad looking eye was focused, we had to tow the line. Another feature, the long very curly hair, which was the very same colour of the eyes, whitish, flecked with grey! In her only lesson with us, Arabic dictation, she researched and came up with such unheard of and impossible words containing the little *hamza*, this was like a very short "a" but difficult to put in exactly the right place, that we only worriedly made it to pass in our Mother language! All is forgiven now Na'am Sitt; you have redeemed yourself so many times since then that I have even consecrated a chapter for you in my book.

Back to the reality of the school. A veritable challenge for us girls was the wide staircase which had to be negotiated several times a day. I am sure we exposed more than mere ankles to the amusement of the boys. The rascals placed themselves strategically at the bottom, always to be looking up. If only trousers and tights had been invented in our days!

Our teachers came from different backgrounds and faiths. There was a youngish Moslem teacher whom we felt very friendly towards. Sometimes, at our insistence, he would conduct a lesson outside in the little garden where we all sat in a circle on the grass. This turned out to be highly enjoyable for all as you can get away with a bit of laughter or if it is a test, a bit of cheating. We really started to think of him as a kindred soul. One day, his was the last session of the week on a Friday afternoon. Excited and in jubilant mood, we stood up as usual when any teacher came in, and then shouted at the very top of our lungs - a bit loudly - sorry I mean very loudly:

"Good Morning Sir"

It was meant as a good humoured joke, but it did not go down well at all; it might have been his off day, or maybe (more likely) he had quarrelled with his wife the night before.

71

For some reason he took the loud greeting as a personal insult to the status of the teacher; he told us off for misbehaving in no uncertain terms. Then he collected all the rulers in the class, and making a sort of a sandwich of two rulers at a time, he proceeded clockwise round the classroom to smack everyone with this piece of equipment. Everyone had to hold out both hands which he hit meticulously. The rulers came down very hard and broke several times from the force he dealt the punishment with, in which case he replenished them from the supplies lying on his desk.

The only one that he excepted from this harsh treatment was a very well endowed young woman by the name of Widad. He did not dare smack her, so he said she was not the type to shout as she looked too much the lady. And that was the last time I ever tried to befriend a teacher!

Another teacher Istath William, an Egyptian Christian, not in my good books at all. In this year of GCE "A" level exams he took our class for the assigned Arabic syllabus which covered a few hundred years of history. Instead of reading the exam period to be Omayan, he decided it to be Abbassyd, so that we received the shock of our lives when unknown questions sprang out at us from the exam paper! We all failed except for two boy geniuses whose hobbies must have been confined to study. After the exam, Istath William apologised to all the class (I imagine the Headmaster must have given him a rollicking)!

One teacher whom I remember with fondness was the Hebrew teacher who taught us the rudiments of the language up to age 11. He wore a "sidara", a black cone of a hat which king Faisal I popularized. He was not supposed to teach beyond the alphabet, the days of the week, months of the year and the festivals. As Hebrew grades did not figure in the net average, everyone grew fearless and I for one never opened a book. But when it was exam time, I felt apprehensive, so asked my friend who was sitting in front of me to let me copy from her paper. She did, but imagine our utter disbelief when the exam churned better grades for me than for her! I promise I felt more guilt than happiness.

This teacher filled the regular lessons with all sorts of stories not necessarily from the Bible. He used to walk up and down between the rows in a leisurely way which made him an easy target for us to stuff his jacket pockets with hundreds of folded bits of paper.

One story that has stuck to my mind concerned the shoes that he always bought from a place near the Shorja. When Orosdi Back opened, he saw some shoes made in England, and asked the assistant the cost - the assistant replied that the price was on the ticket and this said £4. So he started saying as required that it was hugely beyond his pocket and that he had seen them cheaper in another shop etc etc but to his dismay the assistant said "look *Ammi*, we are not allowed to go down on the price at all" "What no bargaining"? Our good man did not know how to proceed from thence to buy! So the manager was called in to explain to him that this was the best way of doing business because it was the "English" way, and that is what the people do in the cultured countries. So, still surprised, but trusting in the better Western ways, he bought the shoes which lasted more than the local ones. And the moral of the story? He only bought from Orosdi Back forevermore.

In the oral exam of the same year, I did so badly that exceptionally the Headmaster wrote a note in the bulletin asking my Father to come to the school. It was the first and last time my Father ever set foot there. Wonder of wonders, he stayed four hours till nightime, ensconced in the Headmaster's room! We had all become worried and the supper was eaten long ago! But it was all to a good cause! It seems my Father had become very impressed with the Head's dedication to his work and to his pupils. How Mr AO stayed behind every evening to see that the teachers were doing a good job, how he made sure the school kept up its excellent reputation, how the parents should be putting in more effort to help the kids. He said every pupil had his own file with all sorts of comments from the teachers and that this file was set to accompany them to university and the beyond. My Father had become his best advocate and on my account to boot! He convinced him to take me in hand (which he did for a few months after that). Between the bills of lading, sorting out the popularity of the dried milk and the delivery to all the shops, wherever did my Father find the time to supervise my progress at school?

Is this sad or funny? American soldiers after the invasion reported seeing hundreds of files and exercise books scattered every which way in one of Saddam's palaces. They had the name FrankIny on them and were very damp but as they thought they were important documents, the soldiers had them shipped to America. There they were made to go through different processes to dry. The problem with their complete restoration is the prohibitive cost which was quoted as five thousand dollars. Our poor Headmaster! As for us, we never managed to see those vital teacher remarks that were going to influence our lives, or maybe the Americans will surprise us with miracles yet. Watch this space!

Whenever anyone was a bit noisy or cheeky, that boy or girl was told to leave the classroom, in which case he or she remained loitering on the balcony outside. Unfortunately, the

With the Headmaster, Abdullah Obadiah, in the last year of
school 1965

From left:
Lisette,Ivy,Laurette,Farrah,Vilma,Nadia,Edna,Audrey,Daoud,
Sabah,Nessim,..,Riad,Selman,Richard,Baljit,Daoud A,Said,
Headmaster,Adel,Shoua and Zuhair

Headmaster was full of energy and always went upstairs on
never ending rounds intent on meeting trouble head-on even
before knowing it was there; he acted on his sixth but well
developed suspicious sense. Anyone found lurking outside was
in for a gruelling lecture. The pupil always came out in the
wrong (of course as the teacher was always in the right), so it
was best to hide in the seat -less, ancient toilets upstairs, even
though they stank of arsenic; there was absolutely nowhere
else. On the other hand, the very strong smell could only be
tolerated for ten minutes at the maximum, so deflated and
defeated, we made our way back to the balcony to anticipate

definite fireworks. The teacher was persuaded to re admit us amid the direst of warnings.

Boys (the girls were more cowardly) who really got up the Headmaster's nose were given a *Lajnat Enthebaat* where a penalty board made up of higher ups convened to decide on punishment for acute misbehaviour -a bit like a court martial; the parents were brought in and there ensued such a brouhaha in the whole school! The criminal boys were usually given the supreme penalty: expulsion. They became *Matroudeen* (kicked out) which meant they occupied the lowest rungs for several days amid stern warnings to them and their parents.The decisions of this Lajna were typed and displayed inside the central board to drive the lesson home to all with any potential to sin. No one lived it down, no, not the parents, nor the siblings. Even today I know who the naughty ones are and remind them when I see them of what the board legislated against them. I promise you that they squirm and still try to defend their corner maintaining that it was all due to prejudice from this or that teacher; but then in this good era of adulthood, it is laughter all the way.

Indeed most of us are (or have become) very proud to have attended the school, the more so as we keep discovering the rich talent that was shaped within its walls. For example Baron Darzi of Denham, the Under Secretary at the Department of Health studied at our school for a few years. He later gained international respect for his work in invasive surgery. Many more insignificant students graduated to become doctors, surgeons, and then there were the businessmen, lawyers and accountants (Chartered of course). The ones who did best in this materialistic world were the ones who could not or did not like studying, disproving their teachers' erudite theories. Everybody needed to hew their particular corner and boast an achievement. But, noone even tried to become a Rabbi, no doubt from an overload of wisdom gained in the past about their own Rabbi.

Another important person distinguished in Iraq itself was Shaoul, a chemical engineer during Saddam's reign; although the National Committee for Prize Allocation singled out Shaoul's invention as the most efficient and the most beneficial to Iraq for that year (a much better cement formula as well as an alarm for the cement oven so it does not run dry; this used to cost the factory thousands of pounds in damages), Saddam's office was puzzled how to give the prize to a Jew in the era of Baathists. But thanks to some exceptionally fair-minded people who kept persisting, justice prevailed and Saddam had to acquiesce and award Shaoul the £5,000 prize money (or £25,000 in today's value). Even though compelled to share it out with his helpers, the honor was entirely his; to contribute to a country's welfare while being a quasi enemy of the State must be so very exceptional in the whole world.

No doubt our future potential was not visible to those in power. One day "they" will realise our vital role in stabilizing society, despite our paucity in numbers.

Dressed in style (notice the obligatory white socks) for the birthday party at the Shemis'

Beni Naji,,Norma,Gracie,Odette,Perla,Dorothy,Nabil Rabee
Valda,Dorothy's niece, Jack Shemtob, a few Kader Shemis

OUR ONLY AMBASSADOR IS NOW SILVERHAIRED

Sitt Semha was born in 1919, and attended a teachers' seminary for four years in Baghdad to acquire a "*Licence fi adaab allugga al arabiya*" (B.A. Arabic Litterature) in 1943. She was assigned in her first job the same year at a secondary girls' school. As the authorities wanted to transfer her outside of Baghdad in her second assignment, she found a job in the Laura Keddouri girls' school – termed the Alliance. (I imagine with the strict social laws prevailing at the time, a single girl was not allowed to live on her own)! Following the mass exodus of most of the community in 1951, sixteen Jewish schools emptied from pupils so that the remainder were mostly shepherded into Frank Iny. With time this building came to contain the whole A-Z of classes: kindergarten, primary, secondary as well as a sixth form. This intelligent woman climbed steadily through the ranks from being a mere teacher to administrative secretary in 1959 and then straddling both the positions of Head Teacher of the sixth form in 1963 as well as Deputy Head Teacher of Frank Iny when the latter left the country in 1971.

Sitt Semha Nessim Layla was a one off; under an exterior of despotism the colour of tin grey, she hid a heart of gold. She proved her mettle in the very dark days when she worked full steam on a last minute.com basis to write for each pupil a complete certificate of subjects studied; it proved a real bonus to him / her when continuing interrupted studies or trying to make a living abroad. When the poverty cases multiplied after 1967 because of the dire state laws she was concerned to notice signs of malnourishment among the pupils; of her own volition she instituted a system whereby she

79

and two of her friends approached the better offs in the community who were capable of donating money; the two ladies (Raina and *Umma lel* Brighty) then used this money to shop for big items of food staples that some people could no longer afford. Thus they bought sacks of rice, litres of oil, bags of sugar, grain. They waited till the kids were at school so as not to embarrass them by overt charity, and one of the ladies would take a big Zanbeel of victuals from her car and ask a lad to smuggle it into the house. Finally, they handed the housewife a folded envelope which contained much needed cash.

Newsmen descended on the school as one of the very few community institutions still functioning: as the Amen (Iraqi intelligence) always accompanied the foreign media, the only way of relating the true state of affairs was through handing the foreigners written bits of paper, this done very furtively. And it was Sitt Semha who suggested to the potential sleuths that they wear long sleeves, the better to hide those notes in.

Once she was in her office at school early in the morning and was confronted by foreign newsmen with the usual hordes of the Amen. She became very emotional as she didn't know how to respond to their questions and began to cry; the very next week she reaped her prize: the dire straits of the community had made it to the front pages of at least two London papers! The same thing happened when a student was asked to take questions from newsmen while standing conspicuously in the middle of the classroom; overwhelmed, the poor girl burst into tears! Thus the community learnt from these experiences, how best to make a conspicuous splash in the media which served to prohibit further kidnappings and worse!

Our strict Vice Principal must have loved the school and the pupils; with obvious pride, she will tell you that Katie Gareh came the first on the whole of Iraq in the 1967 Baccalaureate and that there have been no dearth of other high achievers; softly with confidence, she goes on to read from various lists that she brought out with her from Iraq: of the multiple *lijan* (committees) which outlined the tasks of the pupils and that oiled the rest of the cogs at school: thus the lajnat parking of the bicycles, and lajnat looking after the kids at break times, *al khutaba* (speeches), competitions for the best short essay in Arabic, English and French even down to the lajnat looking after the class cleanliness and décor and the lajnat to monitor pupils in the school coaches. Then she will enumerate all the extra curricular certificates that we had to work for, all the medals and prizes given out at the end of the year celebration in honour of the outstanding pupils as well as to encourage the rest: *wissam al tashjee', al taffaweq, al isstihssan, al sharaf, al amthaliyya, al awwaliyah*. It has taken us almost half a century to fully appreciate the value she has conferred on our learning curve but we all agree now: she is inimitable and did a great job even under obnoxiously difficult circumstances.

In her sixties, out of Iraq and in Israel, Sitt Semha proved her mettle once more: she enrolled in a few Hebrew courses as it didn't feel right for her not to be at one with her surroundings. As she admits it herself, she wasn't young enough to take up tutoring once again, so put herself down for training for a different career. She did a course in the Archival files and wait for this, the director chose her with only one other to work there from among a list of twenty "graduates". It seems that all the rest of the seniors started muttering jealously about Semha the Iraqi and Sophia the Russian! She ended up working for 6 years in that department which is a

81

brilliant accomplishment! The Archives dated all the way back to the birth of the State, and she along with the others had the task of reading whole files, appending a short summary to

Sitt Semha is sixth fm the right, Istath Iss-hak is fifth fm the left, ,Istath Ameen is 3rd fm right (2nd row), the boys are left out- class of 67

each for future reference. She seems to have gained a lot of satisfaction from this work until another director came who believed in the superiority of young blood. She lost her job but warned him, in an echo of her past privileges, that young people will not last more than a few years before they get bored (*ma yessem-khon*). He should have hearkened to those pearls of wisdom like we used to do, but it has gone full circle now. It is Sitt Semha's turn to receive help from her former pupils, while it is very heartening to know that some are standing by like real troopers …carry on Dora.

The old lady enjoys the command of faultless Arabic; very lucid and articulate still, literary Arabic crops up naturally in her everyday language unlike most of us. Her looks have improved because of latent eye surgery and she is easier to converse with due to a hint of a nascent sense of humour! She never knew but it seems her class of 1942 boasted no less than a future Minister! This is how she found out: Frank Iny the school was closed in August 1973 by government decree, and Sitt Semha, after thirty years of continuous employment, was for once at loose ends. She applied to the Ministry and was granted a pension, but there was a sting in the tail. She was required to pay more than a thousand pounds in arrears first. After deliberating how not to pay such a huge sum upfront, she wrote an *Areetha* (complaint) to the Minister to deduct this huge sum in instalments from each pension payment. Clever thinking that! But what chance of any sympathetic consideration could she command with the 1973 Arab Istraeli war still fresh in everyone's memory? She expected to be shoved right to the bottom of the list. But lo and behold she was contacted personally to come to the Ministry on such and such a day. There, a clerk came looking out for her expressly amongst the waiting crowd: "who is Semha Nessim?" he asked. To her eternal surprise she was distinguished in being taken to see the Minister earlier than everyone else, and then His Excellency himself getting up and coming to greet her at the door; with polite solicitude he helped her inside and into a chair. After a lifetime apart and very different fates and fortunes, still the spark of kinship from the teachers' college of their yourth had not disintegrated, and the Minister was exceedingly friendly!

Reminiscing from her Tel Aviv apartment she gets nearly tearful saying that she will recall his kindness with gratitude till her dying day. He took up her case immediately signing her papers on the spot and rebuking a clerk on the phone who might have been recalcitrant (as they were): "How can you not treat Sitt Semha well, she was our colleague from way back?" (*mu hathee Zameelatna men ceneen?*). Seeing the esteem in which the Minister held her electrified the other officials to do the same and her pension money was dispensed forthwith -minus the deductions of course! Subsequently she was paid regularly till she left for Turkey in 1976. With an eye on the changing times, she made a photocopy of the last cheque to show her former pupils so that they will ooh and aah a bit more at her exalted connections in power!

There have been other instances when Moslems have shown their genuine nature in assisting a Jewish friend who fell on hard times because of politics. There was a young lad, an orphan, who lived within the shelter of this well off family for a long time, earning his living by helping out in their factory! When Saddam came to power, at breathtaking speed because of his family connections, this simple lad found himself elevated to Ministerial level, while the same powers that be made his previously rich employers bereft (they ceased to be the flavour of the month). To compound it all, the head of the household had died and the family had no one to turn to: but this man never abandoned them and still visited to solicit their comfort, in the end procuring them through some *wasstatt* (connections) very rarefied passports indeed! It is stories like these that warm the cockles and tell you of true friendships between Jews and Arabs in Iraq, and how regretful that the whole structure is now no more.

Back to our Sitt: she points out the fact that nothing indecent or scandalous ever happened in the school even though it was mixed classes all the way. How wondrous is that? What she does not allude to is even more extraordinary: that there were no lectures or any psychological counselling to advise the pupils against any hanky panky, in fact the whole subject of sex was never referred to at all. The teachers did not issue warnings nor had discussions about any form of prevention or contraception. Might this not suggest that present day schools are shining too bright a torch on the subject, generating even more interest than warranted? But I will draw the line here and not dispense any advice; we all know that both our generation and its beliefs are archaic - and that is official.

On the other hand I can see that from the point of view of the staff, this state was synonymous with less trouble and to be welcomed, only (dare I whisper this) what harm would a few scandals have done? Everyone would have come to school more wide eyed and bushy tailed.

Let's try to disprove Sitt Semha: what about the teacher who kept fiddling all the while with his body parts in front of us girls? Not to be beaten, Sitt Semha has an answer to this one too. After the girl students complained of his behaviour, Istath Abdullah the Headmaster had a word with him and he went to the Doctor; it was all due to a hernia and an operation sorted it all out in no time at all.

I can only wish that we are able to teach the next generation some of those same very common sense principles that Sitt Semha managed to do; even thouh this was mostly done by forcibly ramming them down our throats!

An outing with the parents in Masbah

OF STINKBOMBS & CHEATS

Uncle Theota's was a trigonometry class which was taken by this middle aged shortish teacher in the late afternoons; it was slotted after the main classes had gone home. We were usually in a twitchy mode by then, having endured one class after another since eight A.M. in the morning. We called him Uncle Theota rather than Istath Selim because he always used angles called Theota or Alpha to demonstrate his theories! His mornings were spent working in a business environment which explained why he maintained a very formal tone with us and always came immaculately dressed in a suit with a white shirt and a tie. He gave a star rated performance whenever he suspected a pupil of not being attentive or giving of his best. So we really looked forward to this juicy bit:: with a deep scowl, he seized any books lying on the offending pupil's desk, banged them very hard in front of him, and finally exhausted his tantrum by sending them right up into the very lofty ceiling. There they made a resounding noise as they hit it with a big bang; in addition the force of this impact made them fall again with such a velocity that if they hit someone on the head which they often did, it was quite painful. In fact we all ducked not knowing where this Force will descend from in two minutes flat. Wizened boys like Sameer and Daoud, sitting in the front row, usually shielded their heads behind the narrow doors of their desks grimacing at us all the time to will us to laugh and get into trouble.

To cap it all it was very difficult to take the Istath seriously; he had only one very long grey strand near the top of his shiny bald head; this kept turning and switching sides, remaining most of the time in unsettled mode as he wrote on the blackboard.

Worryingly, this escapade that I am relating gives a whiff of latter day terrorism. Once a boy brought in exceedingly good bombs of the sulphuric acid type and tried to induce his colleagues to join him in the plot. He initially started by vehemently getting everyone to close the windows and the doors... the teacher caught him gesticulating so shouted at him and threw him outside the classroom, as per the typical Uncle Thoeta tactics. Full of youthful enterprise and sang froid the pupil still managed to detonate the bombs just before leaving. If you have never had the pleasure of coming across the path of an H2S bomb, they are like an all enveloping concentrated fart. We inside asphyxiated without air but dared not reveal the plot to the teacher. How can we? That would be telling on a fellow student and we were made of much sterner stuff *Honneur double Honneur*.

Uncle Thoeta turned menacingly It was all well worth it to see him pucker his brow as the stink hit him; of course being middle class, he acted puzzled in a non intrusive sort of way. His body language signifying "you mob have a real problem among yourselves, but people like me are above all that, so it behoves me not to investigate these lowly matters". He ordered us to open the windows saying there was a smell of rotten fish, but here was a sticky situation: our friend was simultaneously holding on to them from the outside for dear life so they would not budge. The final outcome being that we were caught in a stuffed up atmosphere, laughing so hard into our desks that we could hardly manage to breathe the foul air - while tears from the fumes ran down our cheeks and the gas blinded us.

BAGHDAD MEMORIES

Ah! How we survived this plot without the Headmaster knowing is in itself a miracle! The troublemaker escaped unscathed for once from his usual two weeks of "rest" at home, becoming a hero instead. The victory he earned us would live on throughout posterity. And so we kept repeating throughout the ages: Ya salaam, Ya Kamal.

Moments of glory were defined in the few instances we managed to trick our way into good marks in spite of the teacher of course! I will relate just such a light hearted escapade. "Moral Edicts" or *Wajeebat* in Arabic was a subject taught by this elderly Moslem man, Istath Yahyeh. It was a medley of social and religious Koranic rules which, though easy to understand, took a long time to learn by heart. As Mr Yahyeh also taught us history, for his own convenience he gave the exams on two consecutive days. It happened that while he was busy dictating the history questions on the first day, the two boys in the front row looked up to see that he had written the Wajeebat questions on the back of that same paper i.e. right in front of their eyes. So, an electric murmur swept through the classroom and we devised means of stalling the teacher's oral reading of that day's exam to give our friends plenty of time to write down the next day's instalments. When the history exam finished, all hell broke loose as we scrambled to get the stolen Wajeebat questions from the jubilant heroes. That night we sat down to compose the best essay paper in our life from the illegally begotten questions. This was followed by the next day's one and a half hours exam, when our only preoccupation was to bide our time and choose the best moment for substituting the paper on top of the desk with the much better written one underneath the desk. Here's a perfect one I prepared earlier Sir, extracting it proudly but discreetly, a bit like Delia Smith's faultless oven concoctions.

89

But there might be a problem: what if the teacher did not believe that we could all of us achieve such an immaculate standard? We needn't have worried in the least, our good man suspected nothing. Maybe he even patted himself on the back for doing such a good job as a teacher. So, happiness and elation all around. This escapade was repeated periodically with much hilarity and endless plotting (it united the class into a solid fraternity) till the end of the year exams. Hereafter conditions always changed for the worst i.e. became very very tough. Not even God is allowed to rescue the poor students then.

Isthath Yahyeh was religious so didn't want to have anything to do with us girls; that was so lucky! It was left to the boys to take the force of his punishment: while scolding them for their mistakes in the middle of the classroom, he would pull their ears very hard and very often and say: *Ichtishi Yawal Ma tichtishi?* (aren't you ashamed of yourself?)

The school report constituted the bane of our life in more ways than anyone can ever believe. It was a regular and long drawn out process: the Headmaster used to come to every classroom to present to each pupil this important piece of paper personally. He always handed it with a becomingly threatening look. It contained the grades of the exams for all of the twelve or thirteen subjects we were studying during the year and heralded much unwelcome turbulence both for us and for our family; we counted the days when these dreaded bulletins were due to be given out and anticipated the Headmaster's appearance days beforehand. He made a theatrical entrance carrying the fat bundle under his arm and, King of the Domain, interrupted the class for as long as it took. Beginning with the top three pupils whom he praised and shook hands with, and then losing patience as his estimation and respect deteriorated rapidly for all the other less deserving dupes. He finally reserved a really degrading piece of oratory for any of the students with a red mark on their bulletin. It was not always intentional on our part, the exams were dedicated to fleece us, but flimsy excuses did not wash. The rhetoric was very embarrassing in front of the whole class and the teacher, so that more often than not we (the girls) ended up crying silently at our desk. The boys especially if they answered back might be subjected to a more physical punishment i.e. a kick up the backside.

Homeward bound, there were still more challenges in the offing. The bulletins had to be signed by the head of the household, the Father, and so another round of retributions at home. How can my Father who was working day and night to the detriment of his health and with the sole purpose of giving us the chance of a decent education, end up with such ungrateful kids? He, unlike us lucky ones, had never had the chance to study because of the unfavourable circumstances prevailing in his youth. Even more to the point how can he ever expect to hold his head high again among his lucky friends, whose kids always came out in the top ten? My Father would not sign, he said categorically, he was too ashamed of his offspring, his heart was torn, damaged from the eternal suffering brought on by his childrens' unfeeling…the family name in the gutter… this and that disaster befalling soon etc. etc After a few grim days of supplications, when he still refused to look at the offending bulletin much less sign it – the more enterprising and desperate among us might sit down and imitate their Father's signature to get out of the impasse. Or we might even manage to recruit the Mother to soften his attitude. Only there had to be fresh conditions laid down and sworn to! It ended up being another court-martial, and the

91

crime was hung round our necks till the next bulletin's due date. Compared with the soft way that the kids of today are let off, whether they are football hooligans, drugsters or muggers, you can be sure that the nice social workers would not have approved of our treatment at all. What a contrast with the present day when society bows its head and blames itself! On the other hand while searching to find that proverbial rainbow I have concluded that doing battle against the elements year after year, turned us pupils into staunch allies for life.

To remain in viable mode, the school had to tow the line of the various revolutionary regimes. Thus in the summer of 1959, we returned to school during a stifling July to wind thousands of artificial flowers round wire stems. This was done to decorate our school's float as it took part in the revolution's first anniversary. The teachers chose a very pretty girl to dance on top of the float as it paraded in Rasheed Street. Later regimes stipulated a flag raising ceremony and singing of the national anthem once a week. Much later still and going steadily downhill because of the upsurge of political rhetoric, the community ceased to be regarded as a viable part of the nation. To attempt to lose its exclusive and dangerous Jewish character as well as provide it with influential friends, the Headmaster started to accept students from prominent Moslem and Christian families who were keen to join because of the high educational standards. Further down the line, we heard of demonstrations trying to come our way to wreak havoc and worse. That is when the Head put in an efficient system of evacuation so that a mob could find no one on the premises

As our community had numbered many more in the past tense, so they had much more clout in the country; by contrast dwindling numbers meant our generation had to accept a significant drop in power and prestige. There were no alternative avenues but to turn submissive and accepting, and our lives became defined by the Headmaster's threats, our teachers' sombre words, and the latest exam grades.

The curriculum was hard and tortuous; in addition to the official public exams set by the government, it was decreed that the pupils should sit further papers from abroad. Surely this involved studying many different curriculums at once. It was usually at the end of the year when we might make a trip to the Wazeeriya where the British Embassy was located (the French Consulate was in Alwiyyah) and where the certified papers were imported along with qualified invigilators. Difficult was an understatement to describe the multitude of agendas we needed to take on board. The only distinct advantage was that once the entire nightmare finished, we found ourselves on such a promontory, that we could sit the public exams without any formal teaching! That was the opinion of Mr Abdullah anyway who would not touch most of the subjects during the year, but gave us a month before this very important Baccalaureat to do a DIY self cramming Odyssey! Of course the girls were frightened and did not budge from the house at all, while the boys on the other hand had to have their football breaks but put in an immense effort nevertheless.

As there was no formal sex education in the school, teaching plant insemination was supposed to indirectly shed a light on the process. The teacher who taught it was aware of the intent, so stammered continuously assuming we did not have a clue. To spare his blushes, we abstained from asking any questions. On the whole though, we judged his methods to compare primitively to Lady Chatterly's Lover; this book was discovered in a bookshop by an enterprising boy the summer before. He underlined in red all the juicy bits and circulated it very widely among us lot. And by all counts, he should have given a copy to the teacher too.

I must allude to the undeniable change that occurred in our lives and culture after the 1950 mass exodus! Maybe because there were not so many customs to observe anymore as their long-established bastions left! For example in my case I had no senior relatives to advise me or tell me stories of another age, neither did I have anyone around to set me on the path of the old traditions and the old values. This was true across the board, so that the community needed to branch off in new directions; thus new teachers' new businesses and new business partners – It needed to hire alternative seamstresses and craftsmen, search for different landlords, doctors and lawyers. In most of these cases, these people were not Jewish. People started to shed an ancient ethnic image leading them to integrate more into the Iraqi way of life. These changes extended to include the names we were called as well. Whereas in my grandMother's era, women were called archaic names like Chahla, Nasskhia, Gurgia, Farha, Mass'ouda, Salha, and Lulwa these later on became an object of derision to us. My generation and my parents' generation boasted English and French names. Thus Albertine, Claire, Doris, Iris, Esperance and Joyce. In the same vein men used to be known as Daoud, Efraim, Haron, Heskel, Obadia and Saleh, but now they were Danny, Eddie,Freddie, George, Ronnie and Sammy.

Of course the Alliance had the root influence in educating the parents to be open to other languages and civilizations, but for my generation it was definitely Frank Iny; its choice of curriculum and teachers was both very liberal and liberating at the same time...

Everything European began to be perceived as more trendy and advanced, whether in dress, entertainment like films and songs, or literature such as magazines and books. My generation tried to espouse it as much as possible. We imagined the West to be that place of colourful variety, vibrancy, and most importantly freedom of the sexes: how we envied them their ability to mingle and go out on dates without the constant dictates of the parents.

Before they left Iraq, the Jews inhabited places like Al Sunnak, Taht al Takya, Souq Hannoun, Abu Seefein, QanbarAli, Aqd al Nassara…now nobody would touch them, they were considered dirty and antiquated. We presently sought the more open and much leafier suburbs of Alwiyah, Masbah, and Hindiyya. Indeed, in my generation, these ancient places were forever more referred to in a derogatory and derisory way. For example if people are swearing they will be told they belong to Abu Seffein, if I bought an item of dress which is not up to the standard required, my Mother will say it looks like I have bought it from Souq Hannoun, or if a place is too far to reach they will say it is situated in Qanbar Ali; hence advances in civilization! Another welcome change: young couples stopped living together with their parents and raising their families in the same huge house as the husband's Father, even though that must have been such fun for the kids. Instead they needed to purchase a house before the marriage took place or at least be seen to build one to move into! The outcome being that the young wife did not have to submit very meekly to her Mother in law's authority and dictatorship for years and years to come. No chance therefore of re-enacting the notorious disputes between the *Channa wa Martel amm* (the daughter and her Mother in law). The new couples must aspire to set up on their own with a deep sigh of relief from the paternal influence and aim towards some independence.

Kaddouri, Raina and Samir with our family

MALAAB (SPORTSGROUND)

We are gratefully indebted for the endowment of this building to Mr Ezra Menahem Daniel, who also bequeathed all his riches to the community and yes, they are still waiting there; proceeds from their rents can be dispensed on the community as long as they live in Iraq. Malaab means just a playground in Arabic but to our generation it was a home away from home.

The Malaab started as an extension of the Frank Iny and Ezra Menahem feeder school in the Senak, to allow their students to relax and play sport; poor souls they needed to get the blood circulation going after a whole week spent hunched up at the desk. It was a solid concrete building, modern and very open, the grounds mostly roofless except in the two areas of the changing rooms and the snack bar! The gigantic iron doors pushed to reveal an impressive circular garden. All around were strewn fields and courtyards for playing various sports: a volleyball court for the girls which could also be transformed into basketball stadium for the boys in a jiffy. If a boy felt inclined to do so, and was enthusiastic to boot, there was no dearth of occupations : football, javelin, disc throwing, long jump on the sandy area, as well as pole vaulting; while both he or she could practise walking or jogging around the bigger roundabout too. In the Malaab it was freedom without curtailment or limitation, no censure on any of the games, and no buying tickets to participate in any event. The most popular pastime was ping pong as it could be practised day and night in the marble enclosure even while the rest of the Malaab remained dark and deserted! The girls found this game's social aspect to their liking! It was an excuse for the boy to buy his partner a coke and crisps to share together from Ammi Hassan at the bar.

Surprisingly the two and a half tennis courts were no less busy, though only in the daylight as darkness must stop play! Friday and Saturday afternoons in the winter were their most busy; we wore white shirts with either white or black skirts or longish shorts, and snow white Bata trainers (the old kind, they were paper thin); in the summer, we played in the evenings just before twilight and we sometimes had to await our turn alongside the few seasoned addicts and a queue. There was no instructor, and that is why I developed a "wonky" serve and maintained it all my life. There was also a *ta-ssa* (bump) in one of the courts which we had to negotiate carefully and as there were no boundaries, the tennis balls did fly everywhere - so we shouted at all and sundry to get them sent back. It proved yet another way of social interaction and having fun. But once over the high wall, the ball was irrevocably lost so my partner and I took turns to replenish an expensive arsenal.

Just outside the tennis courts, in a darkish corner stood a wooden horse covered in leather for the budding gymnasts; near it a heavy punching bag hung from the ceiling for boxing practice. The little ones might have an egg and spoon race, a potato sack race, or whatever their Saturday teacher came up with! It was all worth it on Prize Day when cups were won by the best players! On those days the "adults" were admitted to distribute the prizes: they were the distinguished guests, the pillars of the community! The varied games took until night time to finish so that the heroes were given the cups under the tall spotlights and the stars: and that is how unknown students rose to fame and heroism, while everyone clapped like mad. Their parents' living room would grace the cups forevermore!

This pattern of going to the Malaab included attending it on Saturday mornings in the winter, when sunny. No, we did not make the most of it, guilty of course, especially the girls, as we liked to gossip and to stand coquettishly around watching the players do the work! It was quite ok to come in our best clothes, with heels to boot! But we did proffer much needed encouragement to the team, especially if it included some of the boys we liked. I imagine that formed the most important impetus for them to win too.

Being handed a cup always proved exciting to the throng

If the players were putting in an extraordinary effort, an injury (or altercation) might follow, and so they were taken to Khaddouri Chinqo's house. He had a knack of putting all the bones back where they should be, whether by cracking, bending or massaging them! Though just an amateur; his manipulations always did the trick, but they hurt! No money ever changed hands though; it was all based on bonhomie and trust!

I often wonder how the Malaab has fared in the later days. Are the same grounds flooded with light at night, is the shop still selling the cokes and the crisps? No ill will towards the present occupiers, but do remember us sometimes. This piece of land used to be our treasure island; can you appreciate how unwillingly we gave it up? We were not even allowed to raise a clenched little fist!

SOCIALISING

I accompanied my parents out a lot in those days, as kids did not have a lot going for them socially. On these occasions, children and teenagers visited their parents' friends; we dressed up very nicely and were under a strict code to behave in exactly the way that the elders expected children to

Jallalleh games and fun

behave. The hospitality pattern was always carefully followed as in Iraq the guest is very important, while the host is expected to treat a guest with even more generosity than members of his own household. The setting more often than not would be the garden which was used all year round. In the winter, you sat in its sunshine during the day, and in the summer, you sat there early in the morning and from evening till late at night. Every household had a *Jellallah* (a huge swing)) which was adequate for three or four people and the rest of the guests sat on chairs in a circle all around it. The graceful ladies followed by their men folk will step in gingerly mindful of their high heels sinking in the grass, dressed in sleeveless homemade clothes saying: "*Messel khair*" with pursed lips. This was a rather stylish play on the more common greeting of good evening.

The hospitality always followed the same pattern. First everyone was offered a toffee from a central silver dish, and the polite guest will not just take the toffee but will make out they do not want the toffee...it is not nice for strangers to think that you have no toffees in your house and need to go to other people's houses to eat toffees. After five minutes exactly, cold drinks with ice (usually coke or fanta) were proffered on a tray, and the same principle applies...as the girl bends down with a little bow to allow the drinks to come to the same level as the guest's face, the guest makes out that they are beyond such common needs: *La, la*: Meir-ci, (French for thank you but pronounced longer) so that the girl has to tout around quite a few times telling the guests you must, you must , you need to drink. Hot on the heels of this, there would be freshly boiled Turkish coffee in dainty little cups on a silver tray, as well as accompanying glasses of iced cold water balancing precariously beside: and the well-bred guest was the one who exclaimed "Oh no, we did not come to bother you and eat, we do not want anything, please sit down! I am so full, in fact I have just had one at home on the way out"; in which case the good hostess will repeat that it does not harm anyone to drink yet another cup of coffee, and that we will not enjoy the partaking unless our guest shared it with us. This altercation ended in the guest, as if forced to do so, taking one from the tray and saying a very dainty "Me-rci".

After the coffee by ten minutes they put out the little plates with a napkin on tiny tables in front of each visitor for the home baked *makhbou,z,* pstrries stuffed with cheese or nuts or dates. The hosts went round and round saying *Abdallek* (an emotive please) with the large serving plates till the guests deigned to choose some and deposit them on their own plates, as initially nobody was hungry. In dire circumstances the hosts threatened their guests saying we will not speak with you anymore if you do not take, or my Mother will be so upset, or even that we will boycott coming to your house forevermore!

In addition, the rule was never to finish the plate completely as *EIB (socially embarrassing).* The stigma held that in doing so you are showing signs of gluttony or even worse, that minginess prevailed in your household! Throughout all the above, the host or hostess kept turning round in a clockwise direction offering *charazat* simultaneously from the various containers lying on the main table. They were mostly fried almonds, sunflower seeds, chickpeas and pistachios. But we only took very few at a time as my Mother thought we might be giving away the wrong signals. After that if the weather had turned cold they would bring forth the *istikannat chay (*tea cups*),* or if it was hot they would bring in ice creams or both, if the guests tarried a while. God forbid anyone should accuse them of being stingy with visitors. On the contrary the reputation that everyone had to strive for always was *Eedayhum maftouha* (open-handed) like the mythical Arabic figure of Hatim al Ta-ee.

Whenever visitors came to a house, they would shake everyone's hands in parting and if there is a young or not so young girl in the house, they will say *be'frahha* to each of the parents, to the girl *be'frahhek.* This meant that we hope to celebrate your wedding very soon. This started when the girl was barely twelve years old, and then continued till she was married. After a few years of this, the poor girl automatically begins to think that she should be getting married as soon as she can to prevent people getting worn out waiting or even that she should have been already married off a long time ago. The more trendy kids took the mickey at this tradition and would say to the girl *B'frakheck*, which means I hope you have a multitude of small chicks. The accompanying peals of laughter took away the tragic element from the disastrous meaning.

This custom is dying out anyway: the girls themselves do not feel that the ultimate goal in life is to get married, unlike previous generations, and why should they? Society has opened its gates for them and they are allowed to go much further afield and obtain a worthy career first and foremost. Only then do the eternal matrimonial aspects need to loom in the horizon.

On one of those outings with my Mother I remember there was a lady who was not really known to my parents but was a distant relative of the host. As we finished drinking the Turkish coffee, my parents like everyone else turned their cups upside down. The rule requires the cup to be left to settle for 5 minutes, so the impressions become solid, only then giving it to someone recommended as knowing how to "read" its filigree patterns. The unknown is called *faal* and the person who knows how to read it is called *Fattah faal* (soothsayer). My Mother after dutifully waiting for the mud to settle and as she was told that the lady was a good *fattahat faal*- a bit like magical powers her skills were inborn -she entrusted her cup to her. The lady looked at my Mother and said "you will be the recipient of good news concerning your family soon; there will be a marriage among your close relatives, although you will not attend it.

Later on she also happened to pick up my Father's cup and without knowing it was her husband, she said exactly the the same words to him. At home now, my parents agreed as to the doubtfulness of this lady's skills, as she repeated exactly the same story to both!

What was their surprise when a month later, they heard from indirect channels abroad, that my Father's brother became engaged to my Mother's sister so that both of the stories corroborated nicely, and that led the way to a lifetime of believing in the "design" of those coffee cups. All Iraqis will have a similar story which verges on the supernatural to explain their total reliance on them too

Reading is deciphering what the shapes are; you keep peering into the cup to catch the light until you can spin a convincing story. No, no, I mean till you can see what the future holds: Birds (a trip is beckoning), fish (money is coming your way), open routes is a project that will be successfully completed, closed lanes: not so successful. Many people together herald an invitation to a party! If there are many many mountains and valleys, lanes and roads, then you say to the poor client "you have a lot of problems on your mind and you had better take it easy, but don't you fret, they will solve themselves with God's help"! I, along with everyone else used to beg to have all the luck read, but recently have begun to realise that it all depended on the amount of coffee the hostess put in the pot to start off with! On the other hand I might be turning sarcastic in my old age. Of course it all makes for an enjoyable social gathering, fragrant too if you don't forget to add the cardamom.

Most girls of my acquaintance also swear by the soothsayer talents of this or that "*Arrafá*" who has predicted many things, or described a future husband even before the girl met him. What lends a creepy dimension to these prophecies is the fact that most of those women are blind but can see very well into the past and the future both.

Still on the subject of the surreal, my parents were once sitting outside at my Mom's uncle's house in his courtyard, relaxing in their big j*allallah* and having a very pleasant time. All of a sudden my Father had this inexplicable desire to go home immediately, even before coffee was served! The astonished hosts tried to persuade him to stay put as did my Mother (it just was not done) but he said they must go back. In the event it was lucky that they did as the young maid had gone to sleep leaving the iron on, and very soon the room where we all slept together – safety in numbers they say - would have gone up in smoke.

As I have hinted before, your life was all about exams. Failing was not an option. At best your parents, if on your side, will have a row with the Headmaster which looks bad in the community. At worst you will get expelled. Where would this leave you? Without this community school, you will be out on a limb so far as friends and academic excellence go!

Most of us had to be clever to survive. When you did not catch on you repeated the class: once, two times up to three. Then the system coughs you out! To avoid such a fate was our challenge, our nightmare and that of our parents too.

At exam time, the only affordable pastime was to puzzle out the next day's questions. You tried everything: sussing out the teacher's hints or psychological give aways, even quizzing older students about former papers. Still the most ingenious method was given us one day after a particularly hard exam where we were sure the teacher wanted everyone to fail. It boasted several brave new and unorthodox steps.

My friends: it was the Ouija board. Who came up with it, I cannot remember. But ten of us who lived not far from each other, walking astride homebound, found ourselves discussing the new method heatedly and later with enthusiasm. To be sure, if it could provide us with a question or two, then we were prepared to walk any distance.

Soon, one braver boy emerged from the crowd as we neared his house and offered it to us to experiment. We espoused it 100%. His Mother was taken aback to see descending upon her a horde of schoolkids, but thought it was an educational exercise of benefit to her son's future. So she made us welcome, even brought us cups of steaming Turkish coffee on a silver tray and then retired to another room. It was a big house and we felt blissfully undisturbed. Our friend acted very much the confident master. He found us a table which turned out to be his Mother's bridge table and then someone said you had to write the alphabet letters on it…no problem, he went and brought one of his Mother's shiny red lipsticks; we did not want to know if he had asked for her consent? A girl proceeded by trial and error to fit all the alphabet letters round the square table and that is how we embarked on the scary procedure .

Through the medium of the cup, we got in touch with a lot of spirits. We asked them questions about the morrow's exams and studied whatever they pointed to; at certain times it got pretty terrifying when the spirit did not like us or said they were killed by some horrible method! However, the friendlier ones led us to some questions! Letter by letter the cup went in all directions on the Board to make up the words of the all important questions. When the cup went very slowly, so we

107

decided the spirit had become tired. We thanked him, and released him by blowing him away! At home in the evening, we concentrated on those particular questions but unfortunately they proved to be at most mere pointers or downright hit and miss! Unconcerned, we continued to convene thus every day to ask for the morrow's exam questions. And then a great uncle got a whiff of the proceedings and stopped them short, saying they were against the religion; so we ceased going further down that track!

Some boys did fall off the straight and narrow, and brought eternal embarrassment and shame to their family...no, I don't mean they stole or shot anybody much less had a clandestine relationship or illegitimate babies, no: simply that they refused to impound their adolescent life to school work and its multiple demands. One was Sammy who, having experienced at one time a much more liberal school life in Beirut agitated for freedom rather than a slavish existence. He was charming with all particularly the girls: it was rumoured that he had girlfriends both inside and outside the fraternity; he was also fun loving, a bit cosmopolitan, a bit spoiled...which attributes put him in the Headmaster's black books instantly. His parents were worried seeing that his nonchalance meant that he had already repeated a few classes, and they were also warned that he might get expelled if he did not do better in the end of year exams. Nevertheless, he assured them that everything was under control.

When the results came out validating the Headmaster's opinion that he was not capable of serious application, Sammy panicked no end and felt unable to face the music at home, so decided to run away. As we lived near, his Mother came to our house to ask if we knew of his whereabouts. At first we were of the opinion that he might have gone to one of his friends for a chat. Later on in the evening, his Mom took the car and dropped in on all the kids he hung out with but they denied having seen him on that day! Everyone started phoning around frenziedly, congregating in our house to give all sorts of theories, opinions and bulletins; we had never been faced with such an issue before! By 6:30 pm his Mother, realizing something sinister had happened to her only son made the Father leave his work to go to the police! In those days the crime rate was almost nonexistent and people never disappeared - so excitement mounted when along with the news bulletin we heard the police giving out data about Sammy's height, the colour of his eyes, where he lived. He had become famous, and his glory must surely reflect on us - his friends! By 8pm his Father was in the front seat of the police car, combing all of Baghdad! This hero's standing has risen quite a few notches in the county and he has become a VIP no less, while his Mother had become hysterical! The bulletins on the radio were getting more frequent and had a pleading tone to them. All of Baghdad, it seemed, was on tenterhooks. We started to remember his good qualities like opening the door and being charming to the girls rather than his rogue ones i.e. opening the toilet in his house where he kept two huge dogs locked up; he did this without any warning to visitors to enjoy hearing their terrified screams when the animals bounded menacingly on them.

By now several parents had taken to their cars as well and started looking around aimlessly. There followed more drama: his sister found a note in his room saying he has decided to commit suicide so as not to shame his family because he could not get good marks however hard he tried! This made his Father instantly go to the radio station and record a speech saying that we, your Father and Mother don't care a hoot about the exams, we just love our son and want him back! Finally, at about 10 pm, a police officer spotted him, sitting on a bench in the open park! (The police officer later swore that they had been through that park many times before without finding him). Sammy said he had been perched on a tree the whole day, eating of its fruit. From his lofty seat he looked on calmly as the police and everyone else drove furiously past: but in the end he started to miss his parents - and a good meal no doubt, and that is why he finally came down! No one could quarrel with such common sense.

When the police at last reunited him with his parents well past our usual bedtime, we felt guilty rather that we had not been more attuned to his hard life. He was given a hero's welcome by all and feted the whole week as someone lost and come back from the other world. Without any further recrimination, his parents quickly removed him to another less demanding school! We had to hand it to him, a very enterprising boy!

Once, in the 1960's, all Baghdad was stunned when Israel Broadcasting claimed to have obtained copies of the Baccalaureat exam questions and broadcast them at 10 pm just after the news bulletin in Arabic! Some friends read me all the questions on the phone nearer midnight, so that I spent the rest of the night preparing entirely for them, ignoring the rest of the material. It involved resolving intricate maths problems and more and took up hours. But it transpired that the government of the day caught a scent of the illegal proceedings so switched them around at six o'clock in the morning (worse luck). When we arrived to the exam hall at eight, we saw that the teacher did not behave as his usual self, saying he was waiting for a taxi to find out the contents of the exam questions. Normally, these were typed weeks in advance.

As the special delivery arrived, he then proceeded to dictate them orally into our textbooks

Surprisingly for such a bashful lot of teenagers, we started having house parties in our middle teen years. Parties meant nearly the whole class congregating in someone's house on a Saturday night where a Mother had put together some food plates, and there would be a bit of western music and dancing. In the whole of the class there was only one boy with a reliable tape recorder and lucky for us he liked to record a lot of songs: there were no records to buy. With a lot of patience, he would tune in on "Voice of America" which broadcast from Beirut, and whenever a nice song turned up, fiddled with the requisite wires and buttons to tape it. George was very good at French, so most of the songs he recorded were French, sung by Enrico Massias and Charles Aznavour exclusively, while the glamorous gatherings depended on him not forgetting to bring in his mammoth tape recorder.

In those days, a girl had to sit down demurely and wait for a boy to take the first step and ask her to dance. A bit unfair don't you think this? It was "not done" at all for a girl to get up and take the initiative. One more rule to restrict an already constricted life

In later years, there was a lot of pairing off, so these parties acquired an atmosphere of predictability. But the atmosphere never was for "painting the town red, it was for dancing in a room along with many others" Even though there was the alternative of dancing closer still, it was all above board as the one room had to contain everything and everybody. I am sorry if I am disappointing everyone here, but my powers of narration cannot be allowed to spin stories more interesting than the actualiy.

When the rock and roll craze was sweeping the world, wonder of wonders, it made it to Baghdad as well! We girls started practising in earnest in each other's houses! It was a time for some great body gyrations.

My parents had a totally different social life; it was much livelier and sophisticated. They went by their own rules, so played cards in each other's houses, went for bingo sessions at the Mansour or sometimes for a dance in alMassbah. But mostly it was congregating for cards and a dinner; all the ladies took it in turn to invite the crowd according to a sacrosanct list. They played poker, concan and pinnacle against token money to pass the time in a social context. Bridge came much later and was mostly for the ladies! Some men did not like cards, so they played shesh besh (backgammon); this popular game involved two opponents trying with the help of a pair of dice to gather fifteen counters into one space. There were times when it got very racy a bit like Ascot without the aristocracy i.e. if you needed a six to kill your opponent's counter, then everyone will start shouting "*walak sheish*" or if you needed a three they will shout "*walak Cei*". If the dice showed a double four, then they will exclaim: "Do jahar". Five was a panj, one was a yakk. These were all Turkish expressions and inherited from *Ayyam al Ossmalli* (Ottomans' ancient lore) via the Dads. The ladies took a lot of care in dressing up according to the latest fashions while attending those get togethers; as for high heels, nobody left the house without them.

IN PUREEM THE PERSIANS DREW LOTS

Purim was that magical holiday bang in the midst of a depressing and demanding winter term. The day before, my Father along with all the other Fathers, made a special journey to the bank to withdraw the new coins to give to us. It was not everyday money, it had to be newly minted never handled, consequently shone shone shone. Fatherly love, Fatherly generosity, and fingering them gently, like a long lost friend, we found that for once, our souls connected instantly with our religion. The money was never for spending no, no; though even better, it was for playing cards. And what a pleasure it is to play cards with someone else's money. For once there was something positive in being Jewish in Iraq. Religion dictated that you play cards, religion dictated that you enjoyed it, that society aided and abetted you. For once religion was on the side of decadence. We grasped the opportunity with open arms.

I will tell you the whys and wherefores and then you can join in the fun. Thousands of years ago, there was a VIP Persian king "Cyrus" with a rogue Minister "Haman" who decided to kill all the Jews, as they do. By a series of clever manoeuvres: there were dances, there were fasts and whatever the beautiful Esther and the old man Mordechai came up with - the tables were turned on Haman and he got hanged instead. As it was all touch and go meaning a gamble, we commemorate the overall sanctity of the tale by playing cards.

The joker in the pack of cards is called Haman who becomes the devil that he was. As for the whiff of strong seduction between the King and his Queen and how it all smoothed the way, we were never allowed to exploit that side of things, as social decorum would not have wanted us to imitate them.

The time before the holiday was consecrated to laying down the battlelines: the only criterion being to be out on the streets all day every day. At school for six days a week purgatory, we knew we had to live out a break like this to the full. Usually each class would be trundling to the same venue, but there were also separate girls only and boys' only sessions. The schedule was gruelling though; for example the first invite would be for 10 A.M. on the morning of the first day. The Mother, bless her , turned her house into a gambling den by disguising the dinner and any household tables with nice tablecloths, putting 2 sets of playing cards on each. We only played *dossa* and *naqsh*, none of which was rocket science. In *Dossa* whoever revealed the highest card in the pile, won the money resting on top of the other people's piles. In *Naqsh* you were given cards with the purpose of attaining 15 or 31 points. But you could also hedge your bet by 'sleeping' in between for a while. The boys tried to show off and didn't mind the higher stakes in poker. Play was exciting, play was emotional, and play was raucous forevermore.

All this mental activity required energy which could only be provided by top quality carbohydrates. To this end, the hostess lovingly prepared scrumptious little somethings: sour sheets of apricot dried in the sun, coconut stars dripping with rose water, baklavas oozing with syrup, manna from Persia, tiny moon pastries filled with white cheese / almonds and dates,: all oh so exotic! I don't know if we ever had the time to fully appreciate such delicacies, or realise how odd it was for us to be flourishing thus under dark skies. We were far too busy mapping out a strategy that would win us piles and piles of money.

Think lucky they say! But if you are down on your luck, you'd clutch at anything. Find a rabbit's claw or something blue or make a bargain with God…

At 1 pm taking pity on our hostess, we take our custom and purses elsewhere. A table of finger varieties greets us for lunch: (chicken kubbas, meat kubbas, fish kubbas and potato kubbas), for sure my friend's Mother has been busy!   Food does help the concentration when you need to make a fortune or lose a fortune! Back to the real business of the day: what is this on the table? An Ace! Who cut this disastrous deal, you, *aya jahesh* never more will we allow you to choose the dealer's pile, you have broken the bank! Now we have to hand in triple the money, our profits gone! Oh for the vagaries of the cards ….hey, it is not just a game it is a social occasion too! Enjoy!

Approximately four o'clock we hurried home to put on another set of glad rags, it was a must to look your smartest in a festival. White socks, new shoes, ribbons in the hair, and for the girls all the gold bracelets and amulets in the cupboard. It was supposed to be a happy parade, a parade for the world to admire.

Later on, we needed our parents to fill in the evening session. That was Pureem's biggest thrill coming up: the licence to go out with grownups at night. To be treated on an equal footing, that was elevation indeed.   We anchored ourselves round the same card table as them and dealt to kill. When I say equal footing it was also combined with a special status: It meant if you were winning well and good, but if you were losing and had a long face, someone might dive under the table and swear you have dropped money and return it to you. A luckier "uncle" will make you a partner and entitled to all his winnings on the spot; another will persuade you to accept money left mysteriously on the table ....adults rounded up my day nicely.

In the event of a major money crisis when for example the tide of chance has been truly catastrophic, the parents could be depended on to add a few pounds to the empty kitty.

The second day it was back to the grind, observing the same religious rites as the first day which dictated staying outdoors, walking mostly. The weather was always fine in the spring while the heated conversation was all about the exciting manifestations of the game. We must have formed quite a cavalcade as sometimes we were required to let the younger siblings tag along too. Out with your parents at night though, you tended not to stay late as school reared the next day like an inevitable destiny! I looked surreptiously at what remained of my money: it reverted to me now, no more gambling allowed.

Purim is such a comedy act. Now that it has finished we must let the main actors exit for another year: first, the old man Mordechai on the back of his resplendent donkey is being led by the town crier; then the plump king Cyrus dripping with jewels on a white richly decorated horse preceded by dark slave drummers and exotic girl dancers. Esther in her sumptuous robe and sword is swallowed (majestically) back into the Harem- you can't help wishing the poor girl had a walkie talkie to the King's chamber instead of having to fast every time she wants to say hello. Haman is dead, but we will blow life into him again next year as he provides the fun element of the festival. Actually all those characters were alive and well two thousand five hundred years ago.

By hook or by crook, God in his munificence has allowed us to let loose for two whole days, with all the

116

religious bodies and an austere government looking on. But shush, gambling is strictly forbidden in Iraq.

There were many ways to flash out what remained of the money: boiled sweets, crisps and cinema tickets. The stern Headmaster inflicted his revenge on us for having had our fling in broad daylight, so instructed the teachers to concoct harder exam questions. Back to studying in earnest.

Today the children disguise themselves and become exotic creatures. Ours was a different era, we did it another way, we did it our way!

We had the money to buy sweets from Abu el Nestela

SKIRTS, BUT NOT TOO SHORT

For the girls, the ethos was all about looking good and dressing even better; the community demanded very strict allegiance to both of these principles:

In 1965 the government of the day was trying to seize on yet some more issues to create a diversion from the real problems of the day. Despite those public relation exercises though, the trend was not religious at all. All the girl friends wore shortish uniforms, and we never needed to cover our heads or wear an abbaya. Normal was practical. My Mother had never worn the veil either, neither did any of her acquaintances or relatives. Middle class people didn't, not in the leafier suburbs where we lived anyway. We girls went to cinemas in the daytime, rode on buses, window shopped; nobody ever mentioned the veil except as part of ancient lore. And we always looked forward to the latest trends in fashion as unravelled every year in the West. Even though acquiring the clothes was nigh impossible, we still needed to copy them somehow. Recalling it all again, I have the impression we must have been quite trendy.

As most of us had curly hair, of course we would have given anything to be born with straight hair! Curly hair was the bane of my life, and I remember one day when I was 10, being sat in front of the mirror and inculcated with the old adage: "*il faut souffrir pour etre belle*" (it is worthwhile suffering pain to become beautiful); briefly my Mother and her neighbour laid a horrible smelling pink paste on my hair, and I had to leave it on even while it was giving me an acute smouldering sensation. It soon started smelling of burnt fuse. I began to cry. It was very lucky my hair did not fall what with it being a

118

German product and the instructions written in that language exclusively. No, we didn't do German. It did make the hair very straight though so everyone patted themselves on the back and boasted of a new expertise.

A quicker DIY method in hair straightening later on was to kneel onto the ironing board and have someone iron it on top of a muslin cloth! Yet another beauty project I remember well was when they squashed a huge quantity of strawberries in the kitchen and slobbered the paste all over my face; it started to sting and I started to want to scratch and squirm but was advised to sit still. This treatment required two whole hours to be effective but was said to prevent the *Baghdad* virus from deforming the skin; it only happened in Iraq and to give it its due, this exotic cure did deliver.

The best beauty aid came to our doorstep in 1956 when a Lebanese hairdresser (Cleopatra) opened a salon in Battaween! Tall dark and very slim, with a dapper moustache and a smattering of elegant French terms, Monsieur Georges reeked of glamour (he called each client Madame or Mlle); all the ladies began going on a pilgrimage to his lair at least once a week. It did not matter in the least that right outside this smart salon the running rivulet in the middle of the street featured schools of ducks minding their own business. As the salon was at the top end of our road, my Mother as well as other lucky neighbours were treated to an extra backcombing session in the middle of the week. In Iraq, it is universally accepted that the Lebanese are ultra capable, so the smart ladies attended the salon to look dazzling. The treatments alternated between a cut with *misenplis* in different sized rollers, or adding colour in a credible shade of blonde. It was sufficient for any lady to say that she has been under M. Georges's hood to go up a few notches in everyone's esteem.

To prove it they related snippets of his hip conversations! Anything French sniffed of the latest chic!

My memories of the salon are not entirely positive. I was marched there as an eight year old to have both long plaits drastically shorn right from their roots. M. Georges maintained that the very short hairstyle that he subsequently gave me made me look very French, which accolade was supposed to be the best of compliments. But I maintain that with my long neck, he made me look instead like a shorn chicken. While the important thing hinged on him saving my Mother and the maid valuable time and hassle in the morning rush! Mark my words it must have been a double conspiracy.

Whenever there was a wedding, the bride and her extended family descended on the salon, and regular customers had to do battle to get in. This is surely one of my favourite stories: it concerns this lady of our acquaintance who was invited to a big wedding to go to. She was very lucky that the hairdresser conceded her a rare appointment view the above *khabssa* (crowd); so, after spending a whole hour under the *sechoir* (hairdryer) on a scorching day, and then another hour to have her hair teased as high as possible and sprayed, she arrived home in such a hot and bothered condition that the first thing she did was to stand under the shower! Refreshed by now, only then could she think straight and realised that she had unwittingly wet her hair, and it was looking very much like its regular silver wire state. How can she go to a smart wedding looking like a *Ghissalla* (washerwoman)? She had no alternative but to head straight back to M Georges and literally beg for another session. He was sympathetic enough to let her wait for another turn in the long queue and luckier still: Umm Nouri's sense of humour saved the day.

If you live in Iraq, beware of the ill wind that can turn social customs against its citizens. On an ordinary school day, a girl brought some woeful news. It seems that that same afternoon in the main shopping street in Baghdad, the soldiers under order of the government had stopped some women accusing them of wearing their skirts too short. Instantaneously they submitted them to the ultimate decency test. The soldiers measured the distance covered or uncovered between the knee and the upper skirt, and if it was less or more than the prescribed height, depending on the geography and the anatomy, and which side you were on, the women were in for the worst nightmare imaginable: each of them had to have her legs painted black. It was very summarily done; you went under the brush on the spot. Think of painting a column twice – Titillation was not a word to be used in this dictionary. Nevertheless, the soldiers no doubt were having the time of their lives while in our class there was no end of consternation. What on earth are we supposed to do, and how to get home in case the soldiers were lying in wait in the surrounding area, eager for once, to implement the law of the land?

In those days trousers had not come into their own yet! You only wore the loose variety when you did PE in the younger classes. All our lives, soldiers were a horror that never happened to us, only to other people, and to have to undergo such shameful treatment! Could we ever face the world again with the memory of the painted black legs? We had visions of them turning up at school, starting the proceedings with the woman Vice Principal and some of the younger teachers. (This part though went down hilariously well with us all).

In Iraq power was at best transient, which made the politicians look over their shoulders constantly, trying to suss out the next plot in the making. Whereas fear of the nastiness of the regime made the public hedge in cooperating with its enemies (the real real bastards). I know this is tortuous reasoning but is the best I can do. While even by the above measures, this latest manoeuvre was quite a bit below the belt! If their sole worry was of a moral nature, then they could have used beige paint or summoned the girl to court to cough up a fine. Travelling by car did not guarantee safety either because we heard that some girls were forced to step down and a mischievous tape produced.

The parents, alerted by the teachers' summons from the only telephone in the school, came to pick up anyone in need of a lift by car, and brought some reinforcing garments for the journey. Our class piled in a beetle car, twelve girls at once. We were size eight all otherwise it would have collapsed! The next day, we let down the waist of the skirts to touch the ground, or borrowed stock that had belonged to bemused grandMothers. As some discovered, a billowing black tent hid the transgression completely, and still does!

Well, I agree, making fun of girls is infinitely more enjoyable than plotting grimly against the regime, so friend and foe alike were diverted by this comic thrill. More important still, it won the approval of the religious leaders. Thank God all these tricks did not last long. Soon enough we were informed through the channels that the all clear had sounded and that there were no more soldiers to jump onto a skirt excuse.

Life hobbled on, never normal, never boring! Politics provided the fun and games to those in need of a lot deal more.

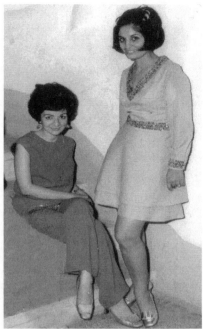

Fashion was freely interpreted in most cases

THE RIVER TIGRIS IS DIJLAH

The River Tigris was that permeating presence winding itself round our lives winter and summer, day and night. It cut Baghdad into half making elegant twists and turns throughout its passage. We passed it going shopping in the morning and coming back in the afternoon; when taking a shortcut from the central congestion of the "City" after picking up my Father on a school-less day. We watched out for the strength of its streams when swimming very early in the mornings, and enjoyed its quieter tides during the day and late evenings in the holidays. Its presence was felt very near in the winter as if it was flooding the city but it receded in a big way in the summer, becoming remote and very distant. On summer nights it came to its own again when people congregated on Abu Nawwass to seek its cool breezes, either walking or sitting in the transient snack bars dotting its shores. It was incredible value for money to buy a tea, a cold coke with a kebab meal some *khubuz* and a salad, and share in the silence of the night with the river gently lapping at our feet.

If the sun was filtering the water you could distinguish tens of tiny fish dancing furiously just underneath the surface. Mid morning heralded the arrival of the many women bedouins to do the housework in its running waters.

As a family, we got into the habit of getting up very early in the morning to swim in Dijlah for our daily exercise. It was really at my Father's prodding, him being a true addict of the river and feeling at home in its surroundings; that's why this routine was close to his heart! My Father as a bachelor with his friends had been even more of a regular: so much so that he had once dived from a bridge as a result of a bet! As luck

124

would have it, he hit a rusty machine that was dumped in the river. His head was slashed and I am sure that his life had

Acrobatics on the river Dijlah in the summer

lurched in the balance too; later on he had to go to the hospital to have stitches.

The river Dijlah coils itself round Baghdad, bisecting it into two halves: Russafaa side of the river where we lived, and Karech where we headed to, our swimming goal. The long summer months stretched from May to October, so that the temperature of the water remained tepid; while the fact that the river bank where the boats were moored was a mere five minutes's walk from our house, proved a definite plus. In those days we all went walking to the shore as a family, while the young kids clutched a plastic ring each as an insurance policy. In later years as we moved house, it became impossible to walk so had to take the car for a five minutes' drive and park it on the embankment near the river. At 5:30 am neither traffic nor parking problems existed! At that hour we could barely open our eyes, at that hour we wanted to stay curled up in bed. But my Father persevered and was not going to give up his favourite sport just because his children did not appreciate its healthy benefits (yet). I don't know how he and my Mother managed to be up so early view an excellent social calendar and quite a few very late nights. Well, let this serve as an example of the achievements that a dedicated soul is capable of.

There were some steps down to the river bank where our faithful boatman was congregating with his mates, ready to take on other families of our acquaintance too. It was the simplest of boats the "Balam" which seated a maximum of 6: we sat leaning against bare wood, there was no other alternative, distributing ourselves almost evenly fore and aft, taking care not to make one side tilt with too much weight. The boats were skilfully but flimsily built so anyone standing was in danger of losing balance and toppling. The young man who owned it rowed seated on the middle plank; he was dressed invariably in a white or striped *dishdashah* which he tucked into his waist for ease of manoeuvre, and clutched the opposite plank with his big toes to balance himself while pushing during the rowing process. He steered the boat by dipping the oars into the water at different angles rhythmically; at other times seeing how we watched him with fascination he let us steer the boat with one oar and assisted us with the other. He made the skill seem so easy, but the heavy oar had a mind of its own and slurped into the water if unattended with an eagle eye; never mind, he took it as a child's ineptitude and laughingly retrieved it from sinking just in time. Later on he donned his *yashmagh* to protect his head from the merciless sun; nevertheless rivulets of sweat continued to drip down his body due to the sheer hard work.

Anyway by now we must have reached a point in the middle of the river where our toes could not touch the sand anymore *bil ameek*. The sun had yet to make an appearance; the

Abu el Balam – the owner of the boat pushed and pulled rhythmically

river opaque and still freezing from the night before. But my Father always made a joke of this initial difficulty as he lowered himself into the river from the middle of the boat: "Lovely" he enthused as he hit the water, "in no way is it cold"! But we had learnt from experience not to believe this promise, so still dithered, shivering at the feat ahead. Further afield came the admonishments in stricter tones: "you should be ashamed of yourselves; everyone is looking at you acting cowardly, *Mu EIB?*" To cut a long story short, in the next few minutes, we were all down there swimming furiously for our lives trying to warm up. Our swimsuits had always been beneath the garments, so hey presto.

By the time we stopped shaking, the sun had come out in its glorious rays; as the positive aspects of the exercise went up, so our complaints died down. From having started as a chore, our hard slog proved its worth when a beautiful beginning to the day metamorphosed itself all around. The pinkish mist of the dawn lifted and as if on cue, the waters became sweet and transparent; as if by their own accord, they parted in front of us into half moons - while the rays of the sun slanted onto their surface shimmering in blinding hues of orange and yellow. The leisurely strokes we made carried us swiftly and rhythmically in and out, in and out. Everything was slumbering still, making us the first to break into a hidden world! Not for long though; soon you become aware of the other boats with their swimmers aiming for the daily crossing towards the opposite shore, *Al Karkh*. Glad tidings these, they signalled the presence of several more witnesses to the adventure, and the enthusiasm built up for an unspoken but thrilling competition: who will be the first to touch land? It took 45 minutes approximately. Both Illead and Odyssey were accomplished once, exhausted, our toes touched a smooth sandy patch which carried us all the way to the bank and formed that day's undisputed plateau of achievement.

The shores we came to could only be distinguished by a total lack of amenities: nobody selling ice-cream, tea or muffins, no snack bars, no benches no chairs or umbrellas, not even grassy patches to sit on; indeed, they were totally barren apart from some fig and palm trees on hills nearby. You needed to hatch a plan to be able to have breakfast, although expediency was very much on the cards because the men had to go to work...so by way of a break we sat on our haunches on the bottom of the river for 10 minutes, sharing the diary of events for the forthcoming day. Then out of the water and towards the waiting boats in a run as it was chilly in the damp swimsuits, from there straight into the towels the Mothers held out for us! Oh for a bit of comfortable fluff to wrap a tired body in, while the adults finished sharing their tea alfresco from the thermoses. Then we took our places once more in the boat which our bo'sun pushed with gusto into the water yet again.

There was more what to do on the return journey: and you could not enjoy breakfast knowing that in half an hour you were back on a main road in wet clothes; briefly we had to scramble or slither out of the swimsuits and into decent clothes somehow. The method was explained to me a few times although definitely it did not suit the faint hearted! You tied a longish towel round you, stood in the middle of the wobbling boat and squeezed the wet swimsuit out. That was phase one accomplished. Then by dint of contorting your limbs still further in all the senses, you managed one or two essential items on and you became decent enough to be able to unwrap the towel. Very few people can do this with their gravitas intact. The real difficulty was the presence of at least another 40 pairs of eyes dotted around the river in addition to *Abu el Balam's* (the boatman) right in front of you so any mishap was not allowed! The manoeuvre became a bit easier when a kind soul held a towel as a shield, which lets one have the freedom of both hands at least, but it was still difficult not to wobble!. For the men, the task was even more onerous as they had to don their work suits using the same method, yes and even including a shirt and a tie (the jacket was kept in the car). Looking smart was sacrosanct in the office.

The night before, the caring Mothers had hastily put together some sandwiches: A simple fare of boiled egg with mango spice, or white cheese with jam or an omelette, all encased in half a *Sammouna*- a lozenge shaped Iraqi baguette - It was not the zaniest of combinations, but swimming makes

129

anyone feel ravenous - so we devoured it, sitting in our cramped space inside the boat. My Mother also offered one to the boatman who took it after primly refusing a few times, putting his hand on his heart in a cordial, diffident gesture. This friendly lad had become very sinewy and dark from rowing on the river as a way of living.

Some more stirrings of life that we now start to notice: trawlers and small ships carrying coal and metals, their waves making our boat go through a mini dance. Then there were the young and not so young fishermen who exchanged pleasantries with our boatman; they were busy throwing nets to catch the sweet water fish, and our boat had to be careful not to get entangled. Veiled housewives in black *abbayas* were washing their pots and their naked babies on the banks, looking askance at us. Their older children organized diving competitions between themselves. The quiet was broken forever when the buses and larger taxis "Furies" hooted on the bridges and started to pick up people on their way to work. Transport could only be affected with much brouhaha. We looked out for the supple Bedouin girls in their colourful jewellery and attire who carried their wares in a column on their head on their way to market. Their backs straight as a ramrod, their bare feet supporting their balance, you had to admire their skill in not letting the tall column come toppling down. Looking back, granted there was no glamour in the proceedings, but looking back again from this far at such a peaceful and powerful tableau, I must re evaluate it as amazing,

On Saturdays the adults could afford to lend more grace to the proceedings; we tarried at the shore a bit longer to eat breakfast with the others, leaning against the boat frames. This breakfast consisted of the same egg but it had acquired a nicer flavour as it had been left to brown for 12 hours the night before. (*tabeet* eggs) Fried aubergines and finely cut salad and pickles added a bit of class to the same Ssammouna. This time around it was Turkish coffee from the thermoses and pastries stuffed with dates and maybe figs fallen from the surrounding trees if in season! The adults gossiped about the night before, whether anyone committed mistakes in the games of Pinnacle or Concan! As if on cue everyone in that generation piped up to give their opinions about how that trick should have been

The Beduin girls (Umm el laban) happily balanced tens of pots on their heads

played, and the culprit would start defending their particular corner. This gossip was perfectly tedious for the younger ones so we occupied ourselves in eating and sharing out the different foods.

And then we might dally until 10am as most men did not work on Saturday, the women never worked and even workaholics like my Father took a few hours off. Going back proved sometimes more exciting; when the flow of the water grew very weak, many Jazras materialised half way out of the water: Jazra is a miniscule island, very transient, its soil composed of submerged sand. Even though a Jazra is not huge (it could be as little as 3 ft wide) , you could sit on it and build a sandcastle till the waves washed it away again within the hour...the sand was so smooth and malleable unlike the rather brittle one on the shores, it was the only place to build the castle of your dreams...at times we would be busy building the ramparts and the waves would start lapping the second floor and so we watched our work disappear; at other times somebody behind would shout in wonder, and we turned and there was yet another jazra, come from nowhere. We waded as the water was not deep anymore, even in its middle; the river   had   changed   character   and   become   more accommodating to leisurely pursuits. Here we discovered sea shells of fascinating hues and took them home, sand and all, much to the chagrin of Mother. Sometimes we did not care to continue our journey by boat and paddled all the way back to the shore. Once the sun asserted itself though and you could feel its blaze, you had to call it quits and seek a shade; but as there was none available, the only way forward was to hurry home

My Father grew tired of seeing my Mother sit in the boat babysitting the sandwiches, the thermos and the towels; so he made her buy a swimsuit and taught her to swim with wooden planks and a ring: for a girl to swim was deemed too risque in her maiden family. She did pick up the skill, so we could consider her as one of us; one very proud moment for her, another small step into the Twentieth Century.

This only happened once, thank God; as my Mother was swimming without any plastic rings or wooden planks, she encountered a *guwwassa* (a whirlpool) and was swept as lightening into its murky depths. We children were familiar with this deadly phenomenon and made a detour automatically to avoid it while she being a novice didn't! A real tragedy was averted as our shouts attracted my Father and the boatman to help in the rescue. The latter threw in his oar and my Father pushed her to clutch it.

As a treat our parents and their circle organised occasional evening swims. At those times, we hailed the boat at 6:30 P.M. after the rays of the sun dipped. It was a different journey altogether; the ethos required us to look much smarter and our Mothers had the whole day to make ready. The food was bought or rather the fish was bought the same evening from big shllow tanks near the riverside, where alive they swam. We picked the ones that kicked the most and my Father bartered for the price till he or the fishmonger gave up; the fish were then slit perpendicularly by *Abu el Sammak* (the fishmonger) with a really big knife! He cleaned off the gills and the fins. They were then given to the boatman who pinioned them with a metal hook to a rope dangling from the boat's anchor. All throughout the trip we could see the dead fish following us with its eyes bulging on its final journey.

Maybe we swam a bit further this time and followed the oars to a largish but a more verdant island in the middle of the river where a fabulous treat awaited us for supper. Everyone was commissioned to gather some dry twigs and bring them to the middle of a clearing, where they were stacked vertically to form a tiny mound; once ready the men would set fire to it! Afterwards when this mound became blazing hot and the flames shot very high, *Abu el Balam* plastered a number of whole fishes *(shabbouts)* i.e.carps on spikes all around it. They smeared them in tamarind and lemon sauce. We all of us monitored the fish cooking, looking with fascination into the flames. The end dish being called the *mazgouf*, a trademark of Iraqi cuisine: Describing it I can certify that the fish was charred never burnt, of a smokey flavour, succulent yet without any trace of fat. We lay them on newspapers on long trestles. Some of the housewives brought *khubuz* which were then warmed on the same fire, and also salads in tiny jars liberally laced with mango pickle and parsley; one religious point about an Iraqi salad is that all the ingredients have to be chopped very very finely! You picked a bit of fish with the fingers, rolled it in a flat piece of brown bread, added salad et voila! You did not need a plate, a fork or a knife to make this meal Michelin starred. The dieticians will agree it was as wholesome as any of the West's top restaurants. Everyone was served, and the helpers too. The feast stretched easily to feed the multitude while we relied on all the stars of the firmament to illuminate a truly a wondrous atmosphere..

A meal is not a meal without dessert and ours had lain buried for hours beforehand; earlier on a great thinker from amongst the crowd would have bought big watermelons (in a deep ruby colour) and dug them beneath the sand right on the edge of the water! By the time we finished the meal, they were freezing! To buy a watermelon is an intricate task: you choose a greengrocer who knows the art of stroking the watermelon lovingly at first, then smacking it harder all over, finally putting it up to his ear to listen to some inner gurglings. He will do this with a number of them until satisfied, he will choose the best one and present it with a flourish to the customer. Another skill was to cut them up in neat slices: someone produced a very long knife and proceeded to distribute them among the throng. Everyone ate as many slices as they pleased; and the calories were too few to warranty counting either.

It was time to enjoy sitting on the *takhtat* (makeshift wooden contraptions) and to look around for example at the miniature lights moving inside the water. No one has invented a better way of feeling a bonhomie than sitting round the embers of a semi doused fire in the dark; you can even be forgiven for feeling romantically inclined! You just need to lift your eyes up to the stars and to the moon, so beautiful!

Very regretfully at this juncture I have to pour water on any romantic overtures you might wish to make. Being seen to be romantic is taboo in Iraq, as idle tongues will wag and exaggerate it all! So if there happened to be a suitable candidate you had to content yourself to being furtively romantic within the crowd, lest the gossipmongers with all Baghdad make mincemeat out of it at your expense. The whole clan will be asked to issue statements the very next day.

The mood now is so relaxed, it is conducive to singing folk rhymes that have been there for eternity and reflect the hopes, fears and stigmas of a whole nation:

> *Ya sayyadel semach, siddlee Bunneeyya,*
> *Esh ajjab enta shee'ee wanni sunniyya.*

This girl is asking a fisherman to catch her fish but wonders innocently: "how come you are a Shee'ee and I am a Sunnee?" i.e. opposite ends of the spectrum.

There is time for everything and now it is time to share jokes: They came from the book compiled by Dr Nourallah in the thirties; he put them in classifications as there were so many, and wonder of wonders not one of them could be called dirty or incited violence either! I will share a few with you to make you feel at home:

A priest had just married a couple: As they stood before him, he began to advise them on how to lead a model married life:

Turning to the man he said: "you must cherish and treat your wife with kindness always and buy her diamond jewellery often" (cool eh?)

Turning to the wife he continued: "You must love and honour your husband and accompany him everywhere, day and night, wherever he chooses to go you must follow"

The poor wife couldn't believe what she was hearing, and dissolved into tears: "Please Father, but my husband drives the rubbish van"!

While this joke reflects more intelligent occupations:

A Moslem and a Jew were sitting together in a restaurant! The Moslem said to the Jew: "how come you Jews are so clever? What do you do to become so smart?"

The Jewish bloke said it is not that difficult: "the secret is that every Friday, we eat the head of a fish. As it happens I have one in front of me, do you want to buy it?"

The Moslem man very enthusiastically agreed to the offer. So the Jewish man sold him the head for ten pounds. The Moslem man fell to and ate it promptly.

It all disappeared so quickly that he paused for a minute and said to the Jew: "that was a very expensive head of fish indeed; I bet your story was just one big lie anyway"

The Jewish man replied: "You see! You are already much wiser. But you never sussed out the lie before you ate the head, did you?"

'Jeha' was a bit like a Laurel and Hardy character, and everybody was ready to fall about laughing whenever any of his escapades were mentioned:

One day people watched amazed as Jeha walked the streets in a very happy mood laughing his head off and saying aloud: "Thank you God, you are a great God, I am eternally grateful to you *Ya Rabbi*"

So some passers by stopped him and asked why was he saying *Hamdelellah* to God?

"Because I woke up this morning and I found that my mule was lost, he has gone forever, bolted no less".

But then people grew even more puzzled as to why he should be thanking God? Surely a loss is a tragedy.

Jeha replied: "I am thanking God because I was not riding the mule, don't you see, otherwise I would have been lost too"

But I digress! As an iron kettle has been stewing all the while on the dying embers, it is time to have cardamom tea served in the makeshift cups; one of the lads is holding the kettle and pours the tea with easy hospitality from a very long spout: *Ashet Eedeiyk (*bless you*)*

Now for the journey home, it is 11pm. The river has become deserted. The cavalcade of boats pushed forward in dark and deep waters, but what bliss while the happy groups break out in song yet again. We pass huge palaces whose foundations cut deep into the water; they boasted very lofty gardens like the gardens of Babylon with huge balconies and verdant plants scattered becomingly all around. They belonged to the King's Ministers. We liked whistling into the void underneath to hear a very strong echo reverberate back towards us. So many boats were moored underneath these Kassers in case of trouble! But their owners did not wake up in time!

We arrive and straddle a wooden ledge to get to the shore without messing up our shoes in the treacherous mud. The boatmen hold out both arms for support: we give them a lot of bakhshish, they have been tremendous; without their good nature there would be no mazgouf and no revellers! On the other hand it is a two way street, they also count on our support to maintain a rewarding life on the river

When I was a mere four year old, my Father already started putting me in the water to float and swim and hold my balance very naturally: then, as a more mature six year old, I

a view from a boat journey in Dijlah

was enrolled with a teacher called Mohammed; he had dark features and skin from continuous exposure to the sun; twice a week, he took our tiny class of six to swim right across to the other side of the river. I am overwhelmed when I think of such an achievement at that tender age. Once in the Karkh, we climbed up steep steps to street level and walked down the main street carrying our black *chube* (a huge safety ring) by our side; there was almost no traffic in those days in the *Karkh*, being very undeveloped compared to the *Russafa*! Mohammed meanwhile was on the lookout for the big barges moored along the river bank. Once he espied a suitable one, we descended to the river shore once more. There he started negotiating with the owner while we all stood around in a circle of sorts, curious as to the outcome. By dint of *Annetein* (two fils) which we might incidentally have in our swimsuits, all of us kids could be given a "jumping" lesson from the high deck of this barge! It goes without saying that I held on to the *chube* for dear life so did not plunge down too deep. Up the barge and down into the water again and again, we practised till we heard our teacher give the order to head back towards the Russaffa.

When I attained the ripe old age of seven, it was decided that it was more seemly to attend an "established" swimming institution called Hai's. As nearly all of Frank Iny went to 'Hai's', I could simultaneously enjoy the company of my school mates during the holidays!

It was more of an afternoon club than a rigid class. Just after lunch when the sun was at its highest point, when the asphalt on the road burnt the soles of our feet and nobody was around except for the proverbial mad dog, two girl neighbours from the other side of the Armenians' knocked at the door. With a miniscule bag containing a towel and a change of clothes, I was all ready to go. We set off enthusiastically on a leisurely fifteen minute walk to the river shore and aimed for the two large *chardars* (khaki tents) erected on the bank, one for the boys and one for the girls. They were absolutely bare but for a long wooden bench which everyone covered with their own jumbled heap of bags and towels! We emerged quickly in our swimsuits to be met by 'Hai 'himself!

Before the first lesson began, he asked me if I ever swam before. I told him about Mohammed and crossing the river twice a week etc. He made as if to listen, but like all other professionals including dentists and hairdressers, he believed that the other guy could never have done a good enough job. So he relegated me back to the beginners's classes. What about my self respect, my standing among my peers, never mind all the rich experiences I have been relating? I complained heatedly! But authority is dictatorial and always wins! Back to the drawing board then: I was allocated 3 cumbersome *karrabs* which are oval pieces of wood wrapped in white muslin to carry round my waist and back, so there was absolutely no chance of sinking; they dug into my flesh and held me so upright it hurt! Fear not friends, for the rainbow was certainly there; after a month or two of diligent attendance, we all graduated free of them.

In the afternoons the river's tide rose: so we went up in a *madda* (against the current) blinking against the strong rays of the sun, all of 50 boys and girls, right to the middle of the river. Then the signal was given to turn around and head for the shore. (Hai never made the swimmers cross the river to the other shore in the afternoons, only the morning)

It was hard without a break, so the coach made enthusiastic noises to prod us on, intoning this typical refrain: "*Yawlad Balboul*": and we would respond with a resounding "Balee! "*Mashuftum assfour*"? (Haven't you seen a bird)? "*Balee*" (yes) again. This silly rhyme reverberated several times till we found ourselves nearer the shore. There existed a very slippery kind of mud there and only careful acrobatics prevented us from falling in it and wallowing in its depths. The mud followed everyone right into the tents and that is why we were entitled to the luxury of a basin of water from the river to wash our feet with. Showers or cubicles for change there were none, alas, and except for the khaki roof and walls, no facilities existed. No one missed them though, we were deemed to have been washed clean in the water so it was just a case of keeping the mud away from the clothes. Anyway, we were too excited chattering about the future promotion that 'Hai' had promised. Next week we boasted gleefully to one another, one more *karrab* will be taken away!

THE FATHEREYYA RAN A CATHOLIC UNIVERSITY

I met the Jesuit Fathers when I started attending their university in 1965. It was still a brand new campus which they built with funds from their native America. Five enormous buildings for the 3 different disciplines accompanied by a library, along with a dormitory for their own use. All were professors in their chosen fields, all led very Spartan lives and no salary was given to them for teaching. They belonged to a Catholic Order which ordained their way of life. Before getting to know them, I had never known what philanthropy and dedicating your life to charity meant.

Freshman first year class of 1965

142

Quite a few were highly academic and set themselves the task of studying Arabic, one of the most difficult languages for a westerner to muster. Good Arabic is literary Arabic which no one uses in everyday conversation, but they did, and although it came out a bit stilted and sounded very foreign as well, we did not have the heart to tell them any different; it was without any doubt a big achievement.

Father Mcdonough, the popular Dean of Business Studies

They taught three disciplines: Engineering, Business and English Literature. Some had an open nature, were more ready to smile and socialize, and we warmed towards them. Others had a remit of leading games in sports or debating societies. Ideally, the Order served to help people to acquire diplomas and skills which they needed to further their lives and the future of their country.

There were some very handsome Fathers to vie with the likes of James Stewart, in which case we would emit a big sigh "Aah, why did he ever have to become a celibate"? At the beginning, there was an element of cynism from people of other faiths; it became our pastime to puzzle out reasons why good looking intelligent creatures wanted to forsake marriage and a life of their own. Where we came from as if anyone needs reminding, everyone but absolutely everyone gets married, it was written in the constitution. In the end we settled for the romantic option to explain their life of dedication: there must have been a thwarted love saga behind it all. In all cases the fact remained that friendly exchanges could only go so far, there was a diffidence between us underlining the fact that not only were they from a different civilization and a different generation, their life also had a loftier purpose.

The degrees that the university conferred were recognized all over America and most of the world except for England where they needed converting. Clearly, my perspectives were broadened by the various activities on offer, i.e. debating, classical music, the frequent trips round the country, as well as by the philosophy of its founders. It contrasted in a big way with that very dull and dour curriculum at school. It felt good to be able to leaf through the latest periodicals…. Before the advent of the internet and e-mail eras, there was a paucity of search tools. Books were expensive in Iraq and the advanced ones came from abroad. The university ran along very orderly lines, the exams and grading very well organised and above board! Everyone knew who achieved the top honours in the classes as the names and the results were displayed on a central board every end of term. Sometimes this read like a Frank Iny roll call.

Students came from a fairly comfortable background but there were also some who could not have made it without a financial scholarship. On the whole people from the different faiths and across the board adhered to campus rules. We were encouraged to strive, to contribute and to achieve, but I suspect most, especially the girls, strove only to pass. It was rumoured by the Iraqi gossipmongers that the majority of the girls were there to find a husband with good prospects, or to while the days till the parents found them one, buoyed by thefact that she went to the "American" university. It became a prestigious place to be in view of its halo of modernity, but for the career minded it also held the promise of continuing their studies in the more advanced West. The girls managed to use it as an arena to show off the latest styles imported from abroad and looked well made up always; for example everyone wore high heels or even very high heels. When the fashion for mini skirts filtered from the West, that is what most of us tried to adopt but some also multiplied it by a conservative ratio. The black and white craze in the sixties caught us unawares as there was nothing parallel in the local shops, but we improvised, cutting black and white squares from patterned cloths and stitching them patchlike into the dresses; and that is how we contrived to wear the designer dresses, no sweat. Trendy fashion was hip and added prestige inside the campus world. Meanwhile, the boys managed to park their sports cars where everyone could admire them in a mini version of the car show!

Friendship between the sexes was not stifled as it was in the country as a whole. One thing which intrigues me still is the difference between the way that courtship is conducted in the East where the girl must act passive and demure, and can only give the barest hint of encouragement, and her counterpart in the West. The latter is cheekier and society sanctions her chasing the boy very openly. East and West are still those vastly different worlds

The Jesuits' further remit was to encourage us to innovate, initiate, choose our own goals and have a say in how to achieve them; this is what happens in America I presume.

145

Unfortunately we were not ready to do that; society did not let us go beyond the "done" thing, traditions still ruled supreme. We lacked the mentality to embrace challenges. On the other side of the equation, we led contented and stress free lives.

The Iraqis love to laugh and gather around to exchange jokes. Accordingly everyone was to be found eating or drinking in the cafeteria in the frequent breaks, later sitting outside on scattered benches in the garden in groups of fours or fives. The garden was there to enjoy summer and winter because of the constant sun. Indeed one of my fonder memories of those times is revising hectically on a bench in a last minute scramble with many other lost souls; the grass still snow white from the frosty conditions of the night before while the sun shone gaily, warm as ever.

The calendar of events decreed several yearly celebrations for the whole of the student body. We discovered that the American way was to respect the student inclinations and wishes and seek to nurture them. When it was time for a celebration, on the initiative of the Fathers, the teachers and student volunteers put out a lot of chairs on the lawn, adding a wooden makeshift stage with a microphone; and hey presto you had space for hundreds of congregants. Isn't it very lucky when you know that it is not going to rain? Freshers deserved a party to see and be seen; a prize was set for the best cake a girl could make. Later classes chose a pop music theme, and still others practised the amateurish Iraqi theatricals in local dress, where they caricatured the more extreme social conventions. Decidedly no mention of politics, as any Iraqi will tell you: that spelled of Armageddon.

Another end of year party organized by the seniors had a much more scandalous theme! They secretly imported in their car a scantily clad belly dancer and booked her to dance for a few hours well into the night. I always thought it was unfair to spring such disloyalty on the unsuspecting Fathers who I doubt were allowed to take part in such hedonistic goings on anyway. They must have been too shocked to remember to shift from their ringside seats towards the back and no doubt joined all of us in suspecting the instability of a few very thin strings upholding the dignity of the dancer. They took it on the chin though and joined in the handclapping. Later on when approached for their opinion, polite as always, they said it seemed a healthy sort of art form! "One question please" the Dean of Engineering piped up: "how come the lady is still fat if she keeps working all those parts to eternity"? Stuck for an answer? So were we!

Sometimes, there were visitors from abroad to join the teaching fraternity, for example, nuns on a pilgrimage. In their traditional attire, similar to a grey or light blue abbayye but with a white collar and headdress, they looked plenty serious. We did not socialise beyond a smiley hello. They were too white, their faces needed desperately to see the rays of the sun. An irreverent pastime was to conjecture how to pair them off with their male counterparts, but to no avail. Both sides were only interested in academia.

My sojourn in those pastures evokes good memories on the whole. Pretty green gardens dotted the four white buildings, and benches placed in the open grounds made socializing feel very natural. It was one of the very few places in Iraq where the different religions met and thrived! Of course constraints still applied: boy meets girl and chats to her in campus, still does not give them a licence to meet outside. It was a little cosmos and reflected all the idiosyncrasies of the Mother country. The campus while spacious was still cosy enough for scandals and gossip. When we were approached by

147

classmates to join them for private parties, we girls steadily refused. The gossipmongers would have had a hayday, it just was not done.

As is always the case, the boys made better use of the facilities for basketball and football than the girls who preferred volleyball. By contrast the tennis courts at the back were visited by both boys and girls. The Fathers organized many a "Sports Day", whole days devoted to sports; a revelation to us.

We found it suited us, a small group of boys and girls, to come and play tennis on our days off as there was a dearth of such facilities in Baghdad. Of course there were the movies and the movie houses, but these were dependant on diplomatic relations which in turn also depended on the politics of the day. If the regime's relations soured with the West, only Eastern bloc films were shown. I think the Jesuits were surprised to see us at first but gave us a wide berth nevertheless. The tennis courts were far from their places of residence and we took care not to disturb their days of rest.

Regurgitating all this some forty years thence, I have come to the conclusion that maybe it was very difficult for the Jesuits to understand the Iraqi culture too. Here life was one big taboo, whereas in the States everything was extremely open, everything was splashed out in the press warts and all! Even if it had a damaging effect on the local beliefs and was blasphemous to the government. They must have decided to carry on with their mission regardless of the many distances that separated them from the locals.

For us they presented this united albeit foreign front summed up as "The Fatheriyya", people of the Cloth; heavily layered in black in the winter, while not so heavily layered in light grey during the scorching summer. The only infringement they made on people of different faiths was to introduce two phrases at the beginning of each lesson "Our Father who art in heaven, hallowed be thy name thy kingdom cometh thy will be done, on earth as well as in heaven, Amen!" Still, people objected to the phrase' allegiance, so non Christians were instructed not to stand up while they were being recited.

Most of the breaks between lessons when the weather was cold were spent lounging together with the girls in my class in the Ladies room, or sitting in the canteen and drinking sweet Turkish coffee! One of them was called Jeehan; she came from a very traditional middle class Moslem family. I wouldn't call her attractive or bright, but we "gelled", and I found myself responding sometimes to her need for academic help. As she was only allowed social interaction with the girls, she could not have that many friends either. Along with the others, we chatted cosily during our time off.

One day as the girls turned their cups of Turkish coffee upside down as usual, I found myself being prodded by all to tell their destiny in the cup and couldn't get away from the task. I have seen the adults do it so plunged in the same vein, using my imagination and never believing one word of what I said; but as the girls were begging me so I jested forth, why not? As Jeehan's's turn came up something must have whispered to me, or maybe it was just psychological empathy. To cut it short I told her what she most wanted to hear! "Jeehan mark my word, you will get engaged before the summer is out!" Her eyes shone as she hugged me and said with tears in her eyes that she felt extremely grateful; "*Inshallah* (God willing)" everyone in the room responded fervently! It is a nice feeling to make a fellow being happy, even if it might prove short term.

Well, maybe I do possess powers in that direction after all! Lo and Behold as they say in the Bible, Jeehan did get engaged and after two months only! She was jubilant and told everyone! Truly I felt I had accomplished a big Mitzvah.

Unfortunately for me, the times were a changing and radically so. It was 1967. By the time Jeehan had planned her big engagement party in May, we ceased to be the flavour of the month. The war with Israel was imminent and there was a lot of enemy propaganda; many people fell for it and avoided us while others were afraid to associate with us and so turned away too; we couldn't wait for the end of the year to get away from the stifling atmosphere.

To be sure Jeehan did have her big engagement party with *dumbuk and mossiqa* (music and drums). I heard afterwards she had invited both forms of her class including people who did not even know she existed, whereas I was relegated to the excluded few.

At the time, this did not go down too well and I really felt hard done by. But never mind. With the wisdom of the years I have come to the conclusion that life compensates plenty at its own pace.

As the war drew ever nearer, so our academic life felt the heat: one clever student in Engineering was told by a colleague in the Party to let him copy during the exam, but within the hall itself the invigilators proved very tough. He developed cold feet and could not open his book wide for the other boy to copy all of the answers. When he left the exam room, while still inside the campus, he was stalked by the gang who managed to beat him up several times. Nobody was strong enough to stand up for justice to be done.

All good things must come to an end. The Fatheriyya were made to leave for political reasons at the end of 1968.

They were accused of spying! The Dean of Science had a telescope on top of his residence to watch the stars he said, but they said he was watching the army barracks next door!

Graduation pictures of the same form (August 1969)

This call came at the start of our fourth and most important academic year! Nobody was ready. The investment from the Jesuits was massive; how they were dismissed in one second beggars belief.

In America now and very frail (most have passed away), they still look fondly back on some of the best days of their lives. They also thought those days would never end. That was the life they chose and thought they would win and never lose. But not here my friend, these shores need to be constantly revolutionized.

Anyway, they were not present at my graduation ceremony - where I sorely felt the need to shake their hands.

MATCHMAKER, MATCHMAKER

Well, this can be a bit of an awkward subject to explain, even though traditionally it is the forerunner of all glad tidings. To live entwined is lovely no doubt, but there are times when we do need to give good fortune *el bacht* a push, and interference here can only be of oh so delicate a nature, while cajoling is still needed on both sides. To carry it through needs a saucy stirring of ethical and non ethical ingredients in a country where superstitions still rule the roost; plus a near depletion of the bank balance. All this lot and you still have to hold your breath for the final curtain, for the magic to appear, for the sparkle and the fizz, and if they don't, it means: God has decided it was not meant to be. And do forgive me for speaking in such cryptic hieroglyphics, but we are given to understand from the sages that this whole operation collapses if anyone dares even talk about it; for mark my word, gossip from evil tongues will ring the death knell for any future denouements!

There now, I have given you enough clues on the process of boy marries girl in Iraq.

Time to spare a thought for the young lady who wants to keep in with a very prejudiced society. Even though she is not allowed to go out on dates, still she has an obligation to marry. Imagine what an impossible conundrum that is.

It seems we need someone here to be in the market for a supply of available men and women. A gossip of thick skin, a busybody no less, to sally forth into the intimate confidences of the Fathers and the Mothers and process their precious merchandise. This person must be adept at manipulating the parents to get them to manipulate their offspring, while all the

152

while oiling the cogs with some advanced marketing tools: the first being flattery while a very honeyed tongue must come as a close second!

Enter Rachelle the matchmaker. She of the white hair and feisty laugh. Her eyes shone as she accosted each one of us, and we knew that once home, she would rush and inscribe our particulars in ledgers similar to those used in stocks and shares. These rose in value as we grew older and more eligible. A chatterer by inclination, she revelled in keeping a sharp eye on all single people; she did not wait for an invitation to knock on their parents' houses to warn of the dangers of letting them stagnate on the shelf. Why, they were becoming less eligible as we speak!

Her job was thus: to the prospective groom: she extolled the beauty of the future bride, real or imagined. Any hint of *sha'er kallabdoun* (blonde hair) or blue eyes and the deal is likely to be in the bag.

To the groom's family: to spin tales of the real or exaggerated amount of the future dowry. It would also look good on the C.V. to mention some rich, important or aristocratic family that the girl can possibly be connected to, now or 100 years ago - anywhere in the world including China.

To the bride: Pass, as all decisions regarding her are made above her head.

Her parents: Reassure them thus about the groom:

1) His career prospects: rosy

2) His character: a real business-chee

3) His house and car: very expensive, parked and waiting for their daughter.

It was rumoured that once this woman gained entry to your house, wild dogs could not drag her out. She has been known to marry angels to rogues, or schoolgirls to very old men. She carried in her satchel many twenty year old pictures of once upon a time handsome men and marketed them with yet another advantage, their experience in life. Even if the first girl or boy didn't quite do, then there was sure to be a worthier one round the corner. It sometimes reminds me of the optimism of estate agents while offering an endless list of houses!

All this work on her part has whetted the appetite and the next step for the prospective parties is to arrange a "sighting". Don't get your hopes up folks; it is still too early for a meeting. The future bridegroom and his family need to check the girl out. To this end, the girl is instructed to walk round a certain corner for example, or may be vetted on her way out of school. She has no inkling at all poor soul of what is being plotted behind her back. Previously, the groom's family might apply to a photographer in Battaween that everyone frequented by the name of 'Nerso'. He agreed with the minimum of persuasion to search through his stock to find a recent or even a decent picture of the girl! If the groom found her to have blotchy skin or maybe of too short a build, then under threat of cancelling the match followed by enough haggling by Rachelle, the parents agreed to hand in more dowry at the appropriate time. If on the other hand, he does find her attractive, and she has an intelligent look about her as she is waiting for the bus for example, the groom's family will ask for a real meeting. This gesture on its own must carry very serious implications, as it means things are looking up.

At this very crucial meeting, both bride and groom will don their smartest dress and be very anxious to please while their whole future depended on the few precious moments allocated to their entire life's desire. Even though it consisted of silly chit chat, there were undercurrents aplenty too. One

BAGHDAD MEMORIES

of the most crucial moments occurs when the girl is asked to serve coffee for the guests. It was not your ordinary instant mix but in Turkish coffee it is a bit more involved as you kept an eagle eye on the progress of the froth at the top. Later on, when presenting it very charmingly on a tray, the girl must show a hint of appropriate shyness and decorum, a respect for the prospective parents in law, an apparent generosity and warmth of spirit, a certain penchant for laughing and not looking dour, the whole delightful character enshrined within a sweet obedient nature. Beyond the impossible? Not for an authentic Iraqi girl! As for the coffee, it should still have the froth visible above each miniscule cup. Those are some of the important skills that the groom and the in laws will be marking mentally as the chitchat continues.

No further doubts now that the bride's beauty and upbringing have shone through. The boy will present his future bride with a trinket at the end of the meeting, signifying his positive inclination to have her become betrothed to him. This might be a bracelet or a necklace, although nothing but really *Kashkha* (high class) will do here bearing in mind the family's reputation. The groom selected it beforehand with just such a grand finale in mind. And here you are folks, joy, pure joy, is going to descend upon the world.

I must not forget to mention also the important conferences and discussions that will have taken place meanwhile on both camps, including all the uncles, aunts, cousins, brothers and even grandparents, as they pool their knowledge of the bride / bridegroom's family and all the pluses and minuses of belonging to their family tree! Everybody's opinion is touted, any relevant gossip about the health of the betrothed and that of the extended family taken into account. Everybody must have a say in this very important matter. Nobody trusted Rachelle as they knew she was out to tie the knot with the sole aim of pocketing the reward, be it in cash or jewellery, re today's estate agents again. But I am not interfering any more, no one is allowed to spoil the nuptials, it is *Haram*. The bible tells us that it is a great mitzvah to bring together a man and a woman to marry so let us all leave them to get on with it.

Within the next few days, our Rachelle is still needed as a go between to take everyone through the rest of the formalities, including the conditions made by the groom's family for the engagement and the wedding receptions (lavish), the bride's trousseau (hand sewn), the bridal bed and its drapes (Fattah Basha) - all paid for by the bride's increasingly fleeced parents; meanwhile, the bride's household buys enough victuals to feed the whole town for the engagement dinner. Only family are invited but then each family has plenty of siblings, aunts, great aunts, uncles. Nobody else is allowed a whiff of the proceedings as evil eyes, jealousy and gossip will nip the plans in the bud.

When the groom, surrounded by his entourage, swaggered in first time through the doors of his intended's house, reeking of perfume, his hair shining with Bryl cream, the seriousness and splendour of the occasion rose several degrees. The bride's relatives went out of their way to make the new family feel welcome. Now everyone comes forward to shake hands and introduce themselves and their position in relation to the bride. Remember up till then it was purely a business transaction. Forevermore they will belong to the same clan and their reputation will be judged to be at one by society! Also, for the first time ever, the bride takes her place on a sofa beside the groom, and everyone will be staring at them both. Isn't she beautiful? (Probably the first time she has been allowed makeup so the poor girl looks too bright and glittery), has the groom fallen in love with her? One minute please; while the shy couple tried to find anything, anything at all, to talk about in the full glare of the curious and the gossiping; I leave the rest to your imagination

No doubt though, romance and magic were in the air that night as the bridegroom broke the eternal cup even before dinner was served. The women in unison went into a resounding *halahels*. Religion already considers them man and wife even though they still live in separate households and are just starting to date! It is still too early for the bridegroom to kiss his bride as the lady is but an acquaintance! Anyway kissing is reserved entirely for the glamorous film stars we see in the movies. The two camps *beitel beneiti and beitel walad* (the girl's and the boy's families) rise in unison and shake hands with each other *Bonne Chance*!

First thing in the morning of the next day, the news has travelled like haywire just as state secrets do! There are many juicy bits concerning the transaction and the couple that have become hitched. Everyone whispered those excitedly in the classroom behind the teacher's back: what the bride was wearing, how many years difference between their ages, how many thousands in the dowry, accompanied by ample comments and criticisms of the lot. The money given to Rachelle was quite substantial especially if both parties felt they were onto a winner as far as their social connections and standing were concerned.

More money was bandied about in the preparation for the wedding. The bridegroom's Mother makes a big order at the Shakarchee, the largest sweets shop in Baghdad and then sends a whole silver tray covered by a white embroidered cloth full of white, fragrant sugared almonds and Turkish delights to

157

the Bride's Mother, on whose shoulders must fall all the work from now on and till eternity. She distributes them in smaller plates to all her acquaintances and family as well as the bridegroom's amid fresh halaheel, with help from her maid and driver both! As for the exuberant couple being feted non stop with more home cooked dinners than they can ever return, one day they may open their eyes wide and blink! Or it might take them yet another lifetime to realise what a potential fine mess their parents could have gotten them into.

But SHUSH! That must always remain yet another closely kept secret in the recipe; in fact you must have guessed it by now: any hint of discord or murmurings is not the done thing at all and must be hushed hastily. With so many expectations hanging in the balance, the marriage can only move forward and with full steam ahead.

To justify the high standing of the family, the bride must be seen in a new dress every time she is invited out. It is also a golden opportunity for any other sisters to step out in the full glare of the public eye so that everyone is alerted: there is a need now for even more suitors. Find them!

The whole town is already looking forward to being invited to the Hennah festivities, probably because they include a *Chalghi* with a *Raqus Sharqi* (oriental dance). In the Hennah ceremony, the bride gets sat on a chair and is anointed with the brown orange dye on her ten fingers by her Mother and Mother in law both; this will protect her against the evil eye. The generous supper is usually laid out in the garden to make the most of the space, with children running around the whole house. More space is needed for the dessert tables so the roof gets roped in as part of the proceedings and adults and children get busy climbing upstairs and downstairs most of the night

My grandparents, Khatoon and Maurice (1926). The newly weds went to Nerso and took a   picture against an exotic background. But he forgot to tell them to smile for the camera.

All this ado forces the hosts to invite the neighbours too and give platters of food to the police who pop in on account of the brouhaha. The whole *taraff* (district) knows by now that the Jews are at it yet again

Supper out, it is now the turn of the Oriental dancer who is waiting in the wings having changed into her scanty kit, her multi bracelets and very long earrings! She will be adding yet another glad, if sassy, dimension to the proceedings! If she is really good, jiggling and jangling very provocatively singly and in tandem all that God has bestowed on her, she will make all the men adore her and the women ogle her jealously. Meanwhile everyone is trying to peep into what lies behind the lacy bits of the uniform!

So, let us all follow the dancer. The Chalgi starts and she is anticipating the beat of the drums. Thus a few snakey turns to the left, and then, as the world and its gravity shift, her erect body gives the appearance of rising; now the whole edifice hurtles down in a semi circle to the right.

Then we are treated to lots more contortions by the individual body parts while the stomach is working hard to acquire the leading part; the arms gracefully swivelling in this supreme art form; the stomach keeps writhing in so many directions, it has become the focus of all the eyes in the room, bringing the rest of the body into the foray: it is by far the main interpreter of this dance. Now hold it as the *Dunbuk* (beat of the drum) has stopped!

This is the essence of the *Eeqa'e* (rhythm). With shimmies, hip gyrations and twirls…not that easy, is it? Then our charming lady climbs a table all the better to show off more incredible twistings of her voluptuous figure. Was that sleazy? Yes, yes! You want salacious? More more! Diving into the crowd, she will invite a man to dance with her, his

alal wehda wal ness
With Giselle, Nadia and Guilda at a henna

primitive attempts at imitating her style increasing the merriment and appreciation of the audience no end in *Raqs el Hacha'a*. The seductive eyes have it, the more she scores in eye contact with the men, the more real possessions she will reap. This ageless and august tradition dictates that the men reward her with folded banknotes while she is dancing, either cheekily stuffing them inside her bra, or yet more cheekily inserting them just inside her glitzier bottom bit. Under everyone's watchful eye, any man claiming to be a man-about-town should be able to accomplish this task without awkward manoeuvring or taking advantage, as we are all decent and it is not the intention to embarrass the dancer. No no, I take this back; the lady is very far from embarrassing.

161

having attained a near professional standard, Sharona
very credibly interpreting the dance

If the evening is up to expectations, people get ecstatic from
their love of very familiar, very dear songs, and end up
throwing money willy nilly in the direction of the stage. This
money will be divided later between the instrumentalists and
the singer. The audience sings with the band, claps with the
rhymes, and all but gets up to stomp the stage. What a fun way
to give the couple a right send off for their future life together!
There will be ample time for the grey matter later, today we
celebrate.

To lend the marriage ceremony its very august message,
all the family, uncles, aunts first cousins and grandMothers
stand or squeeze under the chupah, they are all considered

very important. But then before the ink has had the chance to dry on the *Ketubba*, (the marriage certificate) people are already pouring out their sincere wishes for the forthcoming events of the *Millah, the Shassha, the Pedion* (newborn ceremonies) and the couple have their work cut out for them to fulfil the whole town's expectations.

Tradition again, but this one must follow as night follows day. The bride should deliver the first born within a year, and she can only relax once the all important boy arrives. Otherwise the gossipmongers start to have a hayday in trying to apportion the blame on one or the other of the family's genes. Later on, and with so many children to their credit, and the little treasures having taken over all that remained of their parents's lives, there is precious little chance of remembering the freedom they were once so willing to give up, nor who else they might have chosen had there been any choice. But don't blame the parents, no, no, it is *al Bachet, al Nasseeb, al Qessmi* (fate) that controls all, everything is written in the stars from the moment you are born. No complaints please, somebody might deduce that not all is perfect!

Unsuspected by us, the matchmaker must have been in possession of a host of psychological degrees. If only we could have her cloned to serve our modern men and women who are seeking perfection within that golden cage. The dot com industry is taking them to *cind wel hind* (faraway lands) but they would be better off right here with a far craftier "Rachelle". She will make them jump "Oops" into the chasm without realizing it, sight unseen.

THE REAL UMM AL LABAN

HOME HUSBANDRY FOR THE ECONOMISTS

We needed an incredible number of traders to run a credible household, and so it came easier for us to call them by their services rather than their professional names thus: Abu el nastala(sweets seller), Umm el laban (yoghurt), Abu el 'amba(pickled mango), Abu el qahwa(the coffee trader), Abu el raqqi (the watermelon man), Abu el kebab and not forgetting Abu el sammoon (bread): and there you are, I have shown you an excellent shortcut to the Arabic language.

In those days food was always home made! At any one time, Mother had many things "cooking" or "stewing". On the roof for example, hiding from the direct rays of the sun in the shade of the water tanks there would be various pickles in big jars. In another corner lay big trays of fresh apricots to dry in the searing sun: their natural sourness in chicken, rice and meat dishes adding a definite zing.

A favourite was dubdub jam (pomella) made by boiling the peel several times to get the bitterness out, and then simmering with sugar; orange peel jam with coconut,apricot and plum jams; date syrup was made nearer Passover.

Watermelon was cooling in the summer! After eating it every single breakfast lunch and supper, we saved its seeds, rinsed and dried them in the sun, salting and roasting them afterwards in a frying pan. They became tasty and crunchy and we shared them with friends. As for the watermelon rind, it could be fed to the donkeys! Waste not want not!

We owned a very heavy Hawen (pestle and mortar) of 100% yellow brass. Here the maid banged the Madqouqa for dessert, ground dates mixed with ground nuts.

To wash and starch the bed sheets before the advent of

the washing machine you had an organisation called the

Abu el Kebab fanning the air on his Jaffouf(a bbq)

"Doubee". Every other week, a van pulled outside the house and a very dark man from Sudan, we called him Doubee as well, came in with a huge bundle on his back and a big writing pad in his hand. Meanwhile, my Mother had stripped all the sheets and blankets, towels and pillowcases that needed washing a day earlier. I also helped to count them and write them down in a small book numbering them under columns.

The Doubee verified the numbers and transcribed them into his book, then made another big bundle of them and took them back to his van. Coming back he opened his original bundle revealing the sheets he had picked up two weeks ago, washed, starched with the blue cube and neatly pressed. Then both he and my Mother would tick the items and the quantities off against my Mother's lists of two weeks ago! If something went missing as it often did, he promised to bring it back on his next errand (two weeks hence, what's the hurry?). As long as my Mother was meticulous in her bookkeeping, the system worked very well! The Doubee was always in a good mood displaying incredibly white teeth and behaved like an English gentleman towards my Mother addressing her as *Khatoon*;

Most people owned Persian carpets. They were so well made and knotted that they lasted hundreds of years. They copied intricate Islamic designs and boasted vivid colours especially the ancient ones. They were a treasure and people treasured them and passed them on from one generation to the next! All vied for ownership of the rarer kinds: Kashan (blue or red colours), Tabriz (very fine flowers), Shiraz (diamond motif), and proudly turned the carpet over for the visitor to show the date of manufacture and whence in Persia they came from. Cleaning them could only be undertaken by the strong Kurdish men who descended on us once a year at the end of the winter. They unfolded them from the rooms, grabbed them from each of their four corners and gave them a good shake; they then sMothered them in moth balls and put them inside a sewn gunniya to protect them. Some people trusted them to lay the carpets in the middle of the road for a few hours as treading by traffic loosened the inner dust. In addition, and once every ten years, they needed to be hosed down thoroughly by brushing with soap and water. This last treatment invariably took place on the roof.

Undergoing those vigorous treatments made their colours sparkle even more. They were then stored away till the next winter; the floors felt much cooler as a result during the scorching summer months.

For us children, these practices proved more entertaining by far than attending a live show! First we were sent to spy the band of 4 or 5 barefooted cleaners and bring them in from the street! Then everyone within earshot stood around while the day's wages were agreed upon after a lot of haggling. The men wore colourful garb and headgear; their muscles rippled as they heaved and hauled the carpets back and forth. And then at midday, we bought them a *laffah* (sandwich with khubuz) kebab with the statutory bottle of cold coke! They ate their lunch on the roof, sitting cross legged in company, taking time out to roll out their thin cigarettes from a shiny tobacco tin. When they laughed, as they often did, they displayed several golden teeth.

In those days to prevent the sewers overflowing, or because they overflowed, you had to call someone to doctor them. The Nazzah extricated the dirt from the *ballou'a* which was the top of a huge hole dug underneath the house! One or two people worked together at a time, and they went around the streets shouting a melancholy refrain: *Nazzah, Nazzah Chachma*. The foul smelling black liquid was extracted and emptied into lots of metallic containers one by one, which were taken away by a tired old horse strapped to an even more tired carriage. The pong pervaded the entire neighbourhood. Later on these were replaced by a gigantic hose attached to a lorry.

Heating water for the bath was a lengthy process and dragged on for at least one and a half hours. Outside in the courtyard, there was an element housed in a concrete aperture almost at floor level: my Mother stuffed it with paper, doused the paper with petrol and set a burning match to the lot, so a bang occurred as they combusted.

Mattresses were made from curled cotton which made them light as a breeze. But with time they became damp and shrank, losing their springiness. Hence the *Naddaf* who came to the house approximately once a year, sat in the courtyard, and disembowelled the mattresses. With the help of a lyre like instrument to strum the chord with, he whipped the cotton into its original feathery density with a dull thud of a sound like: "ti ti pam pa". The second day he sewed the newly stuffed mattresses together with a silk coloured sheet on top to produce a duvet so light and bouncy, you had to have good dreams for the whole night! This fascinating profession provided a social get-together for all the neighbourhood children.

To surmount the cold we had Aladdin heaters, blue and elegant. They could warm a room in the bitter winter but if we came too near them as inevitably we did, fingers and clothes got scorched. Moving them from one room to another constantly was a real hazard if any petrol spilled or the flame fell and ignited.

To shine the shoes, the man of the house called in a *Sabbagh*. This was a Kurdish man with a small polishing kit who sported a very colourful knitted skullcap. He used to make the round of houses with a melancholy musical refrain "Sabbagh Kanader" When called in; there was no need for bargaining for once, as his fee was cheap enough. He promptly sat down in the courtyard on a tiny stool incorporated within his kit and fell to. My Father sitting on another chair opposite the Sebbagh put his shoe on a tiny stand (part of the kit). Our man followed this plan meticulously: he first washed the shoes with water and soap by dint of an old toothbrush, wiped them, and then applied two coats of polish, rubbing the excess off each time with a different cloth. Finally he buffed them vigorously to a perfect shine with yet another brush. My Father would have a very pleasant conversation with him while he was applying himself to the task. The profession was regarded as a Kurdish forte.

We did our best to recirculate clothes, not from an environmental point of view, but because thrift management had been the instilled creed in my Mother's generation. For example a "new" dress was supposed to make of me a fashion icon at its inauguration. I wore it for grand occasions like a wedding or henna, maybe a New Year's party in a first class club. The next year it went down a notch, but I could still wear it on social visits out with my parents; further more down the line in its third year, it would fit the bill to go to the cinema or the Malaab- The progression has by now reached the fourth year but it still looked uh decent enough for everyday life. After that, even my Mother had to admit that the deed was done, so we gave it to the rag and bone man who toured the neighbourhood with a donkey shouting (*Attiq lel bei'e*).

Our guests were regaled with *May Wared* (a fragrant drink)! Once a year the Shakarchee (sweet shop) sent a man to grind the multitude of pink roses the gardener had bought into a pulp, all the while stirring them in massive pots on top of a flame. The resultant very fragrant infusion, the consistency of water, was filtered into glass bottles for all round yearly use, topping it with fresh water and ice.

As there was no tomato paste to be had, households bought a lot of tomatoes in the summer (there were none in the winter), ground them and put them out on the roof to dry and thicken.

The government did its bit to combat the *bargash* (flies) and other annoying summer creatures. Frequently it blew a whiff of DDT on the city. At these times we had to stop breathing for a few minutes, and as the air became bluish too, everyone disappeared in a haze.

IRAQI FOOD TO GO

It is a truism that to be delicious, all food has to come from the heart and be equated with love; the foremost ingredient is a sincere wish to satisfy people's taste buds and disseminate happiness. Iraqi food is arranged neatly and prettily on bigger plates and people help themselves from the centre dishes; the pieces are cut small so as to fit in the mouth without fiddling. Read here a lot of attention to detail. To look the part of the hospitable host there should be much more food offered than warranted with no correlation to the number of guests present, not by a long shot! The only valid rule is for the table to be full to overflowing. When we say to people *tafadallou* (help yourselves), people are supposed to scatter round the table homogeneously, never queue!

Quite a few of the Iraqi ladies "who cook" have written excellent cook books becoming our mantra everywhere in the world i.e. Alice Shashoua and Daisy Eeny. No, no! We shalll not forget our traditions, but must need to doctor any recipe suspected of being too labour intensive.

The following is a very condensed cooking book of the most ethnic and popular dishes laced liberally with Scherezade's professional tips:

Kuzzi Muhasha: Take a medium sized lamb, clean it all and stuff it with rice, almonds, kubbas, and satsumas too. Roast it slowly so that all the juices drip onto a bed of rice. This is usually served on a very vast tray.

Pacha: This is the stomach of the lamb, stuffed with a special mixture of rice and mince meat made from its head, mixed in with onion, fresh tomatoes and spices.

Sijjaq: This is a delicacy; made with the intestines of lamb after a very thorough cleansing operation. Inside the mouth of the tap you push one end of the intestines so that water flows into them thoroughly - now turn them inside out and repeat the process. Next the intestines are soaked in salt and vinegar and, sparklingly clean by now, get rubbed with

a grand occasion – Can it be a Henna?

orange peel to acquire an extra nice flavour. A mixture of rice, lamb, onion, tomatoes and freshly ground spices is pushed down their whole length. Then they are put in a saucepan containing tomato sauce and cooked on a very slow fire: the final taste is out of this world – only the very exlusive delis stock them.

Tabbeet: is an exotic dish and no Iraqi Jewish party can do without it. Difficult as well as complicated, it requires years and years of practice. The following can only serve as a basic groundwork. After stuffing the stomach of the chicken with rice and offal, sew the opening firmly shut with needle and thread so that none can escape (you are allowed to leave some pins during the cooking process, but they must be removed later or your poor guests will get a surprise). In a big pot, cook more rice and push the bird in it with chopped tomatoes and cardamom and any unhatched eggs you might discover in its stomach. And here is the climax of this very traditional dish: let it cook for 12 hours on a very low flame while you sleep, until the rice becomes reddish and the residue (*haqaqa*) is blackish; if the colours decide to turn the other way round, forget it, back to the drawing board my friend; to spoil the Tabbeet means you have spoiled our Shabbat!

Kubba: I have remained in awe of this pattie whose manufacture can still ensnare the seasoned cook!

Rice or semolina is ground very fine, and then added to some ground chicken or meat till it the mixture resembles dough. As stuffing, fry minced meat with parsley, spices and almonds; beginning with a piece of dough, you spread it between the fingers and push in it some of the stuffing. Try to close this pattie firmly so it does not open while cooking.

It is only right to warn amateurs that you cannot make kubbas in one day; the process is too laborious; it is so much better to divide the work between 2 days and a few friends.

Kebab: Is minced meat with lots of parsley carefully shaped round a long widish skewer. For an aromatic finish, it must be cooked on charcoal – in addition it needs a bit of animal fat mixed in. Its optimum taste comes out when sprinkled liberally with *summaq* and *amba pickle;* it is true that the real professionals are more likely to be found in Arbil or

Suleimaniya but I have yet to come across a Kurdish cook book to quote from.

Ras el Usffour (head of a bird*):* tiny balls of minced lamb or beef comparable in size to the head of a bird, hence its name, stewed in a sour tomato sauce.

Rice and salads are the staples that accompany every meal. Rice must be of the Basmati or Amber varieties, treated with care and freshly served. The best salad (*tabbouleh*) made up of parsley, spring onion mint and tomatoes added to massive amounts of burgul is the most seriously time consuming dish ever!

I hope I am not putting any one off making Iraqi food, but it is the case that in Iraq time stretched infinite, and the Iraqi housewife's commitment to her household also stretched to fill the beyond, it has always constituted her raison d'etre. For she only ever aspired to be that rare phenomenon: an *Ishat Chayel*

That is why her very grateful husband (we hope) is counselled by the Bible to sing her praises:

"An accomplished woman, who can find, her value is far beyond   pearls
She does good and no evil, all the days of her life.
She buys wool and flax to make many useful things
and wakes up at night to make food for all
She watches over the ways of her household, and does not approve any idleness or waste."

POTIONS FROM THE ANCIENTS

A trip to the doctor was something special and unusual and we waited for my Father to take us in his own time. With no NHS in Iraq then, we paid a fee; again with the absence of NHS rules, visits were allowed to stretch to become an almost enjoyable social occasion.

Meanwhile we made do with a body of alternative medicines which the parents had gleaned from present and past experiences! For example, whenever anyone complained of a pain anywhere in the body, my Mother would advise us to drink from the brandy bottle kept in a cupboard in the rather dark dining room: stomach pains, headaches, colds, coughs it was the ultimate panacea. We only drank half an inch, holding on to our nostrils so as not to take in the reeking smell. That is why a bottle of brandy lasted at least five years. If this did not make it better and the pain persisted, we resorted to *Wared Mawee* (blue flower) which is a very bitter potion made by grinding and boiling the leaves of this flower.

It was believed that perspiring was good for an ailing body, so blankets and water bottles were piled on top of the sick. The opposite treatment is meted out in the West where people are covered in ice cubes to cool down the fever. Wonder of wonders, how is it that both treatments seem to work?

A cold can be made better by dousing the head, the chest as well as the back with Vicks, which must be why the classroom smelled funny in the winter! In the case of an earache, relief can be sought by blowing cigarette smoke into the ear's inner canals! Sadly it did not take the infection away!

175

One other drawback included the likelihood of one or two tiny fires starting in bed from the embers.

As sore throats blighted my earlier life, all the doctors bar one declared that I should have had my tonsils removed a long time ago! But as that one doctor was English and everyone was in awe of English doctors, so I ended up suffering from them for a long time. My Father wound a ball of cotton wool round the wrong end of a spoon, immersed it in a vile red liquid, and then pushed it down my throat as though polishing it. I could not accept this treatment lying down and there were always negotiations beforehand as to what was on offer to compensate for the horrible aftertaste and smell! Agreement was reached only when a few pieces of delicious chocolate were put on the bargaining table.

If anyone fainted or was about to faint, or was otherwise sick, we would run to the kitchen and get the jar of Turkish coffee and put it directly underneath their nostrils. This really worked wonders! In more difficult cases where a bad spirit penetrated into the body this had to be exorcised. The elders advised to tie a handkerchief around the neck when sleeping at night or to put it under the pillow: then first thing in the morning, someone gave you a lift by car and you threw it in the river Dijlah. Coming back from the little outing, you feel lighter in weight which means the spirit has absconded!

Some people had an evil look which boded ill luck to a household; it had to be stopped in its tracks. Strands of hair were gathered from all affected and burnt in a brazier chanting incantations all the time.

To turn the hair into a more fashionable colour the girls might use the henna powder sold in the Shorja. This was real unprocessed henna which turned the hair carrot red in amateur hands. More wizened, we added coffee or tea leaves in "tempering" quantities aiming for that modest glint of brightness which society allowed the young girls to get away with! It was a much healthier alternative to harsh chemicals, but what a mess if you did not get the chemical proportions right! You might end up looking like a *polichinelle* (clown), a favourite word in our household when anyone wore too many colours at once. One little mistake might cost a lot here so I don't recommend it for the clumsy, the fainthearted or anyone who is not Iraqi born and bred.

Exposure to the harsh rays of the sun will cause dry straw like hair: In this case we recommend a paste of *teenkhawa*, a dry mud like substance mixed with water; it did wonders. It was then washed away with "watermelon" soap from Syria which is just about the gentlest soap imaginable; we called it watermelon but it is really made from the laurel plant.

Arthritis was cured by using the E*nkhalla*, which is the leftover from wheat grains after passing through a strainer: first heated in a pan then put in a cloth wrapped in a towel for warmth.

I remember being kept quiet in a corner, while the doctor came often to see my great-grandMother; all the sessions ended with a poultice (*lazqa*).

Rice is that important diet staple, but it has many curing qualities too: for diarrhoea or a stomach upset, the best thing was to abstain from eating anything except very soft freshly cooked rice. If you suffer from a bad cold or are feverish therefore have no appetite at all, the best thing to have is cooked rice with plenty of added milk, a bit like soup but much tastier.

In effect it seems to me that rice along with *maraq* (stew) in our culture is parallel to chicken soup in the Ashkenazi culture. It is used as a panacea for most illnesses.

For skin rashes try eating *numi helou* (sweet lemon); this fruit is neither sweet nor sour but just right, with a lovely aroma. It looks very sunshiny, its colour a delicate pistachio.

To combat the germs in hot weather, my Father made a red solution of permanganate in water, dunked the vegetables and the fruit in, and recommended that they be scrubbed vigorously. Of course the maid grumbled about the extra work and time this involved.

As for any anaemic tendencies, or lack of energy, we were prescribed wine. We loved the Iraqi wine from Mosul, full bodied and dark, it was said to be good for us; but as it was a bit bitter so we added spoonfuls of sugar into the bottle. It was a delight to watch it foam and spill over the worktops, inundating all the empty crockery round it.

God forbid a pain persists and will not let us go to school; then the doctor more often than not prescribed penicillin jabs; these were invariably administered at home by a very buxom lady who also served as the community midwife: Jeddah Rahma. As she came often, and the jabs were very painful to the kids, so the parents capitalized on our dread of her visits. For example, if we did not drink milk or have the regular dose of cod liver oil, they would threaten to tell Jedda Rahma! The poor woman became the perfect ghoul!

And if all the above did not work, my Father would hunt by word of mouth for the whereabouts of Dr Daoud Gabbay (he of the unconvential touch). He was a clever man and had a lot of followers especially in the counties outside Baghdad like Amara; many swore by him while he flatly refused to take any money from a needy patient! He became Abdul Karim's doctor and as such attracted envy; that is why they imprisoned him in the Kasser.

The older generation counselled a visit to the synagogue, turning round its lectern with the Rabbi's hand on your head.

If a woman finds it difficult to conceive, she made her way to one of the four Jewish Prophets to ask help: the most popular was Ezekiel in the Keffel near Al Hilla on the Euphrates. The lady would pray in Hebrew from a book that the caretaker handed her and ask the Prophet to intercede on her behalf. The Moslems viewed a holy Jewish man as sacred too, especially if he was mentioned in the Koran so prayed to Ezekiel as well.

Poor Rabbi Ezekiel, I fully expect His Holiness to have defected completely to the other side by now, as there are no more loving Jews in Iraq to visit his shrine. One notable exception to this occurred in 2003 when Huda asked a Moslem friend to measure the dimensions of the tomb and then sent Him a very nice drape from America; it was her own private pledge to the Prophet to thank him for finding her long lost brother in Iraq.

the Shakarchee distilling May Wared from the flowers p:170

ARABIC MUSIC IS FUN

Iraqi culture and cultural life were heavily influenced by everything Egyptian. Most of the books that we were taught in the curriculum at school were Egyptian and I have to admit they did an excellent job linguistically, for example Najeeb Mahfouz, Tah Hussein – while even the adventure and fashion magazines which we read in our spare time were Egyptian - they had by far the upper hand in literary output. There were also a lot of translated material from the world classics but they felt strange to the indigenous culture. The cinema houses in Baghdad were awash with American, English, and French films with Egyptian films close on their heels. Later on Russian, East European, even Cuban films were given the chance to shine depending on the current diplomatic climate of course. One period I remember well when all films except the Indian ones were forbidden. As per our habit, we had gone as a family to our usual cinema on Friday night; it was playing "Umm al Hind" Mother India. As one horrible tragedy unfolded after the other, we all started sniffling into our tissues. During a breather, I took a look around the audience and saw that invariably everyone was crying loudly, ditto the people on the screen. Then my Father, looking a sad shade of angry *Hay M'ayna Suda (*what a disgrace*)*, said we were leaving immediately because he could not take any more heartbreak. So we trooped out to people's consternation, everyone else becoming stuck in yet another catastrophe. I, too, share the attitude that a film must radiate a bit of a good feeling and dispense happiness - as indeed the modern Indian films do extremely well. Anyhow the diplomatic relations soon resumed thank God and the Western culture became kosher once more! We made the most of the entertaining films before the Zionists poisoned the political climate and deprived the country of its leisure - it had been their fault all along!

For the Iraqi man or woman in the street, it was the Egyptian actors and actresses who became the most popular icons; the Egyptian dancers were phenomenal and much more superior than their modern European look-alikes who are too slim to have anything worth titillating; as for music, every month Umm Kalthoum came out with a new song and people sat at home mesmerized, listening for five hours at a time.

Luckily, there remained one area which was pure Iraqi born and bred: the distinctive Maqam: here the native singers had the exclusivity of the lyrics because the Maqam depicts exclusively Baghdadi society. Its composers straddled such differing periods from the libellous Abou Nuwwas, through to the melancholic Al Mutannabi and the rebel Mohammad Mehdi Al-Jawahiri.

My family and I together with our circle of friends enjoyed those songs a lot both in their ancient and modern mode. Granted that the Maqams, full of wise words held this "wailing" quality which suited the older generation, it was rather the pestatt that we, the younger generation, awaited eagerly at the end. We identified totally with their light heartedness, swinging rhymes, and romantic overtones.

I confess to be pleasantly surprised in doing this research, at how rich in Jewish influences and contributions the Iraqi music was in its fledging years: Jews, doubtless, had been the musicians of the Iraqi people. This state came about originally because the Ottoman government in Iraq was fanatic, and did not allow the Moslems to play music; the Jews applied themselves to learn the complex Arab modes and stepped in to fill the vacuum   In 1932, for example, all the

181

instrumentalists who attended the first Arabic music congress in Cairo, were Jews, (except for the singer Alqebbantchi), they received the first prize from King Fuad. When Iraq Radio was first established in 1936, the entire instrumental ensemble, apart from the percussion player was Jewish, as were almost all the instrumentalists in the Baghdadi night-clubs. Iraqi music is played by an ensemble called Chalgi, and during this period there were only two of them in Baghdad, both Jewish, called Patao and Bussoun.

Chalgi ensemble

The Chalgi plays the following instruments which produce a sharp metallic sound:

A Joza is half a coconut with a fish skin stretched across it, Qanun is a flat shallow guitar plucked with the fingers, Santur is a wired flat box with tiny hammers, Duff is a framed drum, surrounded by tiny bells, Dumbuk is a goblet-shaped drum, Oud is a lute, Nay is a flute.

During the 1920's, the Al Kuwaiti brothers Saleh, a *kamanja (*violin) player, and Dawud, an *Ud* player achieved star status: They formed the official Chalgi for Iraq Radio. Born in Kuwait to a family of Iraqi origin, they received a violin and an oud as presents from their uncle who returned from a business trip to India. They began studying music and quickly became prodigies. Saleh began to compose, Daoud excelled in playing, and the two began to perform at events hosted by Kuwaiti high society. Later on, its ruler Mubarak al Sabah invited them to perform at his wedding. Nevertheless they gravitated to Baghdad as a more central metropolis for music.

Although his official attitude toward Jews in Iraq was unfriendly, still they became favourites of King Ghazi who asked them to broadcast from the King's palace. Jameel Basheer who became a stalwart oud player was taught by the Jewish musicians

Saleh saw that Iraqi music needed bringing up to modern times; it had been stuck in a time warp for too long! So he infused Western elements into it and developed the new music further along the lines of traditional Makamat. The brothers' best songs such as "*El-Hajer Mu Ada Ghariba* about leaving a loved one, "*Khadril Chai Chadri*" simmering tea, "*Ma Tgulli Ya Hilu*", how did God make you so handsome? form an essential core in the Iraqi music and are played daily throughout the Arab world albeit without giving the brothers their full credit. As their reputation travelled far and wide, Umm Kalthoum on a visit to Baghdad in the thirties asked them exceptionally to compose a song for her and "*Galbak Sakher jalmoud*" a romantic song about a stony heart was born. Before that she only ever employed Egyptian artists; this song was destined to become a regular part of her repertoire; even Abdul Wahab when he came to Iraq, sought to learn maqam Lahami from Saleh. It seems an amicable chemistry developed between them and they became close musical companions! Night after night they sat after the performances, played together and taught each other Makamat from the traditions of both of their countries. Sadly they later lost touch with each other: they were living in separate enemy states.

However, upon the signing of a peace treaty between Israel and Egypt forty odd years later and despite the prevalent boycotts, Abdul Wahab found a way to send a message of *salaams* (regards) to his friend of yore, Saleh.

As most of the Jews left Iraq in the early 1950s, the music industry in Iraq suffered a blow. The government of the day vested in its premier Nouri el Said forced two gifted Jewish musicians, Patao and Shemmeil, to stay behind and train al Rajab and one more Moslem in their art. The sons of those two musicians, who in turn were also taught to play, still recall the episode, the heritage and the debt. It seems Nouri was desperate to persuade the Jewish musicians to stay, with the gift of a house etc in Iraq.

Saleh and Daoud were applied to by the Kuwaiti prince no less to continue playing their music in the corridors of his palace; during the mass exodus of Jews in 1951, while the planes were busy taking off with people who had given up all hope of going back to their country, a limousine burst onto the runway of Baghdad Int'l airport and blocked the path of the departing plane - not in an attempt to stop a secret shipment of weapons or arrest fleeing spies, but to deliver a personal message to the musician Saleh al Kuwaiti. It was an emissary from the ruler of Kuwait, Mubarak al Sabah, begging him to change his mind about emigrating to Israel. His departure would be a severe blow to both of the Kuwaiti and Iraqi culture and impact negatively upon the Emir's artistic life. Too late, the whole family were already packed inside the aeroplane and so he declined. Much later and remembering this friendly gesture, Saleh named his second son "Sabah" after the Emir.

Israel's Ashkenazi *"Vuzvuz"* preponderance looked down on Arabic music as well as on the Oriental culture in the early days of the State,; they were both relegated to second class status; furthermore the Iraqi Jews were seen to be laid back as well so they were labelled "pyjamas". Worse, this inferior status was equated with an enemy culture. Saleh and Daoud watched bitterly as the trends favoured music other than their own. These two great musicians and composers were forced in the end to take up basic commercial work to earn their living and what a falling down from their former glories! It was only a decade later that a meagre weekly opening presented itself in the Arabic section of Israel radio. A very small chink to entertain the multitude of adoring ex-fans from the neighbouring countries and inside Israel! Never more could they bask in the star treatment of yore, never more could they consecrate their lives to music.

But there were more woes! Immediately after their departure, the other Arab singers started to claim ownership of their songs. In the seventies, at the behest of Saddam Hussein, they were razed from the cultural history of Iraq! A committee was established to remove the names of Al Kuwaiti brothers from every official publication and curricula belonging to the Academy of music. From then on, the songs that they had attuned with such dedication and love were labelled 'of folk origin'! Such unfair and utter rejection of their art had a profound effect on the artists; it led to Saleh forbidding his children from the study of music absolutely.

Happy news: After sixty years out in the wilderness, the world has turned on its axis in more ways than one. In the freedom of the post-Saddam era, the Iraqis have decided in fairness to re-accord the Kuwaiti brothers their eminent position and are now starting to give fair dues to their vital influence.

As a result their name is beginning to be appended once more to their songs, and they even won the title of "favourite composers" in an Arabic television program recently. Saleh's son Shlomo has collected all of his Father's and uncle's best tunes and compositions on a CD which he has sent all over the world to journalists and scholars. Surprisingly, both Iraq and Kuwait are now contesting their "ownership" to add to their national heritage! And more rainbows are in the offing: Israelis have become much more attuned to Oriental music and the third generation are not ashamed anymore of their grandparents' Arabic culture as they were all those years ago. Indeed they are very curious about their heritage and want to connect with it! We see that Daoud's grandson (Dudu Tassa) has managed to learn his grandFather's songs and is now a singer in his own right. Their talents have merely skipped one generation. If only these prodigies had survived a little while longer.

No respectable family allowed its daughters to enter a professional singing career, *kullush EIB* (extremely forbidden) this time, and as the industry could not function without the gentle touch, there appeared to be a conundrum of sorts. It became a necessary custom to recruit the women singers and dancers from the local brothels. Salima Murad managed to climb this particular fence and attain an exalted rung among her countrymen, who became hooked on her songs (pardon the pun). The government rewarded her by the title Pasha in recognition of her services to music, so she became known as Selima Murad Pasha throughout the annals. This exalted position earned her a lot of money. She married the singer Nathim al Gazali, he of the full bodied voice who was almost 20 years her junior. She was a Jew, he was a Moslem. They opened a disco in the sixties, where he sang all her songs as well as his own with a definite charisma, then travelled together for duos in the West and Lebanon to regale the grateful Iraqi ex-pats amid huge sumptuous assemblies. Nathim put the audience in his pocket the minute he flashed his black eyes and warm smile, being very charming and handsome to boot! His *pestatt* (lighter moments of maqam) became legendary: once he declares his love for the neighbour's daughter so she hands him fresh bread from behind the clay oven, very slyly of course – another pretty girl will not respond to his advances because it is not allowed, but her eyes continue sending positively flirtatious messages in the meantime! That is why he seeks refuge on top of the palm trees where he addresses the local Bedouin girls! His concerts reverbated with happiness and joy to all, they embodied the true spirit of Iraq! Enraptured, we were all very close behind him, clapping and tapping and enjoying the refrains.

Very unfortunately coming back from one of his frequent jaunts to Beirut hosted by his multitude of fans (and courted by his younger girlfriends), he suffered a massive heart attack (1963)upon his arrival in Baghdad. This star of the Iraqi firmament died too young at 43. Selima, a widow now, though continuing with her career as well as with her august status, began to shy away from too much public exposure. Accompanied by her band she kept singing till the end (1974).

Iraqi music is appealing because the singer gets close to his audience in so many ways! You can hear the wavering catch in his voice along with its naked emotion filtering clearly through very basic instruments.

We also managed to attend western disco entertainment, albeit illegitimately. Night clubs did exist, but it was not done for a woman to be seen in them; however an alternative offered itself in this one. My parents had friends whose roof overlooked the gardens of "Sameeramees" nightclub, so they invited us and several other families regularly to watch the show from their rooftop. We took our seats under cover of darkness very near the audience though on a much higher elevation, and behind them. The European dancers got ready for their various acts behind the stage, but since we were on a promontory we enjoyed a complete view of the proceedings. They painted their fair complexion with a white translucent soap which made them highly visible; then they appeared again to the front in their rich costumes and performed their stimulating dances. Nobody hearkened to our presence as we talked in whispers on the dark roof. Though we felt like clapping with the audience, we couldn't, but we appreciated the fact that the entertainment was of a very good standard. The men and women dancers kept going back and forth changing their stylish uniforms, keeping pace with our hosts who kindly plied us with cold drinks and fruit throughout the night. It being a freebie heightened our senses of enjoyment and achievement both

It was such a treat to see these perfect figures in their natural glory, right in front of our eyes too! Once the whole game was nearly up: a friend was so enthralled with the spectacle that he let out a long loud whistle. This resulted in the dancers shutting the doors catastrophically behind them whenever they changed and forevermore. We never forgave the culprit either, indeed he is still being blamed and berated for the loss of such an incredible privilege and told off every time Emile looks him up in Toronto thus: "*Walak leysh?*": "*Walak hichee?*"

We crawled back to our nearby houses at 1 a.m.- still way ahead of the rest of the relaxed audience. They had presumably fortified themselves with some strong locally brewed Araq and Iraqi beer too.

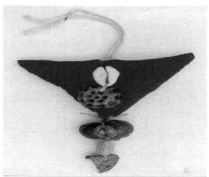

Good luck always came with the Amulet

A FASHION PHENOMENON

How else to explain our addiction to the latest trends when we could have no contact with them? There were no fashionable clothes in the shops, only cloths, none of the latest magazines at the newsagents, no catwalks, none of the gyrating models popular in the West!

The Lebanese expats were credited with possessing a whiff of the French about them and were considered to be Baghdad's trendsetters! When two sisters opened a boutique to import knitting materials, all the well to do ladies flocked enthusiastically to be told what to buy and what best to make. My Mother and her friends started to knit jumpers for their men folk and even crocheted sweaters for all the family! And dresses too. Even I crocheted dresses with cotton or nylon bought from "Abbachi" this trendiest of shops. It was very easy and progressed rapidly since the crocheted pattern contained many gaps; the lining served to hide those gaps later, but at the same time the whole effect looked very elegant and lacy. The dress was made to such short specifications that within a few days hey presto it was done; the secret was in stretching it to the length required by putting a wet cloth and a hot iron on top then pulling hard.

Otherwise there was a lack of shops and shopping; this is why people resorted to making special shopping trips abroad to buy enough clothes for a few seasons taking the opportunity to parade them in front of their envying acquaintance. However, there was an awareness of smart, a positive appreciation of good fashion sense. It tilted to the other extreme sometimes when people were judged exclusively on their finery.

As we were forbidden to travel so had no access to the sophistication of London and Paris or even Beirut! It became a point of honour though to compete with the other Iraqis who could do so and dressed in the latest trends at university or in the clubs! A difficult task at the best of times but becoming yet more onerous in the last few years when, adding insult to injury, the government announced very restrictive monetary laws; our bank accounts had limitations on the amounts we could take out per month.

It is quite mystifying how in view of these worrying times we still did not waver in our vision towards becoming fashion icons. Somebody up there must have heard, and a kindred spirit sent us "Burda"

Burda, a German magazine was a new concept then. It performed wonders: not only did it contain the latest fashions, but it allowed the layman to execute them as well; it contained a pattern for each dress, skirt or blouse. This is how it worked: in a very compact four pages at the back, like a complicated maze, all the patterns existed intertwined within each other.

This led every girl in my acquaintance to anticipate and buy its various colourful editions off the bookshelves
We became quite adept at pinning the magazine with a bit of cellotape to the window and then with the help of tracing paper and a bit of light, we could follow the same contour of that line throughout for the different pieces: back, front, darts, sleeves, pockets. In a jiffy, the complete pattern was "downloaded"! When you think that one single Simplicity or Vogue pattern cost more than the whole magazine whereas enterprisingly "Burda" provided more than twenty patterns at once! The Mothers and girlfriends became adept at sewing the

clothes too. I must salute Burda and its inventors; they were the answer to a lot of praying.

A Burda outfit from the sixties

.

After acquiring the pattern, we made our way to the market and the cloth seller would cut a cloth according to the same measurements that Burda recommended: *"Affiat:"* congratulations, said he, as he cut the length. *"Bil Eeffee"* repeated my Father when we told him later, *"Bifrahek"* exclaimed the neighbour when it was shown to her! Give your Mother two or three days in the summer (in the winter it took longer because of the sleeves) and the dress was ready to parade in front of a very appreciative society. If the Mother could announce truthfully or even a shade of truthfully that "my daughter put the pattern together and made the dress up all by herself" that was considered to be a feather in the hat of the whole family and you could see both Mother and daughter - even the Father, visibly expand with pride at the feat.

192

In my modest opinion, dressing well is not about spending a lot of money, not at all! But I concede that dressing extremely well, no doubt, is. To achieve the first requirement you need taste first and foremost. To illustrate this point I once bought a light greenish cotton cloth from Orosdi for a meagre sixty fils. It was the time when the government was trying to take the merchants' business away from them by importing cloths on the cheap from China. By the time we put in some red and white tipping, the price had gone up to 1.50 dinars. Nevertheless, it turned out to be a very "*chic*" dress. As people admired it, kudos demanded that I pretended that it cost much more. Style is no doubt a very unstable equation but a whiff of luxury sure lends a helping hand.

The downturn in having everyone copy and execute the same patterns of course is that a bit of originality creeps out! But still it is a fact: never did so many people with such meagre resources dress so smartly by dint of a little outlay! I bet Churchill would have liked this.

Thanks to Burda, our sense of fashion never deserted us but grew and mushroomed to lead us into Knightsbridge, Macy's and les Galeries.

As for shoe shops, they were not in existence for a long time. And then trendiness descended as a Lebanese shop called "Harraq" opened with exquisite taste and the most delicate of shoes in all the colours of the rainbow! Before that it was just black for winter and white for summer for the ordinary mortals like us.

Gold was the best of 24 carats and never caused an allergy. Only women wore golden ornaments while heavy multiple bangles, earrings, necklaces, voluminous *hejjels* (anklets) were earmarked as signs of prestige; some jewellery was set in an exquisite blue stone; it was usual to see very poor women going round barefoot, still weighed down with the gold on their person.

OF RELIGION AND RABBIS

As a family we were not over religious, but in a previous era psychologically aided by their extended family , my parents used to be much more observant. Some families did keep all the doctrines for example the Cohens as their standing was much higher than ours in the Bible.

Religious rites were accepted as implicit and no one ever questioned them, sought to ameliorate them or even comprehend them. The real culprit was the Iraqi government where one of its edicts after 1950 said we were not permitted to study our religion, only to learn to read and write it; this meant that we never advanced enough to understand its laws or the sayings of its Prophets. As for the history of our own indigenous ancestors that went back 3000 years and beyond in Iraq itself, nobody discussed it or alluded to its impact throughout the years!

We studied about Ur without ever linking it to Abraham, we were taught instead the history of the Akkadians, the Assyreans,the Sumerians, made to memorize extracts from their languages and cuneiform inscriptions (so difficult this) and which animals or gods they worshipped. We also studied chapters from the Koran and learnt some of its teachings by heart for the Baccalaureat; no matter if it was complimentary or detrimentary, we still obtained a good mark in the exams!

Of course all of the above did reflect on our religious observance, or lack of it; briefly, we tagged along with our parents on two occasions a year to the synagogue: once in the New Year, once on Yom Kippur. Along with the rest of the women, I and my Mother sat upstairs on wooden chairs, my Father with the rest of the men had more comfortable sofas downstairs; the women were not required to read or know what was being read and I cannot remember any book ever being put in my hands! We aped the men down below on the ground floor, whenever they stood up we stood up, and whenever they sat down that was our cue to sit down too! In between we gossiped like mad.

New Year was the time when we traditionally put on new clothes and looked dainty; so white for new beginnings: white dress, white socks, white shoes; white shorts and white socks for the boys too; even the men wore white suits or off white suits (*Shaari*) and light coloured shoes. I would go out to meet my friends in the street outside whenever I got bored which I always was (remember I did not understand the proceedings or the language). The synagogue used to get stifling once the sun came out; that is when the huge off white roller blinds were drawn horizontally over the open middle of the synagogue, and then there were fans as well in the men's enclosure (switched on by Moslem lads, our friends in observance!). My Mother and most of the ladies brought their own paper fans and used them to show off! Yom Kippur was a much more solemn affair notwithstanding the fact that my Mother along with the other Mothers brought sweets and food in their handbags to give to us during the long prayers; these served in lieu of breakfast and lunch as usually they did not have the energy to go home! Everything was difficult even coming on the bus to the synagogue; we could not pay as we were not allowed to handle any money; luckily the friendly *jabee* (bus collector) took it in his stride and trusted us to pay another day: we bumped into him almost daily. Going back to the house at night proved to be an adventure with no lights to go by; strict adherence to the religion that particular day meant no electricity could be switched on. This edict ceased to be later as we became more modern!

It was on Yom Kippur as well that the Cantor spent the whole day lecturing us about how bad we had been in front of the Lord, and how we must do penitence the whole year and not just on that one day. He really contrived to make us feel very guilty. But why, I ask now? Looking back I am aghast that we could be the butt of these charges as our life was so empty of temptations and pleasure. We the young never drank let alone indulged in hedonistic activities as even going to nightclubs was not done. As for the adults: there could be no extramarital affairs (everybody knew everyone else's business view the fact that the roofs were adjacent to each other) while the maids also got to know the innermost secrets of the families that they worked for and kept gossiping about them to all of the other maids. No violence where there were no guns, no immorality because of lack of venues, and lastly utter obedience to the laws of the land because of pure cowardice! We had through no choice of our own become model citizens! If only the natives had copied our example.

One memory from the synagogue that has really made the most impact on my young mind used to be the repetition *ad infinitum* of this catchy phrase by the Cantor while he walked throughout the four corners of the sanctum: *yezeedeb umurle yazeed (*he who donates the more money, will be the one to live longer)! Nadji was trying to raise funds for the synagogue by auctioning each of the prayers being recited;

When we did sit around the table to celebrate Passover, my Father would read the story of the exit from Egypt, interspersed with eating from the usual hors d'oeuvre; (the matzot called jaradeq were much nicer and crunchier then, as they were hand baked in the *tannours* or clay ovens, and not mass produced and dried up like in the West). We put on weight dunking them in the velvety date syrup, ground almonds and nuts throughout the feast; there was also grape juice my Mother strained through a muslin cloth. I would be very interested on those occasions to ask questions, stemmed on by some ancient yellowing pictures in a very ancient book of prayers, but did not get too far. That particular service *Pessach (*Passover*)* was very long and I presume my Father became tired trying to read through the book. My Mother did help a bit especially with the Aramaic which we understood as it was so very similar to the Arabic, but we had to be satisfied with the same bits every year and can't remember ever making it to the end of the exile from Egypt. That was the time when we really missed having an extended family to help in the reading; all the while, my Mother would be diligently bringing in the festive meal to get it all done and dusted. We usually had the dinner while the horses and the men were still drowning in the sea. Once we made so bold as to ask her if she had ever sat down during the Pesach meal and read the whole book! Surprisingly the answer was yes. It seems that when my Mother was still young her younger siblings could not keep awake, so she kept sole company to her Father while they read the whole book between them both! What! Two people on their own to carry out the mammoth task, so where was her Mother? Apparently my grandMother had become so exhausted preparing the food and getting the household ready the whole day that she fell asleep long before the festival or the festive meal began.

Well thank you God a million times for providing the housewife in our days with a lot of helpful technology and gadgets. It does not bear thinking of those poor souls coming out of Egypt with no dishwasher, hoover or ready made foods, how did they ever manage to celebrate the Seder? And in the desert to boot? Where did they buy the cheeses, yoghurts as well as the cakes that have been sanctioned to eat thanks to the new scientific methods and the modern Rabbis? By the way we were not allowed to touch those in Iraq! In Iraq we were made to feel the deprivation of our foreFathers rather acutely.

The meal over, we all piled into the car for a spin round Abu Nawwas on the river to breathe into the fresh air and the atmosphere (well how else to lift the spirits with no relatives to pop in?) Even at that late hour, the promenade was full of families walking and children running way past their bedtime. People were gesticulating in a very lively manner (no one could talk without using their hands), all the while crunching the famous pumpkin seeds. There were men peddlers a plenty either carrying ssammeet (slim baigels) lined very symmetrically on a tray on top of their heads, or sitting on the pavement with a tray of *semesmiyah* (sesame) and coconut sweets. More trays on the head full of *Cherraqs*, Baqsam and Kaak (pastries) and *lablabee* (cooked chick peas) inside the huge trolleys too. The Sudanese peddlers stood roasting peanuts in the tiniest of mobile stands; they sold them burning hot in paper cones. The promenade on Abu Nawwas is long and wide so bear with me, we have not finished yet. Yet other peddlers sold cold cokes, watermelon cut to show an amazing red colour, green and yellow figs:(*lawee ya teen*), *zangoolas* (fried dough) hot and oozing with the fragrant sugary syrup…

We must not forget the parallel commotion on the main road as all the while the cars hooted furiously and continuously - no doubt much more lively this than boring traffic lights had they existed. In the absence of gizmos, the drivers had to wind down the windows either to signal a left or a right hand turn, or to shout and make the usual gestures at the other drivers. They in turn lost their temper so responded in the most colourful of languages *kaleb ibn sitteen kaleb* (son of

Selling Lablabee with a bit of added lemon

sixty dogs), being one of the more innocent swearings. There were plenty more of them but we girls were brought up not to swear. What is certain is that this whole scenario lifted our mood in no time.

I think my favourite festivals were Tabernacle (Succoth) and Pureem. During the *eids* all our friends also stayed home, we had a field day visiting them on foot shaking hands (we never kissed) and saying: Bonnefete. The convention was to stay half an hour in each house, crunching the roasted charazat and eating of the handmade sweets. Pentecost was called *eid al ziyyarah* which literally means "visiting". As the weather was nice during Pentecost (Shavouth), people would go on picnic like expeditions to see the two most famous Jewish prophets in the south, one on Dijlah (Ezra the Scribe, Hasopher) descendant of Aaron Mose's brother – It was he who started

200

the synagogue establishment for Jews to gather in prayer in the foreign lands, and instituted the reading of weekly portions. While on the Euphrates near Chefel (Hillah) was (Nabi Heskel) who tried to comfort the people in exile from Jerusalem.

Both these prophets were revered and held in great affection by the Iraqi Jews! They would light a lamp and circling the tomb kiss it and tell the prophet about their intimate wishes. On the night of Shavuot (the giving of the Torah) everyone gathers around to sing songs after a festive meal,, clapping hands in great rejoicing:

Yal nabbi yal nabbi, uhfuth lee ghayyabee
Wennesh'el shmee' el assal,
Wen ssallee lil nabbee
(Dear Prophet please guard my absent ones
We have come to light the honey candles, and pray for your holy name).

While the very devout continued spilling wine on his tomb for the Prophet to join them in.their festivities.

Inside the shrine are coloured glass decorations

201

It is usual for Moslem men to revere and keep watch over the tombs; these guards come from the older, more tolerant generation; this guard tells us: "I saw the prophet Ezra in a dream, and he told me: please don't leave me alone and I swear I never will". Regretfully the new generation cannot remember / acknowledge us nor even our past presence.

View of the Cheffel from the river

It is very worthy of note that it was right near here that our learned ancestors compiled the very revered Babylonian Talmud; It took the sages over three hundred years of continuous discussions to do so hence the paraphrase "it is good to talk". Here also were established the famous academies of Nehardea, Sura and Pumbaditha, forerunners of the modern European universities.

Nearer the end of the nineteenth century, some influential Moslems claimed that the tombs belonged to their faith since it had minarets on the roof just like mosques. The Iraqi Ministry of Holy Sites recorded it to be so, and upset the Jewish community exceedingly. Hakham Bashi of Baghdad, together with the help of Sir Moses Montefiore from England objected, so the Sultan sent a special Turkish Minister from Constantinople to investigate the matter. He ruled in favour of the Jews. Nevertheless, it became a tradition for the Moslems to pray in the tombs, and the Jews ended up taking turns to wait for the various Moslem prayers. It is now a bit like a Jewish *haram shareef* (a Moslem holy place).

But now these conventions had disappeared from our household, we had a novel way of celebrating the feast of Pentecost: my Father would take the car at 6 am and race off to Bab el Sharqi where he would order Kahee cooked in the brick oven: Kahee is a sort of millefeuilles but the layers are a bit thicker as they are rolled by the bakers one by one and fried in butter; delicious with a bit of sugar sprinkled on top; To mark this special day, we had it with date syrup and queimer which is the doublest thickest whitest clotted cream you can imagine! We each picked one Kahee (they were huge), slobbered everything together and ate it with our fingers in the messiest way possible. All this had to be on the table by 7 am and cleared away soon after so that we were not too late for school. Well it is a festival, my Father said, a bit breathless from that early morning rush, but he, along with us, so enjoyed the providing and the eating and the marking of this festival.

On the last night of Pessach the men picked up long branches of greenery from the synagogue and brought them home; there they would dip them in a silver dish containing water and silver coins: it was a good excuse then to hit people with it saying *santal khadra* (have a fruitful year), and sometimes the taps became smacks and really hurt, but that constituted the fun element too.

Kosher meat and chicken were delivered once a week, or once every 2 weeks and at a lower progression still as "the situation" worsened. The institution was comprised of a Jewish butcher helped by a Moslem lad named Ali, who was well known to the community as he delivered to the houses. On those days our house, my Mother and her maid were all in turmoil! The chickens had to be plucked and singed over the fire as the feather bits still clung to them, and then the head with the eyes stared gloomily at us for a very long time till they were thrown away. The meat came in huge chunks and these had to be hacked away and quartered, the smells emanating from the kitchen were prohibitive on that day. And the sights were not much better: Whenever I dared put my head in, they were either cleaning the very long raw intestines of the lamb or pushing the stuffing of rice and raw meat down miles and miles all along their very wobbly length, cleaning and stuffing the stomach, or getting the blood out of the liver by roasting it on a naked light. Even though I admit that the results justified all this effort, there were too many guts and insides for my liking, so I shied away!

On the other hand we did eat outside the house in some take aways too as did most of our friends; for example nearly everyone upon their return from the *Malaab* ate hamburgers and chips from a kiosk near our house called Abu Yonan, run single-handedly by the owner. Abu Yonan was an Assyrian and he was so deft at making and frying the hamburgers, he acquired an honorary entry in the dictionary; thus instead of saying I would like to eat a hamburger, you just say I want to go to Abu Yonan! Nobody can believe how delicious they were and I can still hear their sizzle.

Some large families used to buy a whole lamb to stuff for Kouzzi Muhasseh; this is a true story of a family who bought this expensive lamb (there were many in the household) and stored it on the roof to fatten it up till it was ready to be slain for the festival. They tied it with a noose and a little rope and placed it on a little roof ledge as the large roof formed their sleeping quarters. One day the Mother asked one of the daughters to tidy up the whole area and the daughter went obediently up to the *Satteh* (roof) to clean it. As there were no lights so it was a bit dark; she pushed the silent lamb thinking it was a furniture item to try to clear the space underneath it. The poor lamb fell off the ledge and was left dangling with the noose round its neck till the next morning, when the neighbours from the other roofs alerted the family to the tragedy. The poor girl had hanged it without knowing! Anyway, as the religion forbids the eating of dead animals, the money had gone up in smoke. She had such a rollicking from her Father, what with the end of the Kuzzi, and them having to "donate" it, and no festival celebrations!

At certain times when we were supposed to do sacrifices in the ancient times Y*om Kippur* my Father would buy three roosters, one for himself and two for my brothers, as well as two chickens (my Mother and myself), and then recite a blessing while circling the live animal over our heads. Neither the cocks nor the chickens liked being handled by the feet by my Father and turned around like so many spaceships, so they squealed lustily with a very ominous look in their eyes. We had to trust that my Father would not let go of the chicken and that nothing will drop on our hair either as we had to make it to school without smelling of chicken droppings. If my

Father's hand dipped by chance, the chicken scratched our head; indeed it made as if to scratch our eyes out as well, and then it was our turn to squeal! What a frightening custom that was. Later on these birds were donated to the poor.

Another peculiar custom required that every time we walked past a greengrocer, we were admonished to close our noses with our fingers and not breathe; until we felt like

Kepparot for all the family

suffocating. It seems as the greengrocer stocked broad beans, and these were believed to be lethal to Iraqi kids, we were not allowed near them or even to smell them. It all sounded a bit folklorish: it was only light years later that I came to understand the concrete medical facts behind such precautions. The Iraqi genes lack the G6PD enzyme, which gives oxygen to the red blood cells, so a severe blood reaction will follow whenever fava beans are eaten. The good news is that deficiency of this G6 enzyme acts as a natural defence against malaria.

As for marriage ceremonies, the circumcisions and the funerals, they were usually conducted by two men of the cloth: the Chief Rabbi Sasson Kaddouri and Nadji Paneeri the Cantor; the latter performed the ritual singings and was also very active in everything else. Unfortunately I cannot recall any conversation with the Chief Rabbi, even though he presided in my generation and my parents' generation both. He served as the communal leader since 1927 except for seven years interspersed in between. I used to see him on many occasions for example on school prize days, weddings and assemblies, although he has never given a lecture or a sermon in my presence. Those Rabbinic activities had been confined to a better past, as I found out later; he had this grand aura and certainly looked the part of a very dignified leader: A long bushy beard of tarnished silver, a very heavy luxuriously embroidered turban that was like a cylindrical cake of the same colour as his cloth while a voluminous serge dishdashah or jubbah covered all his plump figure in an imposing way so nothing showed except his shoes; add to that a pair of dark and heavy glasses and the real man receded to become a mysterious, mystical figure; he was rendered even more august by the fact he had straddled all of the three Iraqi Kings, the Regent, many Prime Ministers, the 1941 revolution, the 1958 revolution and all the successive rulers as they wreaked revenge upon each other, remaining in his lofty position as Head of the Community. Surely this must be a feat. He had become an integral part of Iraq's national identity!

When he travelled outside his house, the Rabbi always took his own coffee cup with him so that he could drink coffee in the public places; everyone knew that the Jews only ate kosher and so could not eat chicken and meat with the Moslems. This issue needed to be resolved somehow when the Rabbi and his entourage went to visit al Najaf to pay homage to a Shiite VIP who had died! In the sombre ceremony that followed, the Rabbi read a psalm in Hebrew and the Shiites stood in reverence and awe. Then his secretary read a eulogy in Arabic, and the whole gathering dissolved into

The chief Rabbi with King Faisal II

tears! The connection was there spiritually, but how to feed such a noble gathering? It went both ways as the Shiites believed the Jews to be unclean so did not want them to touch their utensils. It was even said that a Shiite business partner needed to wash the money belonging to him from a Jew in the river before it became his. Resolving the issue, the Shiites caught fresh fish from the river, built a huge fire on the ground and threw the fish in it. As the Jews always brought their dishes and cutlery with them, so triumph and smiles all around. They had managed to share in the festive meal without compromising their ideals in the Koran or the Engeel!

If there was no dearth of diplomatic skills such a long time ago to resolve all awkwardness, what's the impediment now? However if the United Nations had been called in, their lawyers, translators and speechwriters would still be at it in closed meetings till the present day.

One of the Rabbi's most important tasks was to mediate peace between the Jewish community and whichever of Iraq's many regimes held the power at the time, but never interfere in politics. Politics was a no go area for the Jews of Iraq, this edict was set in stone. To this end the Rabbi always met with the current Head of State bearing greetings and gifts. When Abdul Karim Kassem was shot, the Hakham went to Salam hospital to visit him. He presented him with a Hebrew prayer written on the skin of an antelope and encased in a pure gold tube. Abdul Karim was said to have become overwhelmed with emotion, kissing the gift and pressing it to his chest.

Of course there had been other earlier more constructive times when he commanded more influence, boasted of strong friendships with Ministers and the like and to be sure he had a reputation of speaking eloquently and being extremely charming. Members of the community had alternately described him as being very diplomatic, intelligent and forward for his time; thus he gave Jewish people more chance to integrate with the natives by not demanding that they wear religious garb everyday. He also asked the matchmakers to come to him when a poor bride found difficulty in getting married due to trouble with the dowry; in this instance he would try to make it up by asking richer people to donate; indeed he often advised the community to try whenever possible to forego a dowry.

Nevertheless, he still aroused strong controversy in many cases. In a different age (1929) he was accused of eating

The Chief Rabbi with Abdel Karim Kassem

non kosher meat, or of eating meat and yoghurt too soon one after the other without the due interval which is required by the religion, so the Rabbis took away his title in 1930; but King Faisal I and Nouri el Said both liked him and brought him back as the communal leader in 1932; after the Zionists' led riots of 1949 where he was forced to take part to get the accused out of jail, he resigned (or it was suggested that he should resign) till after the great exodus (the Tassqueet). He always advocated to the Iraqi Jews to stay away from Zionist activities and to think of Iraq as their country first and foremost. No doubt he helped individual cases by going to the government buildings and meeting the officials concerned, writing letters to the authorities about the various rights taken away from the community after 1936, 1948, and 1967 respectively, and complaining when people were jailed unfairly.

But in more recent years especially, as successive nationalistic coups chipped at our presence in Iraq, there was a malevolent tide within the government that swept away any magnanimous considerations of his past good will and standing

He was definitely manoeuvred by the military rule that was in power: he had to take the podium and be on public display whenever circumstances dictated: When there was any doubt as to the Iraqis treating their Jewish minority well, so he was summoned to whoever occupied the high chair at the time to prove to the world that the Jewish community still existed....next time round there was a murder or for example people were being hanged, and the world press descended on Baghdad to write about the community being hapless and helpless, we would see him on television saying that the Jews of Iraq were treated fairly! But then two dreaded Amen men were standing directly in front of him pausing as cameramen, how could he say anything else?

His son Shaoul proved to be his best champion. He wrote a book to show how his Father had served the community well during nigh on six decades. In it, he demanded apology from the people who said unseemly things, and even threatened them with libel! At the same time, he insisted to have due recognition of his Father's long-time service! Shaoul Sasson is very adamant his Father could not breathe a word to the gathered (international) media. But wasn't the wound too deep for such considerations? On the other hand, the Baathists took his son to the dreaded Kasser al Nihayya and what a blackmailing card to play on a man in his eighties! I know there was a lot of hostility at the time and we all felt as though we were being stabbed twice! The only thing I can add is that a man of that age should not be put in the position of a leader, for all sorts of reasons to do with old age! He was only there because no one else wanted to be in the limelight at that time; it was considered downright dangerous!

It might be that that was his way of steering the ship in muddy waters: to calm down those in power forevermore! Hasn't that always been his remit during all those years? And what other recourse can present itself in a military dictatorship?

On the other hand, but, and, however or even a maybe: please understand dear Reader that life was very unfair for all concerned during those days, and the answer my friend has blown in the wind.

A MONARCH CUT OFF IN HIS PRIME

In the pre 1958 days, we had a King. Dashing, handsome, everyone loves the promising aura around a youthful King. Granted he was a bit remote as he lived in a palace on the other side of the river, the Karrech, while we lived in the Russafa, but he was an orphan who lost his Father at the age of four and his Mother at the age of 15 and was ensconced between an English tutor and a strict uncle, which made for a very sympathetic image to us schoolchildren. He smiled benignly through his pictures and cinema trailers (before the advent of television) and he looked the part in smart western or military dress with the occasional white feather. He represented nationhood, the promise of a bright and prosperous future, with a whiff of English peerage: England was seen as being at the forefront of the latest advances, and the seat of culture. So impressive then that he was educated at Harrow and Sandroyd, two of the most prestigious schools in the world, the schools that begat Churchill and other glorious names. As befits a King, we saw him ride in the royal carriage with the young Queen Elizabeth on State visits to England, adding to his stature and credibility. Iraq as a newly independent nation was hankering for global recognition, and he seemed to be the Monarch with the right pedigree as well as an immaculate lineage: both his Father and GrandFather were Kings and his Mother the Queen was also the daughter of a King! Moreover he was the first of his dynasty to be born in Iraq. A young King with a clean slate to devote to his countrymen! Such was his popularity that everyone waited with abated breath for him to take over the reins from the Wassi his uncle, the Regent. Iraqis were predisposed to think very well of him; he will give Iraq a new vista: he will do away with all of the cobwebs, make the desert bloom, the economy soar, and give the poor an incentive to work! Oh, for the amount of happy potential there is in a young King.

It seems strange to say the least that Iraq ended up being ruled by a Saudi Arabian Dynasty that came all the way from the desert of the Hijaz. Their story is definitely worth telling, as it has become an integral part of Iraqi history.

We begin with the last days of the Ottoman Empire, the sick man of Europe. Its territories were too vast for effective rule by Turkey from Constantinople, so that its powers were dying a slow death. Its Arab subjects saw in this decline a window of opportunity to try to claim independence for their people after an oppression of 500 years.

During World War I Britain was fighting Turkey and Italy. Into the arena stepped Sharif Hussein, the Emir of the Hijaz by appointment to the Sultan. A tribesman and a leader of tribes, the Emir commanded a big army skilled in desert warfare. He offered Britain a deal: "We will help you to topple Turkey, but in return give us (my tribe) sovereignty over our holy cities of Mecca and Medina as well as most of Greater Syria". His son Emir Faisal sought to rule Syria which was considered the real jewel in the Middle East.

Furthermore in 1919 Emir Faisal signed an enlightened agreement endorsing the Balfour Declaration. In a famous correspondence with Chaim Weizmann, he expressed the hope that intensive cultivation of the soil by the more modern methods of the European settlers will bring in its wake cooperation and therefore amelioration in the condition of the Arab peasants and farmers. Faisal initially welcomed the Jews emigrating to settle Palestine as long as they did not harm the indigenous Arabs. Meanwhile T E Lawrence notoriously promised the Arabs on behalf of the British Government that they will get the independence and the lands that they were aspiring to.

The Sharif hit Britain's enemies with all his might, assisted by his three sons and their armies, and when the framework toppled in 1918 they demanded their just reward from the victorious British.

Unfortunately for Faisal that was not forthcoming as France would not relinquish Syria. The English did try to make France budge from its stance, but France was adamant that it did not want to abandon its Christian minority! Angered, Emir Faisal left the Paris conference for Syria where he was nevertheless proclaimed a popular King by the enthusiastic Arab masses. France marched its troops into Syria to combat the stalemate, and after a big bloodbath of a fight, Faisal knew that that particular path was closed to him. The British nevertheless were very impressed with King Faisal's leadership and diplomatic qualities, his intelligence as well as his fighting skills! He made a perfect match for Iraq: a Sunni Moslem with a Shiite lineage going back to the Prophet Mohammed. T E Lawrence was Faisal's good friend, and he was an assistant to Churchill in the Colonial office. Churchill concurred with Lawrence and (the very important) Gertrude Bell that Faisal should reign there as a sovereign. So Faisal decided to put himself forward and it is only fair to mention here that a majority - 96% - of the Iraqis voted to have him as their King. The year was 1921

He signed a "Treaty of Alliance" with the English which promised independence in the future. Iraq would receive tutelage in all areas in the form of advice and assistance from the superior British Empire. It really meant that Iraq was still under the power of Britain even after its independence in 1932.

Meanwhile, his Father Sharif Hussein had proclaimed himself, with the tacit support of the British Foreign Office, the Caliph of the Moslems in Saudi Arabia (King of the Arabs). This did not go down well with the Al Sauds who effectively surrounded his army in al Taeef in 1924. After a big battle and a huge loss of lives, he was forced to cede the throne to his son Ali who then removed his warriors further afield to "Jedda". There King Ali was cornered again, starved of food and ammunitions, so he surrendered completely this time to the Al Sauds; his brother Faisal, now well established in Iraq, offered him refuge there. And this is how both King Faisal and his family (his son, two daughters and retinue), King Ali (his four daughters, his son and their retinue), all came to reside in Iraq.

In this context mention must be made of the fact that between them, Churchill, Gertrude Bell and T E Lawrence "owned" all of the Middle East after the Great War and kept dividing it and apportioning countries to whomsoever they pleased. Thus the State of Iraq was artificially made up from joining together three Ottoman localities in the north and the south. Several races who might not have belonged together or seen eye to eye under normal circumstances were required to live together in this new State: for example Shias,Sunnis, Assyrians, Arabs and Kurds.

The English had their troops ensconced in several places in Iraq and their power allowed them to continue to move the strings! Faisal, an experienced statesman, understood that he had to tow the line with the English who intended to remain there for the long haul. Iraq was too strategic, its oil too rich for them to leave. Even though aware of the natives'

216

desire for independent rule, he also recognised that he would not be able to give it to them. Let us not forget that Faisal spent 15 years in Constantinople while young and must have absorbed some of the enlightened Attaturk ideas, while the city lent a permanent sophistication to his personality and manner. He came to Iraq full of ideals from his successful military campaigns; on the other hand realizing the very real limitations of this mandate, he nevertheless tried to do the best for Iraq by encouraging his people to serve their country. All of the minorities remember with gratitude his unaffected speech when he first ascended the throne in 1921: "In the concept of nationhood there do not exist Moslems, Christians or Jews, only a country named Iraq. We all hail from the same Semitic stock and there can be no difference between us, except in the amount we contribute to the welfare of our Nation!"

Very unfortunately for Iraq, King Faisal died in 1933 aged 50 years; too young, his rule too short to reorientate an impoverished nation. He succumbed to the same disease of arterial scleroses as his brother King Ali two years after him. His son Ghazi was thirteen when he came to Iraq from Saudi Arabia and a young 21 when he was proclaimed King of Iraq. In contrast to his Father's diplomacy and tact, Ghazi was reckless and arrogant so that instead of complying within the very sensitive balance of power that his family found itself in he preferred to make friends on the revolutionary side. He was spoiled rotten by his Turkish great grandMother who gave in to his every wish and this is why he did not heed people's various warnings, but instead went along with mistaken and mutinous political activities.

On the other hand Ghazi saw himself as a true Iraqi who wanted the best for Iraq and its people and resented the

English who cheated his Father of the land they promised him after fighting on their behalf. His grades and his temperament did not dispose him for Harrow, and to the chagrin of his Father King Faisal, that august institution quickly gave up on him. But to do him justice, he had many other abilities and skills e.g. horsemanship and car racing. He was also an excellent pilot and an extremely good shot, while his verve, vigour and passion for all things Iraqi endeared Ghazi to the multitude.

He enjoyed spending his evenings with the army captains, sharing their jargon and pastimes in preference to people from his own Royal family. The army treated him as one of their own.

On the flip side, he was also a womaniser and drank too much for his own good. A devil may care race driver, he liked nothing better than doing dangerous feats in his fast cars. Politically to spite the English, he became a Nazi supporter who left all caution to the wind to broadcast anti-English slogans from his own radio stations; in one of the revolutions against the British in Iraq, King Ghazi was caught red handed when the leader of the uprising was found with letters written by the King asking for weapons to fight the British with.

Alas he was thwarted in love. A girl he was attracted to from a prominent Iraqi family was vetoed by Prime Minister Nouri el Said who was wary of her influential Father. He accused him of trying to get a foot through the palace doors. He managed to persuade Ghazi's uncles to interfere. They, King Abdullah of Jordan and King Ali in Iraq jointly ordered him to marry his cousin Aliya who came from Saudi Arabia at the age of fifteen. According to their relatives and friends, their life together was never harmonious and he would leave her with her family and do his own thing on a regular basis.

They had one child, Faisal II the heir to the throne. Alas when the child was just 4 years old, a drunken Ghazi drove his new Buick into an electric post at a very high speed.This fell on him and crushed him instantly.

The Iraqis grieved deeply when King Ghazi died in this car accident. Not only because he was too young to die at twenty six, being so attractive and charming, but also because everyone knew he wanted what they wanted and that was to do away with the yoke of British rule. From there it was an easy step for his friends to accuse the British of killing him. Indeed Ghazi feared for his life at the end. He knew he was out on a limb after having made enemies of the men in power

His death divided Baghdad for decades. While the Royal family refuted the existence of any plot, his friends presented all sorts of theories: there was a slave sitting near him who attacked him from the back of the neck, or that there was a waiter who increased the alcohol concentration of his drinks at the palace, that the electric post was pulled out entirely from its base and not in the direction of Ghazi's head, that no one was allowed to see Ghazi but that he was interned with suspicious speed.

One more thing that divided Baghdad was the succession to the throne. Queen Aliyah and the King's sister swore that Ghazi always said if anything happened to him to leave the Regency to Abdul Illah, i.e. Aliyah's brother and Ghazi's cousin. Ghazi's friends maintained that the Queen lied as Ghazi could not stand Abdul Illah, did not like him and that therefore would never entrust his son to him. Did Abdul Illah command her to do so sotto voice in Turkish?

A few people deliberated this succession, Nouri el Said among them, and decided for Abdul Illah! The outcome among the Iraqis became an intensified hatred for both Abdul

Illah and Nouri el Said who were seen to benefit the most from Ghazi's death.

At the King's funeral thousands and thousands of mourners were chanting: "Nouri, give us back Ghazi's blood". No one dared chant against Abdul Illah but the loathing grew from there.

And thus it was: Abdul Illah with not much beyond a secondary school education became the man at the top of a potentially very rich country. Until then, he worked as a clerk in the Foreign Ministry earning a very moderate salary. He was to rule for the next nineteen years until toppled by the 1958 revolution.

Abdul Illah's childhood had been quite fraught. He was born just before the WW1 while his Father was busy fighting the Turks and did not see him for a long time; then his family went to Syria where his uncle Faisal I was declared prestigiously the King of Greater Syria (Lebanon,Palestine,Israel and Syria)! This only lasted 2 years and he was ousted in a traumatic war; back to his home in Saudi Arabia where his grandFather the King of the Arabs and his own Father King Ali were attacked by the El Sauds while trying to rule that country. They fought valiantly but lost their thrones and had to give up fighting to spare further bloodshed among their followers. Abdul Illah's life could only start to settle at the ripe old age of 13, when the family joined his very embittered Father in Baghdad. He always dreamed that one day he will go back, back to the thrones of his Fathers in Hijaz.

We are told in the annals that Abdul Illah was a polite respectful young man, with very good manners when he was young; He was also very well thought of by his uncles the

Kings, while King Abdullah even offered to make him once the heir to the throne in lieu of his son. Abdul Illah refused.

Later on, the politics of the throne would turn him into a chain smoker, a very frequent whisky guzzler, a solitary being who turned into himself and did not warm readily to others. His immediate family comprising his sisters, his Mother and the young King were paramount in his life as a matter of course and he shielded them constantly. By some quirk of fate he found himself the only man able to offer them protection in a prejudiced era where a woman had to be seen to be sheltered by a man: his Mother was a widow, his older sister never married, his sister the Queen was also a widow after four years of marriage and his nephew the King had absolutely no one else when Queen Alilya died. It was according to her wish that the King finished his education in England and Abdul Illah made sure that the King kept up with the school curriculum while in Baghdad, even during the funeral of his Mother. He was the focus of the family, set them strictly observant standards of behaviour as befits the Prophet's descendants and took all the decisions. With another sister, married to the Egyptian branch of the family who lived nearby, they formed a very close nucleus. It might be that they may still have felt psychologically as Saudis in an Iraqi State.

Abdul Illah was married 3 times but did not have children. The first wife, an Egyptian, either could not get on with the restrictions of the palace life as imposed on its Royal ladies or maybe could not get on with his Mother's equally strict traditions. The second wife an Egyptian too, complained that she could never be alone with him, that there were too many people around; indeed she became irate she said, as she caught him twice in compromising situations with another man! Abdul Illah made known his priority of having both his sister and Mother always live with him no matter what any wife's preferences were. His third wife (finally an Iraqi to everyone's relief) hailed from a prominent and respected tribe. She stayed with him till the end.

He liked going abroad a lot even when he was needed in the country to resolve a crisis, a trait of which the politicians complained a lot.

Another hobby was tending to his stable of very good breed horses; he often spent entire evenings with his guards

Abdul Illah won best Arab Stallion competitions in the Iraqi Royal shows

and army captains, drinking and making jokes, having unrestrained fun. He memorized all the names of his army personnel and used to shower them with gifts from his trips abroad in the early years of his reign (not so in later years). He put his trust in them and thought that they will never cheat on him, but subsequent events showed that he was not always right. Often, he promoted the wrong people who were not honest in transmitting to him the mood of the country. On the other hand he demoted and distanced others who later proved to have been most faithful. Accounts from his close personnel seem to point out to a lack of superiority in any discipline or to any essential leadership quality! His conversations were never witty or eloquent; he muttered a few phrases and quickly got bored. Neither was he very tactful, he let people know when he did not like them, which put paid to any diplomatic potential.

King and Uncle (on all fours) trying out a present of a German "Grant" tank from Egypt

He also lacked the bonhomie, the open mien and the instant interaction which the Iraqis could not do without in a public figure; the young King had it, his lovely spontaneous smile lit up his face and beguiled his love for all and sundry; his was a sunny, innocent and sweet nature: the Regent's moody frown was interpreted as that belonging to a calculating person..

Abdul Illah knew that he was not popular, complaining that the Iraqis were ungrateful whatever he did for them.

A big rupture with the natives occurred during the 1941 revolution when Rashid Ali and his group frightened him into deserting Iraq and it was left for the British to fight the Nationalists in order to reinstate his rule; meanwhile he hid at his uncle's Abdullah in Jordan; thus he was smeared as a traitor to the Iraqi cause; later on he agreed to punish and jail a few of those guilty of the brouhahas (he authorized the hanging of three of them). The Iraqis never forgave him those measures either.

Abdul Illah always deferred to Nouri el Said calling him Sheikna, "our Wise Man" a very experienced politician, certified to be head and shoulders above all the other politicians in the Middle East! Abedel Illah, not skilled at running the affairs of State, was not in the same league by far. Nouri, originally a military, became Prime Minister when King Faisal I arrived in Iraq and elected to this important office an impressive fourteen times during the next thirty years! This foremost politician believed that the only route for the future development of Iraq was to collaborate with the English!

Nevertheless, a schism developed between those two rulers when Nouri advocated dealing harshly with the Opposition while the Regent favoured a more temperate approach.

In 1956, France and England declared war on Egypt. While the Iraqis condemned strongly such an attack on an

Arab Nation, Abdul Illah did not or could not lift a finger to protest or defend it. He never lived this down in the annals of Arab brotherhood.

To be fair, Abdul Illah's entire rule was peppered by people plotting to kill him, plotting to overthrow the government, in addition to his army friends cheating on him. Like his uncle Faisal I before him, he came to the conclusion that with all their different creeds and criticisms, independent spirit and resentment of authority, the Iraqis were nigh impossible to govern.

There is some truth in this! Iraq's boundaries were imposed on it by the British therefore were not geographical; Their newness by contrast, lent them an uncertain nature. This caused frequent border skirmishes with Kuwait, Saudi Arabia and Iran. Moreover relative strangers who did not get on with each other were clobbered together in the new State. An apt example being the Shia and the Sunnis! Despite their fewer numbers, the Sunnis gained the better jobs because of the experiences they acquired during the era of the Ottoman Empire.   Add to those rebellions by the Kurds and the Assyrians who both yearned for their own independence: The Kurds preferred to be ruled by a Turkish State and the Assyrians' bitterness resulted in skirmishes with the Iraqi soldiers resulting in thousands of deaths on the Assyrians' side.

King Faisal II reached his majority in 1953 and there was a big display in the streets of Baghdad to commemorate his coronation. We, along with thousands of natives, slept on the floor of an office in Rashid Street, ready to enjoy the next day's pomp and ceremony: the King riding his cavalcade underneath the balcony, resplendent in white and shiny buttons. The whole of Baghdad came out to celebrate:

thousands upon thousands of people shouted out their good wishes as he stood up to acknowledge them in the Royal car.

Through the intermediary of his aunts and their approval, King Faisal II met and became engaged in 1957 to a Turkish princess: Fadhila Khanum, great granddaughter of Turkey's last Caliph Sultan Abdul Majjeed, the good Sultan. His dynasty was deposed in favour of Kamal Attaturk's Republic. It must be said that the aunts looked far and wide and discounted quite a few princesses until they found the right one to fit in with the King's lifestyle and circle. It is also true that the King was extremely happy with this choice and on his fiancée's brief visitsto Baghdad could be seen courting her with real love in his eyes.

King Faisal was a very well educated monarch

When he got engaged my friends and I listened keenly to the radio for news of the beautiful bride. We were thrilled by the marriage plans and the amount of jewels and elegant words that were being exchanged between the two high ranking families. Slim, blonde and green eyed the future Queen lent an aristocratic air to the proceedings. She and her family were the embodiment of the latest chic in Egyptian high society and cut an incredibly elegant figure. It seems the King had been on the lookout for someone with a fair colouring like hers. His aunts did do the groundwork, but of course he was the one to rubber stamp the match! Romance in the air glammed things up.

Newspapers wrote whole pages about the new couple, with pictures of them water skiing in Marmara etc this being the King's favourite sport. We stood up and sang the National anthem with gusto in celebrations at school and in the games we played: *ja-aal malek quoumouqiam addou salam (*the King has come, stand to attention and salute). A buzz of excitement was definitely in the air.

At this juncture, it might be useful to make a brief comparison between King Hussein of Jordan and King Faisal II of Iraq. Born within two months of each other, the two Hashemite princes acquired their right to the throne through descendancy from the Prophet's daughter Fatima. Their grandFathers were brothers and also Kings. They both attended the excellent Victoria College in Alexandria, and later Harrow School in England. Both of these establishments were run on the lines of the English public schools which seek to develop an enhanced sense of responsibility in its students. History will testify that King Hussein went on to rule his Kingdom very ably from the tender age of eighteen, trying to optimise his country's limited resources with more efficient methods. He was also, from his studies and life in England, aware of democratic rule and human rights; all this helped make of Jordan a progressively modern state. Of him it can be easily said: he was born great, had greatness thrust upon him and achieved greatness too - albeit through a very hard slog

Unfortunately for the Iraqi King, his life was not fated to progress through the same channels. First of all he was prone to asthma attacks whenever it was too hot or too cold as well as when in the vicinity of horses, making him too weak for active military involvement. All of Iraq's powerx were wound up in its army, soldiers and army captains therefore its ruling military junta looked for a virulent interaction from their King in the running of the country; this is in contrast to the system in England where the Monarch is Head of State without real powers: conversely too, this is how the future King was indoctorinated at his English school and beyond!

As Iraq is very much a patriarchal society where physical strength matters the Royal family tried to hide this health weakness of Faisal's from the nation fearing it might impend on the viability of the monarchy. The military could not help but feel that the King was not one of them when he abstained from joining in their pursuits, interacting in their jargon or enthusiastically mucking in as his Father had done before him.

King Ghazi had been a real "Iraqi" in that he was actively on top of all the hot issues concerning the country.

Regretting all of the liberties given to his Father before him though, Faisal's uncle and aunts really turned the noose on him to be a more modest, placid monarch. The young King was expressly given the sort of guidance not to embrace "explosive" issues and not to get into troublesome company which might lead him away from their own traditions and beliefs.

His Mother Queen Aliyah, deemed a charming and popular figure among the Iraqis was also quite able politically and her brother the Regent respected her views and suggestions on the issues relating to the ocuntry. She was known to be eminently sensible. Even though she did not progress beyond private tuition at home and could not speak English very well, she was deemed to be very intelligent by all who met her. The Iraqis also liked Queen Aliya as she was a bit of a soft touch and people petitioned her help in their problems. She used to distribute alms among the needy and the guard's families, answered the locals' letters, phoned and met the deprived personally to help. During her reign, there was some social interaction with the population in her weekly open day (*qeebool*) when the local ladies had an automatic invitation to meet her at the palace. She also started an organisation to improve the Iraqi women's place in society.

But after she died in 1950 nobody took up that mantle. Fate had dealt the orphan King a bitter blow in taking away the best person to coach him into his grand role of King.

King Hussein's Mother Zein al-Sharaf, able and competent, proved an anchor in directing the reins of the Kingdom when King Abdullah was killed in 1950; Attention turned quickly to a very young Hussein and Zein advised him a lot in the early years, encouraging him to soldier on. A free thinker, she is credited with ensuring that the Jordanian Constitution included full rights for women, dedicated time and energy to the Red Crescent and the orphanages therefore raising the profile of the Monarchy amid the people. This analogy shows how poor King Faisal remained tragically destitute.

So Faisal II was raised by his uncle and devout aunts to abide by the rules, and not to deviate. He led a spartan existence, only meeting with the high class and protected friends that his family vetted; he was not interested in wine or women, no, not even in smoking. One of the royal guards compared him to an angel; he swam daily in the palace swimming pool, went downtown to the Belatt al Malek (royal offices) with his Uncle to carry out whatever jobs his uncle set him. Coming back to the palace, he sat with his private tutors to improve his English and Arabic both, in the evening rewarding himself by watching a film within the bosom of the Royal family. He retired to bed as soon as the film finished. By 10 pm the palace was dark, except for the garden lights. Any rare late night event might be confined to the yearly shooting party hosted by his Uncle.

King Faisal 11with King Hussein
a codial relationship existed between the third cousins

The ladies' way of living may be judged to verge on the austere. Very devout, the three sisters and the Queen Mother, King Ali's widow, did not mix on a large scale and only with a very few select ladies in Iraqi society. They could not sit in the company of men except enrobed in an abbaye to maintain their anonymity as dignified relatives of the Prophet

Accordingly, the palace lacked a First Lady to look up to, to set the trends in fashion, style and sophisticated living. To be an arm of public relations if you like! Thus no liveliness, no glittering evenings for the elite, no lavish celebrations for the staff, no famous orchestras or singers, no glamour full stop. People are accustomed to see a buzz round a Royal palace to draw attention to its importance to all and sundry, to attract the tourists at least. This Royal palace didn't do!

King Faisal seems to have grown up very docile, and instead of aggressively taking over the affairs of State as per his birthright, or at least displaying that sort of insistence or curiosity to do so in the future, he very willingly let his uncle continue as before, running the entire show! Except for some speeches and greeting of ambassadors, he did not seem to want to know about the nitty gritty of his inheritance! And that is where it all went pear shaped. People liked the King and hated the Regent, and they were all waiting with bated breath for the King to rule. But unlike King Hussein, King Faisal had a buffer in the shape of a beloved uncle and Father figure, so he did not have to push himself forward and take the bull by the horn. This uncle did try to advise him and be at his side as much as possible but maybe he could have been less protective. As for his impressive educational credentials, true, they could have counted for a lot, but they also caused him to stray away from the country in a cultural sense. While young, the English nanny and Dr Sinderson ruled the roost as regards to his education. After that and until he was 18 years old, proportionately big chunks of his life were spent abroad and maybe that acted in a detrimental way to keep him from close contact with his native culture. On the other hand his asthma deteriorated whenever he was in Baghdad's heat so his health was better off in England and that might explain his frequent sojourns there.

People at close quarters noticed and commented on the King's insouciance. The guards who had the task of security in the palace and who saw him every day were astounded that he never summoned them to have a serious discussion, there were only polite greetings. It was his uncle who talked seriously with the Ministers and the army, had all the important papers piled on his desk, while the King's desk remained sparse. He did not want to discuss politics full stop, or become friends with the captains of the army who visited either.

As the King rode to his Royal Office in the Russaffa, the tradition allowed the citizens to hand in their petitions through the last motorcyclist in the cavalcade. This charming native convention sought to develop a closer relationship between the Monarch and his flock. Little did the locals know that their King, instead of trying to resolve the problem, went and put that same request in front of his uncle the Regent to deal with! The austere generals shook their heads aghast at what they saw as utter dependence.

It might very well be that Abdul Illah seeing how prone Faisal was to dangerous asthma attacks sometimes even reaching death's door, wanted to shield his nephew as much as possible from any emotional stress that will precipitate such attacks! Or he might have intended to give him responsibility in little stages. Abdul Illah himself was fed up with all the plots. Three times he was on the verge of resigning as Regent: after Rashid Ali's revolution in 1941, in 1945 as well as in 1949 in the aftermath of the bloody demonstrations against the Portsmouth Treaty. On two occasions he wrote a letter in full view of the assembled captains of the army and the Opposition as well as his friends to suggest that they find another ruler: how can he put his nephew through that same noose? His "nice but weak" nephew will not be able to take the heat. While the Iraqis admit freely that they do not have a good record in treating their rulers well!

High ranking officials have written that AbdulIllah never aspired to take the throne away from his nephew; indeed that he cared a lot for Faisal's welfare and was very affectionate towards him as befits the son of a much loved sister. But the Iraqis were (and still are) adamant that Abdul Illah wanted to deprive his young nephew and become the King himself, being jealous and selfish! While this same Abdul Illah postponed becoming an Iraqi national hoping to be called to become King of Hijaz one day.

Hatred was raging against the monarchy from a lot of quarters because of their abeyance to English policy. The Royals also became the butt of incessant enemy rhetoric emanating from Egypt's Nasser, who accused them of selling their souls and Iraq's soul and all of its people's aspirations to capitalism, a very general but deeply condemning term.

It seems that for several years the Royal family woke up to the fact that they were not very well liked! One of the King's aunts was quoted as saying to a female acquaintance that the family would not mind leaving the monarchy to concentrate on the happiness of the orphan King and his

233

bride, even if it meant living in a small house! Certainly Abdul Illah knew of the many plots to topple him. Indeed in the wake of an almost successful plot by army captains, he confided to an aide: "maybe we should let them govern, they are all excellent captains, devoted to the nation; they know me well, they must know my limitations, maybe I am not very capable".

Things went from bad to worse for Abdul Illah. It came to a head when Nouri el Said, his staunch ally, offered him half a million pounds to leave Iraq and accept an ambassadorial post abroad. All the Ministers and the public wanted to give the King a chance to show his personality, a chance to get close to the affairs of State, to make decisions. Abdul Illah refused. People close to him have suggested that he was waiting for "a big bang" so that he would have an excuse to take all his family away, out of Iraq, never to return!

Abdul Illah was not a callous bloodthirsty man, and his was not a killing strategy for his enemies. When Shafiq Addas was accused of being a spy in 1948, he kept dithering from signing the death warrant, saying "I know the man is innocent". He also felt guilty for signing the death warrant of the three revolutionaries in 1941 (the Golden Triangle), but the State demanded it! In later life, whenever he discovered military personnel had been plotting against him, he did not order their killing, and contented himself with excusing them from their duties or exiling them to an outpost! Later regimes would become much more bloodthirsty towards their enemies.

Meanwhile everyone (King Hussein, the Shah of Iran) was warning him of the plots being hatched. Other Heads of State counselled him categorically in 1958 not to go back to Iraq; they even gave him the name of the Free Officers who will put the revolution in motion! One of those Officers was

Abdul Karim Kassim a favourite of Nouri el Said. Abdul Karim swore to him his allegiance to the King as late as May 1958, and Nouri el Said certified it, he trusted him. On the other hand, as Abdul Illah began to get reports that everyone was spying and cheating on him even among his personal guards, he stopped trying to keep track, all names were confined to files and left to gather dust.

On the 14th of July 1958, the Royal family were set to fly off: some to Turkey to consolidate the Baghdad Pact, some to go on to England to purchase the trousseau for the much anticipated wedding; and this is when the revolution burst upon them. This tragic story, often told, will never lose any of its drama! How a bomb was thrown at them just after 5 a.m. which made the upstairs rooms burst into flames; how the King, taking a call from his aunt just after 6am, told her serenely not to worry as it was "only" a revolution and they were trying to initiate talks with the revolutionaries! How Abdul Illah refused to give his guards the order to shoot at the revolutionaries for a whole hour when he still had the upper hand, which doubtless would have squashed the revolution in its prime! On the contrary, not initiating fire made for dire consequences: It gave the revolutionaries plus the truckloads of criminal thugs and cut throats that they had released from a prison en route, time to receive vital replenishment in the form of tanks etc. The command not to shoot encouraged the rebels to come progressively nearer the palace guards and confront their captains aggressively into giving up their arms!

An undisputed fact here: Abdul Illah could yet have saved his family with no loss of life! Until 7:25 am he could have escaped from the back doors of the palace though the Khurr river and the western desert to Jordan! The last attempt of escape was offered him by a loyal sergeant who risked his life amid the hammering bullets to bring his Opel car to the entrance of the palace, dashing in and begging the Regent to escape through the (still) unguarded track behind the palace! How the Regent refused still, neither to fight nor to escape. He kept repeating to everyone that his primary objective was to avoid bloodshed at all costs, and to initiate negotiations with the rebels.

After that Abdul Salaam's cries from the radio to the population to converge on the Royal palace produced hundreds of fellaheen from Baghdad and its suburbs; the surrender of the Royal Guard denied any escape later. The Royal Guard never deserted to a man but Abdul Illah himself kept them from shooting at the demonstrators gathered outside, till their captains told them to hand in their guns and go back to their barracks! Once this was accomplished, the five Royals and two servants were on their own

Probably remembering the respectful way that the Egyptian revolutionaries let King Farouk end his rule and board a ship with the accompaniement of gun salutes, or his own Father's exit from Jeddah after relinquishing his crown to Al Sauds in 1924, Abdul Illah must have expected the same decorum to be extended towards his own family! It has been said of Abdul Illah by a member of his family that he was a sensitive man, a bit like a poet. Maybe that is why he never reckoned with the black hatred that built up against him and Nouri el Said.

Twice he sent his army personnel with a request for negotiations, promising he will leave Iraq and never come back, but such a request was given short shrift by the colonels. Instead, the attackers started swearing venomously at him and the rest of the Royal family. In the second stage of the barricade, he offered to give himself up to the revolutionaries just so they let the innocent King and women go free. Turning to the King, he suggested to him that he should resign. Abdul Illah tried to keep a cool head to negotiate, but he turned deathly white in view of the roughness being displayed towards him. When the armed colonels were sufficiently near the kitchen door, they ordered the Royals to come out of the burning palace. Abdul Illah was the first with one hand in his pocket, and another holding onto a white handkerchief on top of his head! Queen Naffissa was King Ali's wife, in her seventies, very devout, and devoted to her grandson Faisal. She scrambled ahead of him down the steps leading to the garden and held writings from the Koran on top of his head, begging the generals not to touch the orphan, for he had never done anything wrong in his life. Then Princess Abadia the King's aunt followed, and Abdul Illah's wife, the kitchen chef and one more domestic.

There had been lots of rumours since that the revolutionary council, as late as May 1958, had planned not to kill the King. But then other sources say that both Abdul Karim and Abdul Salam made a pact that they must be gotten rid of so that there was no chance of the revolution failing.

The final moments were not much later in arriving. Someone swore at Abdul Illah, and one of the guards told the former off for swearing at a Royal. There followed an altercation, and then Colonel Ubussi came from behind and in retaliation fired at the guard, and then continued aiming from the back with the same burst of his machine gun at the group of five as they stood petrified under a tree! This acted as a trigger for many more rounds of ammunitions fired from those creeping ever closer - at the hapless group.

It was said that this Colonel was confronted one day as to why he had killed the Royal family and he said some sort of madness came over him. Within the year he retired from public life, and then committed suicide in another country.

In view of the fast surge of the populace towards them to get hold of the dead people, the armed colonels acted quickly. The two women: Abadia the King's aunt and his grandMother were taken away and very summarily buried in the grounds. Abdul Illah's wife Hiam was extremely lucky; she escaped with an injury and a captain pulled her away from the scene. As for the Regent and the King, they were put in the boot of an ordinary pick up car which tried to speed away. But the throng surrounded the car and would not let it move, they wanted to wreak further revenge. So Abdul Illah's body was slithered and thrown out as a decoy, while the body of the King was raced to the hospital. There, the doctors declared him already dead while the nurses burst out crying as they beheld their King's blood spattered body. The Colonels were at a loss what to do with it, so they dug a hole nearby and smoothed it so well that nobody but them knew where the King lay for decades afterwards.

The animal mob had a hayday with Abdul Illah's body, they pulled it around the streets, crossed the bridge with it, finally stringing it on the door of the very same Defence Ministry where the leader of the 1941 revolution had been hung.

The Rihab palace's big subterranean space was subsequently turned into a jail with well equipped torture chambers, during the reign of the Baathists. The rumours abounded, but people knew that whoever went in very rarely survived intact. It had been built as the palace of welcome by Faisal 1, but came to be known as the Palace of the Grim End among the Iraqis.

Much later during Saddam's reign, the King's remains were re buried in the Royal cemetery in al Adhamiyah where his Father King Ghazi, his grandFather Faisal 1, his great-uncle King Ali, his grandMother Hazima and his great great grandMother Bizmijihan were also buried. Saddam Hussain refurbished this cemetery to make of it an outstanding monument in honour of King Hussein's visit when he arrived to lay a wreath in memory of his own two great uncles, the first Hashemites to settle in Baghdad.

It seems the boy King continued to hold a fascination for Saddam Hussein, who was only two years his junior. Guards told how he would come to the cemetery to gaze at the remains of the former King1

In fairness to the memory of the Royal family, theirs was not a life of grandiose luxury and Italian marble, their palaces did not aspire to be much more than big houses; only the King, upon attaining his majority, as well as the Regent, were paid salaries, their style remained modest and they did not need to cheat their countrymen of millions to smuggle abroad like subsequent military leaders did; quite the opposite, their real revenues came from stretches of land owned by their grandparents when Emirs of Saudi Arabia during the Ottomans. Abroad, they the King and the Regent jointly owned one stately house: Stanwell in Salisbury, England. This was acquired so that his Mother Queen Aliya could supervise him while he was studying in "Sandroyd" boarding school in the years 1948-1949. It was sold for an insignificant sum in the sixties and is now no more. Any other lands and shares belonging to the Monarchy in Iraq have been confiscated.

<u>TASSQUEET (DE-NATIONALISATION)</u>

Ezra and Nechemia were two prophets who returned from Babylonia to help in rebuilding the Temple and Jerusalem a few centuries B.C. Aptly that is the same name given to the operation that took the later generations of Iraqi Jews to Israel in the years 1950-1951.

The Tassqueet has become such an incredibly important word in the annals of the Iraqi Jews, that many portents have been added to it since then: I believe a good beginning will be to try and translate this word accurately:

The root of the verb is *saqqata*, which means to make unusable, or broken; in this particular vernacular it is applied to a passport so means foregoing or giving up of a nationality no less. As the above construction of "Tassqueet" implies a passive mode, does this mean that the Jews let go of their Iraqi nationality passively?

And yet there exist other modes of the verb whose echo are still heard even now in the everyday conversations of ex pats which point the hand to a premeditated action; so how willingly did these other Jews give up their nationality?

No doubt a sort of conundrum can be detected here. Did the Iraqi Jews cede their right of belonging to the country of their birth passively or actively? This will form the subject of my immediate investigations: a whodunnit of sorts if you like

This is the one journey that I had found myself so far incapable of undertaking; indeed it seems to me that I have been trying to put it behind me intentionally! With noone to question in Iraq and no evidence to look back on... All the more so as I never met up with any of those involved, how could I when they were all transported to Israel? It has been decreed since 1947 that anyone caught corresponding or communicating with Israel was committing a flagrant sin. It follows that all contact ceased with the transportees the minute they boarded the plane.

Being only three when this big bang happened, my memory did not extend so far as to ask about anyone's welfare. That is why there could not be any future scenarios. Instead those thousands of actors and actresses vanished into thin air becoming personae non grata in the country where they had once lived and thrived.

With my Mother's family before their flight
The Tigris forms the background on the roof of the Kasser
Jamil,Doris,Yvonne,Abbood,Claire,Sassoon(grandFather)
Bertine,Maurice,Khatoon(sitting in the middle)Joyce,me

Ah for politics in Iraq. The wheels never cease churning to herald yet another political dynasty; the different creeds sometimes fare better but at other times can also expect the worst. The life of the Jews used to depend on which half of the Koran is being given precedence at the time, the complimentary one before Medina or the not so complimentary one after Medina. The Sunni/Shia/Kurds's welfare followed the religious makeup of the latest government, while the Christians have a saying that Sunday always comes after Saturday.

In the scheme of things, as I realise now, twenty years is just a drop in the ocean, much too brief a period for the earth to move drastically: and here I am yet another persona non grata in the country of my birth. History is right when it proclaims *plus ca change plus c'est le meme chose*. The ghosts of this old story have come to haunt me, in them must lie that unbroken thread that exploded twice within two decades, 1950 and 1970. As I go back and dissect the Tassqueet into its primal elements, I may yet find the logic behind them both? While the political scenario in the Middle East is that complex and convoluted, even God seems to have given up on it. Still people will point an accusing finger at His Holy Books: who else is left to attack after a century of everyone attacking everyone else?

The Tassqueet can be summarised thus: Within one year, approximately 130,000 Iraqi Jews ascended an aeroplane and left a country where they and their foreFathers had lived for 2500 years. They left on the strength of a £12 one way aeroplane ticket, to a country that they have never seen. Officially all that they were allowed to take were a small suitcase and a £50 bank order

The magnitude of this event is beyond statistical figures. Rather its human scope must point to profound tragedy and homelessness; even though the root causes were political, doubtless the poor emigrants found themselves as pawns in a game of Russian roulette, treated as a human cargo by forces more powerful than they; in this game the only action allowed them was meekness!

These emigrants responded to a Law promulgated by the government in March 1950 "the Denaturalization Law"; it stated that all Iraqi Jews who wished it, could register their name, give up their citizenship and be flown outside Iraq; even though not mentioned explicitly- its name is contraband in the Arab world- the only place the *Mussaquatteen* could go to was Israel, no other country would accept such a multitude of people without a passport, visa, work permit or money.

The direct impetus was given to the Law by a meeting in 1950 between the Prime Minister of Iraq at the time "Al Suwaydee" and the Head of the Jewish community "Heskel Shemtov". They needed to find a solution to the fact that thousands of Jews were entrusting their lives to smugglers in Basrah near the southern borders in order to leave Iraq. It not only made the emigrants prey to those smugglers' whims so that many were killed and mugged on the way, but if caught by the border guards, caused them detention and worse. Lastly these two august men were worried that illegal smuggling contravened as well as downgraded the Constitution and the State. The *Tassqueet* Law came into effect when the Regent signed it in March 1950.

Upon its promulgation, circumstances became doubly difficult for its candidates, the native Jews. Apart from the complicated psychology inherent in "giving up a whole way of life a land and a country", registration and filling the forms with all the red tape took a long time! Wherever possible they tried to liquidate their assets in an earlier form of a car boot sale even though these could only fetch a mere fraction of their value. A few managed to sell their houses at this same lowly rate, while others bequeathed them to Moslem friends. Following that they waited around in synagogues and community schools for months in Baghdad till there was space in the officially designated aeroplanes to take them away; the multiple powers that be starting to wrangle meanwhile. There was also an issue regarding the choice of the company supplying the aeroplanes, while the biggest culprit in processing this airlift speedily was the Israeli government itself. It kept repeating that it could not increase the quota allotted in its absorption centres for the Oriental Jews.

Only hard work could help the poor emigrants in 1950

The following essay can only offer a synopsis of the whole picture due to the complexity of the issues.

1-When Britain submitted to the UN the fate of Palestine in Feb 1947, several Arab leaders among them Iraq, declared that the fate of Palestine would have an impact on the future of the thousands of Jews living inside its countries and that Zionist success would threaten the survival of those Jews. Thus it was that with one stroke of the pen, good and loyal citizens, who were the original natives a long time before the Arab arrival to Iraq - these Jews became marked to bear the brunt of deeds of people from far away whom they had never had any contact with. They became ostracized by the government from then on. Even if their leaders wanted to disassociate themselves thereafter from the events in Palestine and continue with their peaceful lives, they were always deemed to be right at the epicentre of the storm.

2-This only aggravated the mistrust that the Jews had held since 1941 when, during two days, the government let them be attacked by decommissioned army personnel and other mobs without ordering the police to fire to protect them; echoes of this mini pogrom never ceased to ring dire warnings. In its aftermath, there grew divisions in the community. Many people became affiliated to communism so that they could work for an Iraq where everyone was equal. Community leaders were of the opinion that this glitch would never happen again as quite a few years of peace and prosperity followed and thus they counselled their flock to stay away from politics. Still others were so ashamed of their inability to defend themselves during this pogrom that they called for help from Israel to train them in self defence just in case.

Israel responded with emissaries whose tasks were three fold. The first arm was called the Shura, aimed to train those willing to handle weapons and store them secretly within the Jewish quarters in Baghdad for the future possibility of self defence. The second arm was educational in the main: to teach the Hebrew language, Jewish precepts and train the youth for physical pioneering work: it was documented that the Iraqi Jews shirked from getting their hands dirty. The third or last arm helped smuggle people who wanted to leave from the south of the country (Iran).

3- The Iraqi government sent volunteers in conjunction with the Syrians to help the Arabs of Palestine in their war against the Zionists both after Nov 1947 and May 1948. When they returned they demanded repercussions against the Jews! Hastily ratified laws saw these downgraded natives fired from their government jobs and excluded from university places; while the merchants among them had their import licences annulled along with their rights to sell property; the three Jewish banks's licence to trade in foreign currency was also cancelled. Furthermore it was decreed that only two Moslem witnesses were needed to incriminate any Jew in the courts however august his standing; this led to prosperous Jews being arrested solely to extort money from them; in short the community began living one of its blackest periods. To drive the nail further home, prominent figures were made to donate whole buildings and huge sums of money to the Palestinian cause.

4- Anti Semitism from Nazi literature and books arrived from Germany during Iraq's Nazi era; they were taught to the masses during the Imam Husseini/Gaylani days of 1941 and continued in circulation beyond.

5- In Jan 48' the Treaty of Portsmouth was promulgated, which preserved some British rights in Iraq for yet another number of years: in the communists demonstrations that followed against this treaty, a lot of Jews took part because they believed that a prosperous Iraq needed to have independence from all the Capitalistic powers. This political stand might have targeted them by Abu Nadgi, the nickname for Britain and its omnipresent powers behind the scenes in Iraq, as potentially non desirables who needed to be exiled. In another dimension hundreds of communists were thrown into jail, a large proportion of whom being Jews.

6- Jewish merchants were very active commercially and were trying to open trade routes to the Orient. These might have clashed with Abu Nadji's commercial interests in the region at the same time threatening Britain's preferential trading rights. With such an impertinent ambiton, those businessmen may very likely have driven another nail in the communal coffin.

7- After the return of the Iraqi army, everyone started looking for a scapegoat to blame for its failure to conquer Israel. This is why in August 1948, a very wealthy merchant Shafiq Addass was tried and accused of dismantling and transporting unwanted military parts from Iraq ostensibly to Italy but later on to Israel. The media went hysterical and declared that his treachery had been the decisive factor behind

Israel's winning of the war. As he and his prominent Moslem partners had obtained prior permission from the Minister concerned before buying the scrap metal, the accusations were surely fabricated! Addass was a man with very high ministerial and royal connections who donated generously to national charities. But the rulers were afraid of army revenge if Addass was not hanged and fined the five million pounds ordered by the judge. This savage act attracted scenes of barbaric rejoicing and rang the knell of doom among the community's members. They concluded that any of them could be the next in line for a similar maltreatment.

8- As mentioned before, there were emissaries from Israel inside Iraq: by 1949, they numbered quite a few. In that year of fierce demonstrations the police were looking to uncover communists' cells; some informers led them to some of the Underground's secret arms caches. The police wanted to get to the bottom of the Underground movement and tortured the suspects brutally, extending searches, jailings and abuse to many houses of entirely innocent Jews. As there followed a world outcry, the authorities sought to placate the community by saying they could send a doctor to see that torture was not involved. The Underground organised demonstrations to demand a cessation of hostilities towards the community and to let go of the jailed emissaries. The leadership of the community did not believe in agitating and sought not to take part, but the crowd of demonstrators forced Hacham Kaddouri to go in with them. He was wounded while the police intervened and arrested 42 people; Still the Underground accused him of siding with the Government. They actively sought to end his rule by declaring a fast day as well as a meat ban in Oct 49 which between them dangerously emptied the Lay Council's coffers.

Even though the community supported this last measure, it still ruptured into political divisions whether to side with the Rabbi who wanted the emissaries to take their weapons and get out of Iraq, or with the emissaries themselves who were telling it that its future lay in Israel; a deputation was gathered to put the community case in front of the Minister to rescind the discriminatory measures of 1948 which were playing havoc with people's existence, but the Minister refused quoting the Israeli government's actions causing thousands of Palestinians to become refugees. Following this the Hacham sent his first ever memorandum to the government to lift the persecutions but this did not help in the least. He resigned that same day and Mr H. Shemtob was elected to fill his role.

Following on from the above events, the government declared that it will go back to treating its Jews as equal citizens like before, and the crisis passed. The searches equally stopped to the relief of all.

9- On the other hand these same happeningso started to make the government eye the community as threatening public order and internal security: these in turn encouraged nationalist elements like the Istiqlal party to demand instant repatriation of the Jews and sequestration of their properties. Another pogrom could happen and the government had to avoid this by all means.

Furthermore, it was suspected that Israel will readily exaggerate any future persecutions to divert world opinion to its own ends. The net result made the government realise that the Jewish question had ceased to be under its exclusive internal domain.

10- View the "still unlifted" discriminations, a lot of illegal smuggling through the south and into Iran continued apace; the Jews gathered in a transit camp in Teheran cemetery nicknamed "bahashtaya" (heaven), during the last quarter of the years 48 and 49. The Iraqis asked the Iranian government to close this route and hand over the illegal emigrants but the Iranians wouldn't because of the money being paid to them and diplomatic pressure from abroad. This led to even more brutal searches to uncover the leaders of the Underground that were helping with the smuggling.

11- Commodities went up in price because of the war and the economy stagnated because of the lack of its vital Jewish input. Its merchants shied away from undertaking fresh commercial risks to import the necessary goods.

12-The emissaries were convinced that the Iraqi Jews did not see the complete picture and that their place in Iraq had ceased to be, that they couldn't afford to wallow in an Arab culture which had become the enemy's. To this end they expected them to renege on a whole way of life. Most of the Jews however cherished their Arab culture; it was the only one that they had ever known. Moreover, some of them had been to Israel or had heard accounts that the European Jews led a totally different life from theirs. Hence the quandary that arose on their lives' future direction.

When the Tassqueet Law was published on 2/3/1950, the Jewish community presumed at first that it was just like any other political manoeuvre, publicised to hoodwink world opinion. When they became convinced it was genuine though, most of them especially the ones who experienced various hardships, welcomed it wholeheartedly. The Zionist emissaries, who also suspected at first that it was only a ploy to flush them out, were relieved as well, the more so as they did not want to take any more risks smuggling people via Iran; It has been estimated that in the three years before this law was announced, fifteen thousand Iraqi Jews were smuggled clandestinely, some were caught and tried, some managed to escape, some were caught and tried and escaped again.

The emissaries managed to sit in on the registration committees to organize all the proceedings for the exit; at the beginning they wrote leaflets saying they were opposed to registration unless the exit routes were determined and people knew what will happen to their property. But the jewish civilians became convinced that they will get a good standard of housing in Israel so started to register nevertheless, taking it for granted that they could still manage their assets while abroad by handing over power of attorney to an Iraqi resident.

Iraq did not want to enter into any secret negotiations with the Israelis, but the Underground agreed with the government that the mode of transport would be in the shape of an airlift! As the government further stipulated that the aeroplanes must fly to a country which enjoyed diplomatic relations with the Iraqi regime, so Cyprus was chosen as the interim airport.

Mossad from Israel suggested "Near East Transport Co". Owned jointly by the Americans and "El Al", it was seen as advantageous to have as its vice president an acquaintance of "Iraq Tours"'s, a travel company; It transpired later that "Al Suwaidy", the Prime Minister, was on its board of directors too; this agency promised to obtain exit visas and look after all the necessary transportation details: they knew that there would be a lot of money involved if they could effect this transaction right to its end.

The British, while giving the travel agency landing rights to Cyprus - nevertheless voiced their reluctance to establishing any transit camps there. They suggested sealed aeroplanes, which had the added advantage of not allowing the emigrants the scope to change their minds or alight on the way.

The first batch was flown on the 19th of May. Later on an unwelcome backlog started to develop. There were a lot of people who had registered and only a minority flown; there were three reasons behind this backlog:

Israel had just become a state and this entailed an instant rush of immigration from European Jews. It was operating by force a system of quota from each country, and it had given Iraq a maximum of 3000 persons per month. It prioritised taking in people from Poland and Romania as they were deemed to possess more of the pioneering spirit and the hard work ethic which the Iraqis lacked.

Nouri al Said returned to power and needed to expedite things; having a huge number of people hanging about in the streets was not to his liking at all. Voices from Iraqi leaders, press and parliament as well in other Arab countries, started to call for a halt to this exodus which might be providing the enemy Israel with much needed manpower. But Nouri retaliated that it was more likely to inundate a nascent economy with too many mouths to feed.

The other reason why not many more people were flown out was the delay in the complicated red tape: every registered person had to go through many departments to prove that there were no rent arrears, income tax or property tax, school fees or any other outstanding debt to an Iraqi national. It was only after his name was officially published that the individual could go ahead with packing, leaving the country within a stipulated fourteen days.

In the meanwhile five hand held bombs were thrown at various Jewish and American venues in the capital…they only killed one person. They served to disquieten the Jewish community even further by providing proof of hatred towards them; it translated into a more increased urgency to register for denationalization. By November 1950, 83,000 displaced people had registered and only 18,000 managed to be flown out. Nouri el Said, Iraq's sagacious Premier who was getting increasingly fed up with the unexpectedly slow rhythm of the operation, agitated for the Great Powers to intervene with Israel to increase its monthly quota. He even asked King Abdullah twice to allow them transit via Jordan so he can deposit them on Israel's borders without further ado. He was convinced that the presence of thousands of potential immigrants constituted a threat to national security if they were targeted by extremists for attack. They had forfeited their passport and with it any hope of protection from the State and the laws of the country. In the meantime they were adding to their suspicious status by trying to salvage trifling money from liquidating their assets.

The Zionist emissaries were panicking at this sorry state of the immigrants. Israel kept saying it could not handle such a quantity, that it did not even have basic tents for them, and that it would have to put them out on the streets.

Nouri now threatened to put them in concentration camps- and as the legislated period was expiring rapidly, at the 11th hour, Ben Gurion had to relent and say he will accept all and to fly them into Israel promptly. The Iraqi parliament voted in February 1951 to allow the aeroplanes to take them to any unknown destination (giving the nod to direct flights to Lod); the Rabbis said it was ok for the aeroplanes to fly from Baghdad on Friday evening provided they did not arrive to Israel on a Saturday. These measures allowed the 81,000 registered so far to be transported much more speedily in the last four months; the airlift had to be extended till May 1951 to process any stragglers.

All in all the operation was running smoothly when Prime Minister Nouri threw in his bombshell: he froze the assets of all the Jews who had registered up until then. The banks closed simultaneously for three consecutive days to prevent any money or asset transfer. Many were arrested in streets, their effects confiscated, their cars seized and searches conducted in their houses for jewels etc. Some Jews who had just registered without having time to liquidate any of their effects, found they were forced to sell their blankets to buy food. These measures began to be reflected in the refusal of the postal and telephone services to serve them and a negative attitude towards them from the locals.

The Prime Minister in justifying this stab in the back declared he was blocking Jewish property pending any future steps taken by Israel vis a vis the Palestinian properties.

During this period bombs were thrown at various venues in the capital; a coffee shop near the river, the American Bureau, Massouda Shemtov Synagogue, a Jewish firm in Rashid Street, (it did not explode). It was perceived by the government and fertile public rumours that the Zionist emissaries threw them to provoke panic among the Jews and hasten the registrations. In June 1951, some of these emissaries were caught and hanged.

Many researchers have advanced the theory that some

They tied our beards together

anti semites might have been throwing bombs too in the meantime! It is true that there were sporadic bombing of establishments in the thirties with the Nazi tide at its zenith.

These same researchers point to the fact that the Israeli emissaries in that era had fallen on their faces in a manner of speaking: with their lines of communication sorely damaged, their funds rapidly depleted, their people being tortured and hanged: theirs were dire straits indeed! Yet they still had to try to provide the homeless amongst the tens of thousands with vital food and shelter.

Was it plausible that they would jeopardise their positions still further by throwing bombs and leading thousands more people to become liabilities round their necks?

To confront those speculations that have yet to die away within the community and beyond, while not wishing to deny people any of their beliefs and concern about the

255

bombs, it is best here in conclusion, to state that the community had no other way of reacting to the various persecutions from the Iraqi rulers at the time. After the petitions for clemency failed, there was no choice but to abandon camp soonest, either legally or illegally!

What criteria convinced me to conclde thus? It is experiencing personally very real limitations on the right to live as a normal citizen twenty years later. There were obviously no bombs nor emissaries then but the oppression could still not be tolerated. It dictated the exodus of the rest of us till all Jewish presence ceased to be in the land between the two rivers.

COUPS & REVOLUTIONARIES

The first eleven years of my life I lived without the shadow of violence or political unrest. Baghdad to me was that quiet town where life was repetitive, a bit archaic maybe. And then there was the revolution of 1958 and after that God decided to compensate. Revolutions and bloodbaths vied with one another and took turns so that life was never dull, on the contrary!

One of the endearing aspects of life in Baghdad is that everyone sleeps on the roof of their house in the summer; it is sweet to gaze at the stars, the air becoming blissfully cool after the heat of the day. Somebody brings up an earthenware jar full of fresh water (*Tengayee*) to the roof in the early evening, and by night time its water has become cool and refreshing through evaporation from the hundreds of its holes. Much later at night, you look around and the neighbours are making their way upstairs after enjoying the evening with their friends in the garden. A silent companionship reigns then. I found it comforting to see the people adjoining our house go through the same rituals as we, signalling that all was well in the world. The rub occurs in the morning, when everyone gazes at each other in their night attire, their hair all tousled up or in curlers, barefoot and still yawning; some of their day gravitas must slip then. Staring at people was not the done thing, so we did not tarry on the roof but climbed quickly downstairs.

It was our custom in the hot summer months to go swimming. On the morning of the 14th of July 1958 we woke up a bit earlier than usual at 5 am, to the sound of gunfire; there was also an enormous smoke coming from the other side of the river. One or two aeroplanes were circulating

257

overhead; they appeared to dip whenever they reached a certain place there. In those days life was so peaceful that we could not puzzle it out so put our swim gear on as usual.

But this dawn proved different. People on the roof were gesticulating to each other, and then we were told to switch on the radio, so we trooped down to the one huge box we had downstairs. From the radio emanated voices of military broadcasters shouting full blast how the Free Captains had terminated the evil regime while one military order after another (*Bayanat*) were being read in extremely agitated , hoarse voices,the lot being interspersed with military marches. Then we understood that the planes we had seen dipping in the distance towards the Eastern side of the Tigris *al karrch*, were the ones bombing the Royal family's palaces along with its Ministers'. The man shouting on the radio was calling for the death of all capitalists aka everyone in the government and the Royal family, describing how the troops had surrounded the palaces and were waking up the Ministers to shoot them on their deathbeds. Later on I came to realise that those events marked the beginning of the deterioration of the world as I knew it. Our family was mesmerized into inaction. During the course of the morning the main road near us became clogged with military carriers and personnel due to the soldiers' instructions to re join their units. Everyone was then invited to switch the television on to see how the jubilant crowds descended on the two palaces and were tearing the capitalists'and their associates to pieces. By now they had also become traitors, murderers and worse. Not everyone had a TV in those days, we had just bought ours and it was still skint in programmes; that is why the transmission was confined to a few hours a day. But the television served the revolution well; everyone could see that the monarchy was well and truly gone, while the bloodthirsty mob pillaged the palace bare, appropriating its belongings to themselves and to their own houses. They were displaying the frenzy usually reserved for a pop concert, even killing the royal pets. After that the government asked the civilians to keep an eye on all the Ministers who could be hiding and help turn them in, which people did. It became the new national pastime.

The new leaders promulgated a curfew every evening and night time to consolidate their base. We were allowed a few hours during the day to do the shopping provided we did not congregate in the streets or on the pavements. As darkness fell and all movement stopped outside, Baghdad became that eerie city. Our neighbours would sneak in noiselessly to our house via the back garden, climbing on a chair and straddling the common wall in between (*the terrah*). Then the adults among them would sit around smoking and analysing the political situation endlessly; we children meanwhile played backgammon and monopoly in the darkened garden as no lights were allowed either: instead, we made do with a few candles.

As it was summertime, there was as usual nothing to do during the long leisure hours, so the television was turned on constantly. The view was always that of inside the jails, and we watched mesmerised as the former glitterati and ex Ministers awaited their trial. They had formed the aristocracy of the nation, people with the best education gleaned from worldwide institutions. The cameras were focused on them in pyjamas and prison garb doing such minutia as brushing their teeth or cutting their beard in crowded circumstances, with no privacy. Their dignity was taken away long before they were disposed of in the mock trials that followed.

When these former leaders of the nation were tried, the

military judge turned moral icon, never let them enunciate a decent defence. He would interrupt people as old and as frail as his Father and tell them to shut up or point out constantly how idiotic and silly and evil they had been. So that without pinpointing the finger in the exact direction, something dimmed forevermore in the national perception of justice.

The most symbolic event of the revolution's birth was the big fire where somebody put a match on two huge oil drums in a refinery in Baghdad. This fire burned for weeks and at night lit up the entire city. In the day, you could chose to ignore it, but sleeping on the roof at night you could see and feel the heat wherever you were; and if a wily gust of wind fanned the flames towards the houses, one collective sigh of terror was emitted by the mesmerised audience: the ones nearer the fire even had taxis waiting downstairs to escape forthwith if their own roof caught fire.

Other disruptions were to our curriculum. I remember in 1957 making a circuit around Baghdad on a school bus to be taught all the street names. In 1958 all those names were modified to include something about the revolution or the names of its leaders; so we had to relearn them for the public Baccalaureat in 1959

Life went on, life always goes on and some of it was merry and some of it was bright! The sun did shine on the revolutionaries, albeit with a violent tint. Abdul Karim Kassem, who had triggered the violence of the revolution, was resurrected as a good man, a sincere man who aspired totally for Iraq's wellbeing. Rumours were rife that he had intended to spare the young King's life. Indeed he came up with a lot of beneficial reforms for the nation during his four years in command. He made Baghdad beautiful by gilding it with roundabouts full of flowers and greenery. He ordered celebrations where floats would go by decked with flowers and children and music. He introduced weekly assemblies at school so that pupils could sing the National Anthem and give respect to the new flag (to the refrain of *Ashal Zaeem* Abdul Karim). He gave poor people land to build houses on and treated our minority decently. To be sure he came from very modest roots but he remained modest throughout his reign too, in contrast with later tyrants. Initially a teacher, he gave it up to graduate from the military Academy in Iraq as well as to complete a year's stint in England earning many medals for his war bravery. A rare leader who did not line his pockets with money from the Iraqi people, he died poor. On the other hand, Abdul Karim was never allowed that clear run. Already in March 1959 people noticed the aeroplane strafing Baghdad; in an attempted revolution, al Shawaff wanted to annexe Mosul. In 1959 too, his best friend Abdul Salaam attempted to plot against him, while the Baathists including Saddam Hussein tried to kill him. Stunned, the multitude heard him struggling from the hospital bed to make a speech to reassure the nation, having been within a hairbreadth of dying. But he forgave magnanimously Abdul Salaam, freeing him personally during the *Eid* celebrations.

To start with, every household was expected to display several large, framed pictures of his and Abdul Salaam's in nearly every room of the house! Then, as one or the other clipped the power struggle and disappeared from the political scene, the family alternated between hiding hanging or even tearing them up!

Finally, his opponents did succeed in killing Abdul Karim with a death squad inside the radio headquarters and the active partnership of the CIA. After a very peremptory military trial in which he was condemned to die as a traitor to the cause, he addressed Abdul Salam with the words: "Remember when I pardoned you? Don't kill me either". Abdul Salaam did appear to hesitate for a moment but the Colonels counselled him against being faint hearted. Abdul Karim requested to die with his eyes open to watch his murderers; promptly they laid his corpse outside the radio quarters on the street, so that his supporters had no alternative but to put down their guns. That night, the former leader was displayed in all his regalia on television, looking quasi alive…but then a sneering soldier pulled the head up and then everyone could see the trickle of blood on his neck. So on like the rest of the country, the way forward was to resurrect Abdul Salaam's pictures from the attic.

After two years, Abdul Salaam was also killed in a helicopter crash going from Baghdad to Basrah! Rumours had it that it was a bomb by the enemy, but then the official version stated otherwise!

By then we were becoming inured to hordes of people in power being killed with bullets or hung or worse in successive plots; it seemed that every revolution became more bloodthirsty than the previous.

One of the great banes of our lives were the exams in our school, and when the agenda was particularly gruesome, we prayed for a political mishap to win a reprieve from the teachers. And wonder of wonders, often enough there was, along with a postponement; there were so many disruptions to ordinary life. There was a time when the school was not allowed to function as the teachers were accused of communism. We sat at home for months and but for the inventiveness of our Headmaster Abdullah Obadiah, bless him, who was always afraid in case we relaxed from the school's work dogma, we would have missed out on large chunks of curriculum for that year. So he devised a network of students and staff to smuggle homework to the older students, and smuggle it back for marking. He would have been prosecuted if caught but could not allow us to waste precious time during the term.

Very sadly, we never resurrected the daily swimming in the river. Dijlah became strewn with debris from the smashed windows of erstwhile palaces all along the Tigris.

The Ba'athists came to power Feb 63 and toppled four days before John Kennedy's assassination in Nov 63 and that is how I ended up having a day off for my 18th birthday. As usual, it was declared a national holiday so no one went to work and the government had a hayday catching the people from the previous regime. As a curfew was also in effect, our neighbours stealthily popped in to kill the time with the most favourite Iraqi pastime of all: politics! Amid thick tobacco smoke and aroma of cardamom in the Turkish coffee, they discussed and opined, crunched the *charazat* that gave them the brainwaves very necessary to analyse the "situation"! Why not, they are proven to be rich in zinc, copper and iron. Everyone listened to the foreign broadcasts, and that is why we, along with the whole nation, tended to be very well informed about world politics (*Professeur Loggeyya* in sarcastic mode). From a young age we understood that the Iraqi media only conveyed what the rulers wanted the nation to believe in, which is why we switched on the BBC World Service or Voice of America. They were only really clear at night so we slept with the transistor under the pillow.

As there have been indirect rumours from the government that a new law was coming out to forbid Jews from leaving the country, of passports "closing", so people anticipated it and took the opportunity to get the last flights out of the country. Most of them never returned as the "situation" worsened progressively. Consequently, anyone who travelled was seriously fussed over, with weeks of dinners and lunches beforehand as though he/she was going to the moon. An autograph book was circulated and we all wrote in it about our love and regards for the departed and then took pictures and made copies for the masses at 'Nerso'! I was taken in my teens a few times to the airport in a cavalcade of relatives and friends to say goodbye to acquaintances; there were absolutely no facilities then, people congregated to discuss the sad occasion helping themselves to *Tabeet* and *kubbas* from steaming cauldrons brought in to mark the occasion! And then, as if on cue, children, old people, the lot burst out crying the minute the hostess announced it was time to leave for the departure lounge. Everyone started to kiss the family in a "you're lost and gone forever" kind of way which was the reality in those days. Sometimes, years down the line, we did meet again but it always had tobe in a different land.

It was decreed as early as 1950 that Jews were not allowed to join the military, so that in the event of a hostile atmosphere or an attack there was not one pistol between the six thousand of us either in Baghdad or Basrah. One of my fellow students, who continued feeling loyalty for his country whatever the circumstances, decided that he was cut out for an army career, his heart lay exclusively in that direction. He went to a military base in the north of Baghdad and told them his ambition was to join up and become a pilot. They fell about laughing, summarily dismissing his request as a bad joke: "Aha, so you want to take a Mig 21 to Israel just like Munir Rofa did"? They howled sarcastically! In 1966, this very skilled pilot took a much prized Russian aeroplane to the Iraqis' arch enemy Israel to study and decipher .This might have helped them win the 1967 war as Egypt's air force was mainly made up of Migs at the time. But Munir, a prize pilot, had been ordered to drop bombs on the Kurds and did not think it ethical so decided that he must find a way to leave Iraq. His story is all cloak and dagger involving the highest of officials and led to him acquiring a new identity abroad together with his family. Anyway this friend was advised "you are lucky we are not booking you in here and now, do not dare show your face anymore". Wasn't going there too risky in the first place Farouq? I know we were bored stiff from doing nothing the whole day, still....

When the Ba'athists came to power and started shouting about their hatred for the Zionists, the religious bodies and the newspapers following suit, we could see that the equation was entering a new phase. Our situation progressively became much worse, slowly but surely, even as we passively contemplated it from the comfort of the living room. And then we teenagers seeing all the vitriolic and violence on television would approach our parents with requests to leave the country. Our parents who remembered the days before the independence in 1932 and all the troubles before and after as well as their golden era in the meantime, were still optimistic They loved Iraq, and always hoped and believed in the eventual return of the good old days. They kept repeating that all the virulent speeches were rhetoric and once the regime stabilized and no scapegoats needed, they would leave our minority alone. Their favourite expression was: "Wait". Wait to finish school, wait to get that all important certificate, wait for this Minister to come or this Minister to go. From this vantage point of 40 years on, I would say they were taking a serious risk with their lives and the lives of their children. But it is a fact that when you are in your forties and fifties you tend to cling to the lifestyle you have, and it is difficult to disregard what you have achieved: meaning that off with the old and on with the new is almost impossible. Anyway as they pointed out, there were no passports to be had.

Basically the community should have never accepted the doctrine of no passport and should have taken steps to avert it, maybe by contacting the United Nations human rights charter straight away; but the elders always advocated leaving politics alone while the Rabbi tried to help individuals by visiting dignitaries and writing affable letters to find a solution. There was no more to be done, there were no democratic processes in the country. The head of the household has an iron clad grip on all decisions and so we bowed to my Father's will and sat still and waited some more: for things to get better, for the fairly moderate Al Bazzaz to issue us with passports, for the UN to send a representative to talk to the ruling junta, for the cholera epidemic to abate from the south and open up the erstwhile smuggling route, for the war to stop raging in the north. And so it went on and on and on. We cooked our goose while talking about the various alternatives in the meanwhile.

Newsweek and Time were eagerly deciphered for a page about us that the censor might have forgotten to cut. Israel had an Arabic broadcast which all the Iraqis listened to even though it was illegal, and we listened to its 12 A.M. and 1 A.M.news bulletins which were the most detailed. News was our bread and butter, and there was such a dearth of real news in Iraq. Once again the papers were not allowed to print anything critical of the regime.

My Father had once sacked a junior employee; young, excitable, he swore revenge but for a time could do nothing more than ring us and bang the phone threateningly. With the revolutions, bloodthirsty mobs came into fashion, and he gathered one made up of hundreds of men and led them to my Father's darkish *khan* in the centre of town. Its doors were always open for deliveries from the docks and for entry by the other tenants who worked upstairs in individual rooms or *offissatt*. Brandishing the familiar loops in their ropes, they wanted nothing less than to hang him; this employee knew that my Father stayed there after hours often on his own well into the night, working. Very luckily, and acting on a tip from a friend in the warehouse, my Father managed to escape just before the mob descended. He went to hide outside Baghdad in view of the fact that his own house was not safe anymore till the mob gave up. He made a hasty will to turn everything over to my Mother just in case a worst scenario developed! I never knew where he went as they were afraid I would "tell" if interrogated.

In those days, and unwittingly, children turned their Father in by saying the wrong thing. A pupil at school might tell the teacher that he saw his Father maltreat Saddam's picture when nobody was looking; this teacher would shoot that Father into jail immediately. Terror reigned and everyone was petrified of potential purges.

LAST DAYS OF THE STRUGGLE

The single factor that made us realise that the knell had sounded for our stay in "the land of the two rivers" was the very visible hatred emanating during the trials and subsequent hangings of eleven Jewish people in the central squares of Baghdad and Basrah – January 1969 was and still is documented as the blackest month in the annals of Iraqi Jewry. The trials could only be heard through the radio and even then: it was amply apparent that the weak voices belonged to tortured individuals who were forced to sign whatever the bestial judges laid before them. One boy's certificate of birth had to be doctored to attain the age of 18. As for the lawyers appointed by the court, they were as jelly, and had no intention of sparking ire by attempting a defence, let alone a cogent one.

It was doubly aggravating as we were dead certain that they were family men just like our own Fathers and brothers, who lacked any prowess to become spies, absolutely. Mention must be made of the valiant efforts made by their wives and relatives to go to various Ministers' offices and homes, to waylay them early in the morning to beg for a reprieve. The Ministers all maintained that it was out of their hands.

Picture an agenda for national rejoicing in the 20th Century! Dancing music, loud and deafening, trolleys with drinks and crushed ice, sandwiches and cakes a plenty! Free rides on the buses and trams to entice more people to come and celebrate in the biggest square in Baghdad! But celebrate what? The piteous killing of scapegoats in line with Roman times when they used to throw the disadvantaged to the lions! People were jostling, a beatific smile filling their faces while

268

even the President of the Republic put in a "victorious" appearance! The only people they could conquer were hapless (very decent) individuals uprooted from within the bosom of their (very decent) families; I can still hear the broadcaster shouting himself hoarse on the TV! But didn't the religion advocate respect for the soul once it has departed?

Fourty years have passed and still I find it difficult to resurrect these atrocities. This episode remains a black one for us and all of civilized Iraq.

Doubtless martyrs each and everyone, their destiny was the final proof needed that our covenant with Iraq had been violated, ruptured and there was no way forward except by a complete parting of the ways.

Tragic isn't it that at the end of a 2500 year almost uneventful sojourn in the land, we had been transformed into that fifth column, whom everyone feared associating with! People we had shared good and bad times with avoided crossing our path so as not to say a mere hello!

From the window of our upstairs bedroom overlooking the local park, we could see the men in the little corner stall, ostensibly selling soft drinks, crisps and cigarettes, but in reality being paid to watch and report our every move to Central Quarters. We spied on them just as they spied on us and could see them using walky talkies to report on any movements from our house! As we went to visit friends by car, they followed. What really hurt is that there was a time not long ago when they were like neighbours and went out of their way even to deliver the cokes personally into the house. At university there was more of the same; colleagues we had called friends were now keeping an eye on us, indeed innocently asking us probing questions to report our "activities" to the party. We were a threat to the regime, us, with no phones, no military training, no jobs, not even one gun to cower behind? More humiliations were to come, this time by post: We received two very polite envelopes from the

Iraqi Jews reading Kaddish on the departed souls
of their brethrens

two social clubs we belonged to (Alwiyah and Acropolis). They threw us out simultaneously curtsey of government instructions. As for the Malaab, it was taken over soon after the war; there was a big lock and chain on the iron doors.

Those days, our last in Baghdad! They eked out far too slowly, without any pattern; we existed, waiting for the wheel to turn...

The school was functioning still thank God as the Headmaster had the foresight to recruit capable boys and girls, ex-students in their twenties to take over from the teachers who had walked out. My Father and I were glued to the radio all day, listening to the foreign news broadcasts approximately every quarter hour. The transistors came into their own at night and so we continued thus till the early hours of the morning.

These ancient and very valuable scrolls, stacked very indifferently, were discovered in the basement of an Intelligence building (2004)

It was the only way of finding out if the government was taking note of the international public outcry on our behalf. My Father was home as they had taken over his office downtown while his import licences were given to others, my brother was home as he was forbidden university, my younger brother was studying with an eye on imminent threats to attack the school and as for me, after obtaining a honours degree in Business, I enrolled with some friends at the French Institute! Why, you might ask? Well, the alternative was total stagnation!

Rumours abounded round us, some claimed that very soon, we would be incarcerated in a special district outside Baghdad; other rumours that the French were making an international conference to get other countries to bail us out, rumours that Alain Poher and Saderildeen Khan were both doing their best behind the scene. The French especially proved a credit to their humane charter. Then there were the not so good rumours that this and that member of the community has been haphazardly picked up: Meir Basri , a bastion of the community as well as being a very well respected author and poet with an immaculate record of serving the Iraqi cultural and industrial scene for decades, was accused of talking to an American journalist and summararily put in jail! When his friend Anwar Shaoul, a well known and esteemed poet in his own right, heard of this latest travesty, he composed a heartrending poem in Arabic which he sent to the authorities. The following is as near a rendition as I could manage:

"Even though I was brought up obeying Moses' creed
I enjoyed life thus protected by the clemency of Islam
And nurtured by the eloquence of the Koran.
So that happy or unhappy
Still I must remain faithful to my native country"

This (excellent) poem was published on the orders of the Minister of Internal Affairs in the Iraqi periodical "Al Jumhurriyyah" and Meir Basri was set free immediately.

When the religious cantor Nadji Paneeri was jailed because his son was rumoured to have escaped through the borders, a captain in the army happened to visit the jail. He knew Nadji well, as Nadji had attended his house often to circumcise his sons in happier times. The captain not believing his eyes, shouted at the guards to let the white haired man go.

To demonstrate the grievousness of it all, some "shopped" previous university mates, with the result that university girls and boys were taken to jail and freed only after the intervention of the French and a £500 bail. In the street, the Baathists' grey beetle cars would be prowling the streets, picking whoever they wanted in their cars, so even a walk around the neighbourhood could prove fatal.

Another casualty was our erstwhile neighbour Edouard who 'disappeared' one day while walking very near his home. His distressed wife did not know who to apply to who could provide succour as all the usual channels were there no more. In the end she knocked at their neighbour's who commanded a high position in the Baath party. Lucky for her in Moslem lore there is a saying: *'haqqel jar al jar''* which means a neighbour must always be there to help his fellow neighbour. He immediately despatched people to look out for him and located him in prison. Edouard was released back into the bosom of his family that very same day.

There is always comfort in numbers so friends and neighbours popped in while out walking: unfortunately there was nothing on the horizon but more doom and gloom. Inactivity and worry can kill. One day we picked up all the lemons and the oranges in the garden, squeezed them, added plenty of sugar as a preservative and bottled them in the fridge. My friends and I used to vie with each other in reading Time and Newsweek magazines from cover to cover and then quoting them for days on end!   Yet another day my Father collected all the pictures which had any trace of family in the West, put them in a tin and sloshed petrol on them; My Father was very crafty, he did it while we were not looking; we would never have consented to having those valuable memories go up in smoke. But, it did make sense from his viewpoint, as a family member living in the West would be proof enough to drag the male of the household away, accused of being a spy.

The mood was very sombre, like caged animals we waited for whatever destiny spewed out. But it was fear that was the hunter, fear of every ring at the doorbell that was not greeted by recognition from our Tibetan puppy "Whiskey". He became that most trusted of barometers, all six kgs of him. Highly intelligent, he knew our friends, so, from his habitual perch at the window ledge in the bedroom downstairs, he assessed the intruder at the gate: if he then bared his teeth and a demonic look came over his soft grey eyes while his tiny silver frame shook from violent barking, then it was a sign that it was a stranger and we all collapsed in trauma: it must be the secret police come to ransack the house and take my Father to *Kasser al Nihayya* like they had done with so many of our friends. People who went there usually disappeared till their family was told to collect them in a shroud.

'Whiskey' never abandoned us, no no! He loved each and every one of us and was a devoted dog till the end! He spent his days running like lightening from the top of the outside garage down the stairs into the garden, executing a complete crescent to reach the front gate and be there to greet us, his best playmates. It was we who abandoned him so callously upon departure! There was a silent consensus that we could not afford to risk an animal bark to lead the police to our whereabouts, while Whiskey could stand a better chance of surviving away from us. Certainly he had a more preferential right to a passport than us!

The media were competing to show us as the worst creeps that inhabited the planet. The television had those comedies with the archaic Jewish names, and I remember this old man who was portrayed hiding under the bed every time there was a loud noise. Come on! Even allowing for the various hiccups and maltreatments we were subject to, our generation and the ones before us had attained a very acceptable even superior position in Iraqi society; indeed we were befriended by many in government and high places. We proved ultimately that given half a chance, we could take the bull by the horn: we did not baulk at leaving a country where the welcome mat had vanished.

On two occasions there were strong rumours that the government wouldl be granting us passports to go wherever we pleased. Our spirits lifted and we bought suitcases and stuffed them with our best clothes to make a good impression abroad. Alas we only proved to ourselves that we had been mugs to be taken in.

My friends and I kept asking ourselves: if they do not like us, why not let us go? Some Western Heads of State repeated in a similar vein:" Let them go to others who will cherish them and receive them with fraternal affection"; by others here they meant themselves, they were offering us unconditional refuge in their democratic countries.

And then, amid all the doom and gloom a door nudged a wee bit open! News came back through the grapevine that one of our neighbours had escaped to Iran through the mountains. This electrified everyone no end, and dared us to map a future of deliverance! Even though uncharted, fraught with danger, it would still be infinitely better than being led to the slaughter like so many sheep! All of a sudden, the young people recaptured that spring in their footsteps. Others depressed, needing Valium tablets every night, brightened considerably as if by miracle. At last there was something optimistic to talk about.

Until 1967, escapees made their way to Iran with the aid of a smuggler to row them through Shatt al Arab and Hamadan, it came to be regarded as a very smooth and trusted operation! The North on the other hand was very much an uncharted territory, not developed like the South. It was full of mountains and ravines and roads were very rare. News also filtered that Max had had a very harrowing time through the mountains before making it successfully? So what, we scoffed! For everyone Max had become the hero, his bravery emblazoned a trail to freedom. Maybe we too should try? While the sages shook their heads and counselled to wait and see how things panned out (as usual) we, the young had had enough of waiting; danger, uncertainty did not matter, what lay ahead did not phase us, material issues be damned, better not have enough to eat but be free!

For once I was glad I had not thrown my school atlas away: the border was so near to Salah –el- deen, why, it was nudging Rawanduz by an inch!? We just needed to keep nagging my Father till he abandoned, like us, all caution to the wind.

Of course the nearest and easiest foreign country was Iran, it was moreover the only alternative to escape to; Jordan, Syria, Saudi Arabia and Kuwait would in all likelihood have handed the illegal refugees back to the regime; the Turkish border is too mountainous and faraway and did not constitute a viable option.

The Kurdish people (24 million) have long lived in the mountainous areas inside Turkey, Iran and Iraq. Unluckily for them, those were the very same countries that at one time or the other fought to annihilate them or kick them out! No one was willing to forego a slice of their land for their sake. Here is a bird's eye view about the people that will help us to attain freedom. The Kurds form the largest minority in the world without a recognized homeland. They come from Indo-European stock and some are startlingly blond featured with blue green eyes: mostly Moslem, their religion does not assert itself in an extreme fashion nor do their women wear the hijab but rather join their men folk in all aspects of work; they are indeed trained to carry guns! Way back in 1921, amid the ruins of the Ottoman Empire, the Treaty of Sevres almost promised them a Kurdish state but Atatürk fought against it and the US sided with him. In those days, they were mere border guards, but now have become a well trained and disciplined guerrilla force who struggle for their people's rights. Their fighters are called Peshmergas, which means: the ones who face death!

In 1991 the United States created a haven for the Kurds in Northern Iraq to protect them from annihilation by Saddam Hussein. The two controlling Kurdish factions have now signed an agreement to share in governing the Kurdistan nation: the KDP(Barzani's party) control Arbil the capital, with Dhouk in the northwest while the PUK(Talabani's party) control Suleimaniya in the southeast; at present, Iraqi Kurdistan is attracting international investment with a view to developing it as a modern and touristical place. Hotels and aeroports are some of the facilities built recently which we have never witnessed during our lifetime in Iraq.

Their parliament elected Massud Barazan, the son of their famous warrior Mullah Mustafa to be the President of Kurdistan and his nephew Nechirvan as the Prime Minister.

There was always a lot of smuggling between Iraq and Iran: for example good brands of whisky and beer which in Iran are banned and therefore expensive; they were much cheaper in Iraq even though rather frowned upon. The smuggling was a lifeline to the remote Kurdish villages when trade limitations were imposed on them. Food, washing machines and people were processed through borders which consisted at times of a tiny stream– the Iranian border guards were bribed, the landmines negotiated while their heavy rubber boots proved capable of scaling dangerous cliffs

Mules were used to traverse the treacherous mountain faces and narrow passes. They were prepared for their perilous mountain journeys by pouring alcohol into their drinking water; this ensured that the mules could not run away when an ambush occurred and made them more docile and less excitable. The many ranges of the Zagros Mountains extend from Iran and into northern Iraq. They contain sheer rugged peaks which can reach up to 14,000 ft, and are separated by steep canyons and gorges. Rivers tumble violently into the valleys from rocky faces. Winters are severe, and temperatures might sink to minus 25 degrees C. Heavy snow falls in the winter and remains on the higher summits most of the year.

The mountains contain many breeds of animals, some quite dangerous, such as brown bear, eagles, wolves, foxes, and leopards and striped hyena.

Following are plucky (but true) stories of escape through those very same mountains – executed neatly and spontaneously in the modern version by our daredevil heroes.

STORIES OF SMUGGLING A LA FRESCO

Max relates his pioneering attempt :

In March 1970 two events occurred successively which signalled to me that a dawn of freedom was in the offing! First as a direct result from the International Conference for the Deliverance of the Jews of the Middle East, we were allowed to move about without impediment in all of Iraq; this was happy news indeed. A second auspicious development was a cessation of enmities between the Kurdish faction of Barzani and the government, which meant that there was no more fighting in the north! With good planning and luck it might be possible to go very near the border with Iran on an innocent holiday trip to the summer resorts. This, I was certain, was an opportunity to be grasped with both hands.

Seizing the first available chance, I took my car for a jaunt to reconnoitre, persuading a friend to come with me. We headed north. We still worried in case we were stopped, and what sort of excuse we could come up with to justify such a trip. Looking around us all the time and then at people more intently, we tried to identify a friendly soul, or anybody that might lead us to a friendly soul; after turning round for hours, I spied a Kurdish man by the name of Daoud, recognizing in him the person who had bought my used car a few years ago! He was leaning against a Cocacola stall on the main road. We stopped and approached him! After the usual greetings, we gestured to him to join us to the side, and sotto voice, tried to broach the subject of a smuggling operation via the North! It seemed he had heard of Kurdish people who were cognisant of routes across the mountains, but he gave us the impression of being too afraid of the authorities to undertake anything on such a big scale! The most he could do was promise to ask his people and come back to us. I gave him my address in Baghdad since there were no phones, and we had to leave it at that.

I waited for ten days to hear from him, afterwards came to the conclusion that this lead was not "taking".

I made myself go to the North again several times after that (Salah el Den, Rawanduz, even higher up to Jindian in the mountains) without telling my friends in Baghdad as that would have led to a lot of risky gossip; I peeled my eyes looking for Daoud all the while but in vain.

Then one night, there was a sudden ring at the doorbell! Saida my wife shouted from upstairs not to open as it was suspicious for anyone to come at that time of the night! But I was pleasantly surprised; it was a very furtive "Daoud" who came in after making sure that there was no one loitering outside! My mood lifted at once: would my efforts come to fruition? He said he had been discussing the issue with a friend who knew the area well as they smuggled "things" between Iran and Iraq; they were from "another" faction which was against the Mullah Barzani, but believed they can take us across to Iran even though there will always be risks. It seemed that I had to make a decision there and then, so keeping in mind that next year this alternative might not be open still, what with the laws changing every minute in line with the regime's vagaries, I had no choice but to embrace their offer! So I said I agreed. His friend wanted most of the money in advance though, as it was a hazardous enterprise and his group had to go into a lot of preparations in advance. I okayed that as well, went one evening to his house, and paid a hefty sum of money in lieu of a "ticket" for each member of the family. Anyone could have followed me or seen us talking the meanwhile so there was a risk in any further delay. That is why we agreed to meet at a certain point in the North the very next day! Accordingly I passed by a taxicab company which promised to send us a taxi next day for the purposes of *Istiyaf* (summer holiday). Afterwards I went to tell my wife Saida to get ready for the impending journey.

Of course Saida was concerned as to the identity of my smugglers as I only knew them very fleetingly; she reminded me that we were trusting strangers with our lives as well as our two little girls'. But my mind was made up; I felt this was an opportunity such that I have been waiting for forever.

Visiting my parents for the last time that evening, I tried to act very normally deciding it was better not to warn them of our imminent departure! My Father was getting on in years so there was no point in getting him worked up in advance! I left the task to my brother to tell both of them the next day. The fear that the government might visit the crimes of the sons on the entire clan weighed on me heavily, and I discussed it in detail with my brother. In the past it has shown its capability of doing so by taking close relatives to prison and torturing them to investigate the whereabouts of a business partner etc,and my Father being eldery certainly wouldn't be able to withstand any such treatment! It was not fair either to my brother to leave him under potential harassment, but on these two last points I had to trust in God!

09/6/1970: Up at five, Saida and I tore ourselves from our last sleep on the roof; that hour was the best one of the whole day, the air so invigorating, the atmosphere so very still Our neighbours from both sides were soundly asleep under their duvets - but we were on a life mission. Carrying the sleeping girls who were six and four years of age into the taxi, we went back into the house for a lighter cargo of suitcases;

Then we turned the door locks, glanced furtively around for Big Brother and decamped with no more ado. The last thing we needed was to have the *Amen* (intelligence) hot on our heels!

The taxi made good progress, and passing through Kirkuk and Arbil, reached Salah el Din in the mountains by 10 am. It dropped us off at an empty house to meet the Head Mullah, to whom I handed the rest of the money. They intimated that my wife and I had to change our names to Arab sounding ones, so in a trice Saida was Suhaila and I, Max, became Abdul Kader; our daughters' names had to correspond, so we called them Suha and Kalda.

Huddled in a different taxi driven by the Mullah, we passed a Kurdish village, Harir, in a plain, and then on to a beautiful waterfall " Gali Ali Begh"; its surrounding area is so green and lush, I found myself longing to relax in its shade just I used to do before losing my status in the country. But we bump into a patrol of Iraqi soldiers who give us some very curious glances, alas; we have to leave the area quickly. We drive through narrow mountainous passes; meanwhile the smugglers, following a discussion in their native Kurdish, decide that it will be safer to follow North rather than go East! (This is where the trip became more circuitous as East is the most direct route to Iran). We ended up veering north even though North was a totally uncharted territory, first because the Iraqis deployed less security forces there and second there was less chance of bumping into the Peshmergas who might have spelled trouble for our smugglers. It seems luck had a lot to do with what sort of smugglers you ended up with; whether they could command the best routes, knew the terrains and the border guards well, or whether they were treating the emigres as guinea pigs and leading them onto dangerous terrains solely to make money. The Peshmergas were the veterans of the mountains but our people belonged to an opposing Kurdish faction.

Shallal (fountain) Galli Ali Beg

Evening: Diana army camp was crammed full of trucks, armoured cars and Iraqi soldiers, and we stop to be searched! We cross our fingers and pray fervently that they would not home in on us. They search the boot and examine the driver's identity card, then at the last minute get detracted by another more important looking convoy so they signal us hastily on! A big sigh of relief! That is the last Iraqi stronghold behind us.

In a night clearing up in the mountains, we get to meet three more smugglers, these are loaded with authentic looking pistols and rifles; I too, am given a dagger. They have brought us Kurdish clothes to make us look like any other indigenous family; both girls look very cute in all the colours of the rainbow, and I am so relieved that they are treating the journey so far as an exciting adventure! The smugglers have brought five mules with them, and these beasts are standing mutely by awaiting our leisure! These animals look as ugly and brainless as they are reputed to be, and we do not empathise with each other by a long shot. But of course we will be eager to love and cherish them forever if they carry out their agenda! The little girls have never seen a mule and are delighted- so brushing aside my negative feelings I exert myself to get on top of one, copying the smugglers' movements; Hamid lifts up Suha on his mule, and little Khalda shares one with her Mother. Throughout the night we climb up and down various slopes, getting trained simultaneously in the art of mule riding. We entrust our hopes and aspirations to them and they soldier on like true troopers. The smugglers keep shushing us as any noise can spell disaster.

10/6/1970: At dawn, we see candles flickering up the face of the mountain, our smugglers fear they might be Iraqi soldiers; we have to veer hurriedly again to the North towards Turkey; unfortunately at this juncture, Suhaila and Khalida fall off their mule . Even though Suhaila is in obvious pain from her back, she bravely decides to continue – our thermos of water is broken as well. Another few hours sees us utterly exhausted so we cover ourselves with some blankets and sleep fitfully on the ground.

11/6/1970: Paradoost Mountains in view and Hamid insists to continue due North. Turning a corner on the narrow mountainous lanes, we are confronted with seven Iraqi men armed with rifles and pistols. Suhaila saves the day by riding her mule very nonchalantly past them and we follow mutely. Miracle of miracles, they do not stop us,

Next another challenge in the shape of a perpendicular mountain face. The agile guides place the girls on their backs, and start to climb it expertly. Suhaila and I do the best we can, donning special rope mountain shoes "gaiwas". Lucky we are fearless and young at hearts still (noone can be allowed to doubt this fact).

We climb all night to reach the top of the mountain at dawn. At 6000 ft high, the ice cold wind freezes our limbs; again we have to sleep on frosty ground. Khalda's face is swollen by an insect bite, the poor child cannot see. I give her an antibiotic pill - lucky that I brought some medicines.

Northernmost Iraq showing the two escape routes taken by most of the crowd

12/6/1970: Some Kurdish people on mules appear from nowhere and team up with us to share the last leg of the journey. Together we climb down a very rocky slope (hairy even if we had a tightrope, on the other hand wouldn't have known how to use it anyway); a snake rears itself from among the rocks but the Kurdish woman deftly kills it with a stone

Midday: We stop at a waterfall, the sun is scorching. Lunch of boiled eggs from kind companions, as our own food supplies are exhausted.

Night time sees us on top of the Kohi Zur mountain (I estimate it to be 14000 ft high). There we sleep in the shelter of a downed Iraqi Mig. It was dropping bombs on the Kurds a few years ago and they managed to shoot it down.

13/6/1970: We awake to a vista of majestic mountains between the Iran, Iraq, and Turkish borders. Negotiating one of the most dangerous mountain passes, Suhaila's mule trips, dislodging stones and opening up a chasm, which nearly plunges both rider and transport into the valley beneath; with bated breath, we watch the seasoned mule put on its thinking cap for a length of time: the smuggler raises his finger to his mouth to enjoin all to complete silence so as not to interrupt any active brainwaves. The mule having planned its strategy negotiates a calculated jump which deftly clears the chasm: my wife has escaped certain death. A medal for both.

Later on we meet five Peshmergas riding on their mules; we tell them that we are in desperate need of food and drink! No problem they say, and cheerfully point us to a Kurdish outpost ahead. What a relief it is to indulge in a good meal at last, our first ever since leaving Baghdad! Ditto for the bath! We sleep on minimal mattresses, the fatigue and fresh air knocking us out for six

14/6/70: Rested and satiated, we continue riding in the snow near the top of Zouzan mountains; the smugglers point to a village further down the incline: a glimpse of our very first

Iranian village, our goal! With a sense of purpose and an air of jubilation we get there at around 8 pm at night.

Hamid's friend being one of the border guards guides us through a safe crossing of the boundary. We ask our smuggler to book us into a hotel like establishment and give him a prearranged signal of safe arrival to transmit to the folk back home.

In the scramble of registration at the hotel, what with many people talking different languages, someone mistakenly tells a guard that I am an ex-army officer from Iraq. As Iraqis and Iranians did not mix (in fact they became arch enemies during two upcoming wars), all of a sudden the entrance of the hotel is swarmed with armed police; I cannot believe it but they have come for me; I get bundled off into the border prison and solitary confinement. Trouble begins in earnest: "Please God, haven't I had my share of problems already"?

Saida gets on the phone from the hotel room; she tries to contact my sister who has been living in Teheran for the last twenty years: she and her family form our only hope of succour in the absence of zero identities. Very unfortunately no one answers (they are away on a trip we understand later). Here goes our only lifeline! Desperate, Saida now tries to contact some refugee associations and seek their help! Meanwhile I can only continue rotting in jail, petrified that I should be handed back to the Iraqi authorities. I keep walking back and forth all day long, and must have lost ten kgs in that week from the sheer agony of it all. To add to it I do not speak Iranian so no communications with my gaolers.

After repeating the story of the escape and persecutions several times to all and anon, Saida finally strikes gold: a Jewish charity decides to send its representative from Teheran to validate my story! The key turns in the lock and an old man enters and confronts me suspiciously asking for proof of my religion! With my back to him and my life hanging in the balance, I recite an important prayer from the Holy Book in Hebrew (the Shema). At last he believes my story, hugs me and expresses joy that I have managed to escape from a real hell! He takes it upon himself to explain it all in Persian to the authorities who nod their heads in what seems to be hours on end. Utter relief, they have agreed to release me, shattered but vindicated. I rejoin my anxious family in their hotel, and we all board the train to Teheran!

There are a lot of officials and Jewish organizations to meet us, we are celebrities all: the first link with a victimized community! It is vital that I inform the authorities on the borders to anticipate a clandestine exodus from other Iraqis. I do this forthwith, even before attending to my needs and those of my family's. They promise not to make life as difficult for whoever of my braver friends makes it or climbs it across the border.

The only adage to go by is "Trust the Donkey"

<u>Shula's escape, at 16, was a joint family effort</u>

My brother Basheer had remained good friends with a Moslem boy from his school throughout the darkest periods. This friend had heard through the grapevine of a Kurdish chap with connections to smugglers who was willing to take members of our family over the mountains into Iran; lucky for us that my Father knew this friend well so could trust him and rely on his promises too. Although the smuggler demanded a steep sum of money per head, we nevertheless managed to come to an agreement that suited all sides: after paying the deposit, the rest of the money would be paid up by my Father in Baghdad upon receipt of a token from us via the smugglers, signalling our safe arrival in Iran. My Father would know then, without the need for further communication (the Amen intercepted all letters and phone calls) that the valuable merchandise has been delivered safely.

Thus nine of us siblings and cousins, including my married brother and his wife, plus my two younger sisters who had clamoured to go last minute, agreed with two taxicabs to pick us up from the house in the early hours! My Mother prepared a breakfast which none of us could touch! She could not decide whether to be happy for us because we were escaping or whether to be afraid because of the unpredictability of it all! As for us, we only dreaded lest something or somebody might foil the plans and we would reamin stifled in Baghdad! At that time, new regulations had come about as the result of an outcry by international organizations and the Pope's intervention, so there were no impediments to us going to the North for a vacation; for once we were on a par with other citizens.

As the idea was to pretend to go on a very short trip, so we took only the clothes on our backs; (one girl, being very fond of her bracelets and knick knacks, did take her jewellery in a pouch but all the crowd frowned on her; she could attract suspicion from the soldiers as well as attention from greedy thieves); the journey to Mosul went off quite smoothly and we were required to stay with friends of this smuggler for a whole day! Cramped conditions but we had to make do (and very strictly warned not to go outside). With midnight came the order to gather our belongings and decamp.

Under the cover of darkness two oldish cars came to pick us up, this was accomplished swiftly! Mosul, a bustling town with a mix of Iraqis, Kurds and Assyrians sits on both banks of the Tigris. It is called Umm al Rabi'ain, the city of the two springs, because its autumn and spring are very similar. It proved to be the last point of civilization and the cars headed towards the more mountainous, deserted areas. They stopped a few hours later and the smugglers signalled us to get out: there were smallish, greyish mules waiting for us, standing around munching the grass. We were taken aback as we had only ever seen mules going about their business carrying loads in the streets; we had never but never ventured closer to ride them or get familiar with their character! Well, here we were upon to embark on a huge educational curb - there was absolutely no other way of carrying on with this dark and uncertain journey.

The smugglers showed us how to get on top of a mule, where to put our feet and how to start prodding without hurting. And that was that. Good job there were no bags or baggage but only ourselves to worry about! Mutely, the cavalcade of mules followed each other, and negotiated one steep incline after another. Our only thought was not to slide and fall off as they inched higher, sometimes in a perpendicular fashion. With continous instructions from the smugglers, we managed to stay on top of the mules sitting on a sort of a carpet like saddle! The cavalcade kept going forward! Although the moon was up, it was quite dark and very scary! We could only proceed at a mule pace and worse luck, they told us that the mountains were surrounded by Iraqi troops! Very often there would be the glare of searchlight suddenly illuminating the mountain, and when this happened we were ordered to flatten ourselves on the mule so that no human shape was visible! Flustered and trembling with fear at the impossible and unfamiliar circumstances that we found ourselves in, we latched on to the donkeys' reins frequently so as not to fall, while the only thing that kept us going was the rush of adrenalin; we were forced to trust and obey the guides' directions, even though there was no chance of communicating with them linguistically.

At one point, the girl who was carrying her jewellery fell off from the mule, crying out loud when she hit the rocks and broke her nose; though painful to watch, we had to go against our instinct to help! We couldn't afford to stop to sort her out. We encouraged her to get on with it as much as her strength allowed, and it was only much later when she reached Teheran, that she could go to a hospital and have an operation! To top it all, she mislaid her precious pieces of jewellery in the darkness. We could hear her crying her heart out. The ride on the mules continued, eerie and very scary, we never knew which mountain we were on, and still do not! The Kurdish guides spoke no Arabic, while our lives were in the hands (feet) of the mules.

Thank God the mules only dislodged stones and followed the narrow paths safely, it was best not to look down the steep slopes and weigh the possibility of the mule faltering in its very next step. By 5 am the dawn started to break in the mountains around us, we re discovered the glorious sights and sounds of the North of Iraq. Such virgin country, such untapped vistas, all bathed in the pinkish rays of the early sun. It proved to be such an uplifting experience looking down at both countries (Iran and Iraq) from that high vantage point. One day these lush mountains will be developed by other people, other generations, we did not belong there anymore; If only we could take one last farewell picture. But I bet the smugglers did not approve of such frivolity and it goes without saying that noone had thought to bring a camera.to achieve everlasting fame!

We reached the borders soon after. We had been riding all night and the journey had taken a lifetime...How our seats were sore, and hunger had us by the throat. All this evaporated when we became convinced from frantic signals by the Kurds that we had crossed to terra ferma: Any suspicion of the guides vanished too: they had opened up a future where just forty eight hours ago there was none. We would have hugged them, but it was enough to be eternally grateful - so we gave them an embroidered handkerchief as agreed, to take back to the parents.

My poor friend was waddling along, stooped and her legs arched: it was the effect of being on a mule for the whole night! That was when the incongruity of it all hit us and we had our first laugh for ages.

Our guards exchanged more conversations on our behalf with the other border smugglers (they ruled the roost up here) and so we were led into a tiny almost deserted town on the border. There, even though all of us shared one very crowded room, still we had the most satisfying sleep of a lifetime

<u>Amid freezing conditions, Linda made it - but her younger
brother's proved too onerous</u>

I had been busy trying to chart an escape plan for myself
when I was faced with some very significant developments!
Certainly the whole community was shaken to the core when
news filtered that approximately a hundred no less of our
friends were apprehended and caught by the Iraqi police near
the borders; subsequently investigated, they were accused of
trying to escape to Iran and thrown into jail. My Father being
a lawyer, found himslef involved in the proceedings and
managed to bail out quite a few.

.After striving hard and obtaining excellent marks in the
1968 Baccalaureat, I, along with all my classmates were
confronted by a very bleak future; the Six Day War brought in
its wake among others a government decree that forbade us
entrance to university, in addition work opportunities were
closed to us as well! My life became so empty and utterly
devoid of purpose that I uncharacteritically became very
frustrated and suicidal. The only redeeming course had to be a
(risky) escape to freedom.

My friends could see that my spirits were sinking fast, I
cried for no reason and my weight ballooned! Throughout my
life there had been always something to strive or plan for, now
there was nought! I spent the day between the four walls of
the house, bemoaning my fate and blaming my parents; all of
us teenagers accused our parents bitterly for the stagnation we
found ourselves in.

And then my best girlfriend suggested I join her and her
family for a trip to the North: her family were putting their
trust in an unknown smuggler; but my cautious Father did not
allow me to do this as he deemed it too hazardous.

Subsequently an older friend of the family also offered to take me with him through different channels! This was again bulldozed by my Father who advised me to wait till he could trust the smugglers better (if only they came with a university degree saying BSc in smuggling). I recognised this excuse as the mantra of the older generation for years past and present, so rebelled and argued that we could not sit still like sheep while they decide when to lead us to the slaughter! I insisted that I must chance it and now was the best time. I really believed my Father's attitude was cowardly, that he was wrong. In the end I went back to this family friend and said I was game to take a risk; when my brother heard that I had chanced on an opening he created such a scene with the parents as to bring the roof down; he was adamant that he could not stay one more minute in such hell! I was 20 and he was 18. My parents exhausted all arguments trying to persuade us to stay put. Well, after all, it was our own life that we were gambling with.

The plan called for us to disguise ourselves and head north by bus the very next day. From there to make our way to the Kurdish smuggler's house and await further instructions. I put on a huge black abbaya and my brother bought himself a second hand coat from the market so we both looked nondescript, piling the warm layers underneath. In addition we were each allowed a small battered case. My Mother and Father were utterly devastated to lose both children at once, but they knew the battle had been played out and there was nought further to say.

Early in the morning, we scrambled into the taxi from the garden door, it sped eerily! It passed Tahrir Square with its nightmarish scenes of two years ago still fresh in our minds; the taxi reached the main bus station which accessed all routes, so we alighted and boarded the Sulaimaniyah mini coach. At this point my brother nudged me to the presence of another Jewish family of our acquaintance in the same bus; of course we studiously ignored each other for fear of suspicion.

The bus had to pass six checkpoints in total all manned by Iraqi soldiers; at every checkpoint, my brother would turn pitifully white while they boarded and asked for identification papers. Of course if they knew we were Jews, they could have told us to get off, our destiny, the purpose of our trip to be investigated further. Our luck held for once and they only approached the other passengers. The driver of the mini bus, blissfully unaware of the crucial time factor, made all passengers come down for an hour to have a snack and a drink at the roadside café and to stretch their legs. The journey to Suleimaniyah takes hours and the bus passes superb countryside but I was knotted up with worry from inside and could not relax enough to enjoy such beauty; I even ignored the book on my lap.

At last we reached Suleimaniyah and alighted: There was a prominent Kurdish presence in the town, but it was an Iraqi enclave nevertheless, with the ever present threat of Iraqi soldiers. It was imperative to continue to keep a low profile.

The smuggler was supposed to meet us here in this bus depot, dressed in a dark suit proffering a red flower in his hand; but, where oh where was he? We panicked, trying to appear nonchalant; we scoured all the passengers in vain. Luckily I had a brainwave then and remembered that the smuggler lived in the only house made of mountain stone near the Mosque; so I suggested we take a taxi. On the other hand, my brother was adamant that all taxi drivers were spies for the security services, so yet another altercation followed between us! In the end I won, and we hailed a taxi and instructed him to take us to the Mosque. Imagine our consternation when this driver began asking searching questions about our reasons for being in the North? We feared he would report us to the police straightaway. All of a sudden, I spied the Mosque tucked in among the narrow lanes, and adjacent to it nestled the single storey stone house! I stopped the driver, paid him and gave him a big *baksheesh* with the innuendo that he must keep mum about us.

The smuggler was waiting outside and welcomed us into his small house. He led us upstairs. What a surprise! Here were the same people we had recognized earlier on in the bus; now they were leisurely ensconced in the room, playing cards and listening to the radio. Seeing them so laid back had an electric effect on us and we felt some of the tensions disappear. After all, we have crossed stage one and were safe and sound! The smuggler had already told them we would be riding on mules, and they saw the funny side of the future adventure! If only I could phone my parents to reassure them that so far so good.

We made ourselves at home! The smuggler soon brought in steaming trays laden with meat and vegetables and deposited them on the carpet in front of us; they were followed by fruit baskets. We were ravenous, not having eaten since the night before.

The little boy (Benny) sat himself on the cushion next to mine and greeted all Linda's jokes with wholehearted infectious giggles! What luck, he diverted me from my gloomy thoughts. Meanwhile my brother and the rest talked politics the one subject we were all well versed in, it came with the territory. As everyone became carried away in analysing the doom and gloom in the country, so the smuggler came to caution us: the noise we were making could be heard by his visitors downstairs.

It was 7 pm and time to embark on the next stage of this journey! We trooped downstairs with our suitcases and placed them in an open army jeep, and squeezed on top of them as well as we could, there was precious little room for the crowd of us. In the front sat a driver with an armed Kurdish man. He had on the usual tasselled turban and wide trousers while a knife protruded from his belt. The driver drove fast making very good progress we thought with relief; and then the vista of the high mountains was upon us. Not familiar with mountainous territories, we never dreamt that the driver would chance driving through their steep narrow lanes in his little jeep. But he did!

It was very dark with no light to guide him except the moon. We hazarded a look to the left and there lay an ominous valley, to the right and there most of the narrow lane was obscured by large branches from the trees. With fear gripping at our heart, we still had to concede that the driver was very skilful at manoeuvring the car. On the other hand the stench escaping from him left no doubt that he had been drinking and that became another additional worry; we also noticed that his clothes were uncouth to a degree that marked him as a contraband bandit or worse. To top it all, he was bent on unsettling us even further by turning his head often and saying he feared that the security police might be on our tracks! We started to seek help from God.

This long awaited escape journey began to sour and turn quickly into a nightmare. Then we started to implore him to go slower but he was as a man driven! The force of every winding turn threatened to eject me from my position in the open jeep, so I had to clutch onto my suitcase for dear life. I started having forebodings about falling in the valley, turning into an unknown corpse among many others no doubt. And what about the additional guilt of dragging my brother to such an appalling fate? Now I wished with all my heart that I had stayed home; to cap it all it was freezing in the mountains. We huddled together at the back of the jeep. That driver must have known the cliffs like the back of his hand, otherwise I would not be alive to tell the tale. Anyway this journey from hell took all of three hours at least, and we were deposited at a clearing at the foot of a mountain. What a relief that we were still in one piece. Indicating that we should not make any noise, the smugglers collected our identity cards and disappeared, taking the jeep with them.

Four more Kurds dressed in rags were taking over; all we could see were their smouldering eyes while their gleaming swords dangled by their sides; they not only looked like highwaymen, they must have been highwaymen too. Unfortunately, we neither of us spoke the other's language, so there was no use trying to establish some sort of a rapport with our potential saviours. Soon one of them disappeared behind some trees and came out pulling half a dozen mules. Not handsome creatures by a long shot, nor robust enough to exude some much needed comfort either. The highwaymen gesticulated that we should grab one and get on top. I began to reflect regretfully on the missed opportunities of my life! If only I had ever learnt to ride anything: a bicycle, a horse, or tried harder at sports. Too late for such thoughts though, I might as well conquer riding a mule in one minute flat seeing how my life depended on it. This explains why, when it was my turn to mount 'my mule', I promptly fell giving a shriek which broke the silence of the night. One of the highwaymen repositioned me, riding astride at my back to steady me.

The animals started picking their way up more mountainous terrains as only mules can do: very gingerly, feeling their way twice over every inch of the way. (No one could have suspected that they were almost tipsy from the alcohol mixed with the water they drank earlier)

On and on we climbed up the rocks during the last hours of the night: I was shaking from extreme cold: luckily I remembered I had brought with me in my handbag a small flask of whiskey for likely aches and pains, and managed to fish it out to drink from. But no sooner did the smuggler see it than he very roughly snatched it and downed in one gulp (maybe his nerves were more stretched than mine); even worse, the effect of drink made him rest his head with great familiarity on my shoulder. I tried to fend him off with no avail; the rest of the party were all wrapped up in the precariousness of the climb and paid no attention to my pleas for help. My brother even snapped at me to shut up else strangers might attack us. I started crying in silence. This state of affairs lasted hours amid a dark and threatening silence.

All of a sudden, we heard a gurgling stream and could just distinguish its crystal clear waters. To cross it, we needed to get off our mules. An easy step that, but lo and behold, it proved gargantuan as the smugglers gesticulated that our feet were now on Persian territory! We hugged each other: At last, it was all worth it, even down to the nightmarish journey. How good it is to breathe freedom; much elated, I was ready to give everyone a very loud rendition of the Arabic songs that I excelled in, but the smugglers intimated there might still be enemy ears about. So we trudged on some more with the little suitcases albeit with a much lighter step, till we came across our first Iranian security checkpoint; there the smugglers exchanged some words with the guards and they let us pass. That is it, we thought with relief, the odyssey has ended! Still, our smugglers would not let us go, they demanded more money for the hire of the mules. How could we argue that we already handed over all of the money in Baghdad? In what language and according to what contract? It seems we had fallen in amongst a greedy gang of bootleggers. Desperate by now to get rid of them, we made up the money between us and handed it over.

We bought petrol with the Iraqi dinars that we had for the hired coach to take us to Teheran. (The station said they preferred dollars to our dinars, it seemed like a tough new world). We drove on excellent roads for three days and finally reached Teheran! There we were welcomed as survivors by refugee associations who took us to an excellent hotel in town (thanks to some philanthropists): we were traumatised body and soul, sunk low by fear of everything and anything.

Looking back I do not think that it entered anyone's mind our dire need for rest and counselling. At the time we were too busy celebrating.

Taking the" clients" from darkness to light, these mules were made for climbing

Selman says that his train journey proved much easier

One day during the Seventies (I was in my early twenties), Na-eem rang our doorbell. He had heard that I wanted to get out and advised me to be ready to leave on Thursday: accordingly I went to buy a suitcase and packed a few bits and pieces. On Wednesday at 3 pm he came again; there had been a last minute change and the car would leave without further ado in two hours' time. Oh well I said to myself, what difference; there were only my parents to say goodbye to.

It turned out that I was the fifth passenger in the car. The other passengers were Kaddouri whom I knew to be a good and a kind man, as well as Eliahou with his wife and son.

We drove to the train station which at that hour of the evening was empty; Kaddouri and Eliahou went in to buy tickets from the manager's room. Imagine our consternation when, instead of the five minutes necessary, it took them a full twenty minutes! We sweated it out in the car the meanwhile and I thought help me God have we been nicked already? Kaddouri emerging a bit pale and shaken said to me not to worry and he will tell me about it later. Just as we boarded the train, the station master came running after us: "take good care of them", he shouted to the conductor, "They belong to my kith and kin". We smiled at him and thanked him for such friendliness but inwardly thought it very suspicious view the times.

The train having left the station, Kaddouri began to tell me what had happened. It seems that the family that was accompanying us were called "Manni" by name, this is bona fide Jewish. Fearful of being thus identified on their way to the

301

North, they had the brainwave to change it to "Matti" by adding a tiny dot to the "N" when they acquired their new identity card from the swimming club. This was a promotion indeed, as the family Matti was quite well known and respected in Iraq. Eliahou's Arabic version was Elias thus: Mr Elias Matti, a stamped identity card guaranteed not to arouse suspicion of any kind. What a chance in a million but it seems that the station master belonged to the same family "Matti"! He fell all over him, asking him the name of his Father, what church, what priest was his confessor? Elias tried to deny having a family, he was an orphan he said, he never went to church; but the station master would not let him go easily but on the contrary insisted on taking him back with him to meet his family and have dinner at his house. None of us could afford this hospitality, not with a dangerious mission beckoning! Finally our man had to promise that he will be in touch as soon as he came back from his ten day summer holiday. He gave the other Matti his defunct phone number from the good old days.

As this was the first time in my life that I had been on a train, I remembered my geography lessons at school and excited. I identified all the villages we were passing by in the romantic light of the moon: al Meqdadiyya, Chemchemal, Khan Beni Saad, Shahraban; The next morning, the conductor of the train regaled us to a first class breakfast, obeying the orders of the station master. The khubbuz was hot, the qaymer very thick and the chay almost black.

Thus fortified, we reached Arbeel. Na-eem had told us to proceed to a village by the name of Galgal so we looked about us for a taxi.

Suddenly I felt a strong grip on my shoulder, and heard a booming voice behind: "follow me all of you, I know exactly who you are and I will take you with me". I turned around feeling sure that the secret police had traced our whereabouts and we were done for. I was confronted by a very confident blond looking giant. We had no choice view the fact that he was armed to the hilt other than to follow him meekly to his car. Little by little though we started to realise from the tales he was regaling us with, that his was a kindred spirit who had served jail under the regime, been tortured and was now very much willing to take risks to save the beleaguered. So we began to trust him.

Soon, his car was ascending the narrow mountainous lanes, which could not have been more than three metres wide. We felt secure that he seemed to know them like the back of his hand but beseeched him to go slower than at breakneck speed. We could see the deep valley stretching hundreds of metres below! When a car beckoned from the opposite way, the driver climbed into the mountain face to avoid a clash. The only signal between the fly-by-nights was to hoot non-stop as they approached a bend. There were also three Iraqi checkpoints along that mountainous road; I was lucky to possess an innocuous identity card with my name Selman issued by the Engineering union, while in Rawanduz all the cars and the suitcases were searched thoroughly. We reached the village Galgal near the border Thursday night.

In a snack bar there we recognized some more people. Our cavalcade numbered twenty three now and lo and behold we needed to get into the one tiny jeep! My legs lost all consciousness as heavy people piled on top. After a few hours' the Barzani HO beckoned, full of peshmergas with lanterns. All around were frighteningly dark mountains. Here a much more spacious lorry picked us up, thank God, for a few more hours of uneventful climb. Then we arrived to the border where the Iranian guard lowered a chain to let the lorry pass.

The Kurdish peshmergas took us on foot to a motel sort of place where we all slept huddled together in one room (I was afraid to sleep on my own in case of attack). In the morning Iranian officials came to interrogate us to confirm that we were not spies- spies have never looked so happy- then hopping on to the latest designer coach for Teheran.

Massoud Barazani in military attire and relaxed surroundings

Ezzouri is a daredevil, he tells us how he tried to go it almost
alone

I was still in my early twenties but Iraq had already
exhausted all future prospects or hope for a decent life. I had
made up my mind to leave a year ago at least, but we had been
thrown a big whammy with the arrest of a large contingent of
Jewish folk who were trying to escape. That put a real spanner
in the works and we all agreed that a halt was called for. My
Father knew I was getting impatient and cautioned me not to
attempt anything on my own (all the parents had the patience
of *Ayyoub (a prophet)* but I grew very reckless, waiting felt like
another death.

One day while he was away from home on business, I
decided to waylay him and try my chances by myself! Quickly I
threw some food and belongings into a small suitcase and
informed my Mother that I didn't believe that things will get
any better, that I was that fed up I didn't care a hoot what
happened to me and was leaving this minute. (Bye Mother, I'll
be seeing you one day).

Accordingly I rode by bus to the cemetery near Sahat Al
Tayarran and there looked about me for some time till I
identified a Kurdish man. I became friendly with him and
talked to him about my problems, man to man. He must have
identified with some of the persecutions, and in accordance
with the adage, the enemy of my enemy is my friend, I
detected flickering sympathy. As he had a car, we fell to
bargaining and he agreed to take me to Shaqlawa in exchange
for the petrol money. I got into his car there and then, it was
10.a.m. I warned him against using the main roads and so we
negotiated some scary mountain passes to avoid being stopped
by Iraqi soldiers. Shaqlawa is way up north and we arrived
there at 4 pm: so that ensconced in this small Assyrian village I

305

looked on with glee at a very satisfying start to my wild escapade.

I booked a room in a primitive hotel and let it be known that I needed to get to Teheran as the regime was not treating me fairly! Soon after a tough Peshmerga in traditional attire with a dagger by his side, knocked at the door of my room and suggested I accompany him further north. He sounded quite sympathetic and promised that he will get me out eventually with help from his friends in the other enclaves. He never mentioned money so I warmed to him. He gave me Peshmerga clothes to disguise myself in, so I made a temporary and necessary transition into a handsome Kaka.

Later on we went to Salah el Deen in his jeep, then to Jabal Al Asfar where the Barazan had his Headquarters. I hid in one of the caves there for a few days. Then this Peshmerga and I started an arduous exercise of walking by day and hiding in huts at night to get closer to the borders. This went on for 10 days and we became good friends. Then we met up with more escapees from Baghdad some of whom I recognized: I was introduced to them again in the snowy mountains as Kaka Ezzouri, a Kurdish smuggler! And boy, were they bowled over by my enterprising spirit. Joviality revived our spirits but there were also tragic tales to tell! One of the ladies was stuck in Iraq after leaving her children in England to claim land left to her by her Father. Needless to say Marcelle was never even allowed a glimpse of this land. And then there was another family with two children whom they carried on their shoulders; one of their relatives had been hanged and for them life under Saddam had become murky and void of meaning.

I still remember the weather was freezing as it was the depths of December and we were deep in the mountains. Soon after, a large Jeep became available and we piled in and headed for the near borders. Our luck was in as this whole area was controlled by the Kurds, so the crossing went on relatively smoothly. We reached Khana on the borders soon after and stayed in a small hotel there for the night. In the morning, we took a mammoth train journey to Teheran.

Narrow river amid some of the gigantic mountains

<u>Esperance was in a hotel in Salah el Deen with her family,
with the genuine excuse of breathing in the cool summer air</u>

Just before breakfast, we heard heavy vehicles outside. All of a sudden the lobby was full of tens of the dreaded Iraqi soldiers in khaki and machine guns. They received information from security cells in Baghdad that a lot of Jews were trying to flee from Salah el Deen and they had gathered in the hotel opposite ours to wait for the arrival of their Kurdish smugglers. We kept repeating that we were mere vacationers in a different hotel (which we were) but to no avail, our goose was cooked too. The receptionist was asked to reveal all Jewish sounding names of the guests in the hotel which he did instantly.

Everyone trooped into the lobby: the soldiers were not really rude, but there was no mincing the grave charges of an illegal escape! It never occurred to them that that would have been the best way of ridding the country of the unwanted element, namely us

Before leaving with our escorts, we had to pay the hotel bill too. What a monstrous mess. If only we had some bombs in our pockets to throw - like others do. The world media would have been at our side in an instant...Wishful thinking!

We realised the regime had a carte blanche as far as fabricating any wild accusation against us; it all hinged whether it saw a need to consolidate its rule still further or make a more decent splash in the media!

They told us to gather our belongings for a small investigation. While we were boarding the large army pickups, they stopped the men joining us saying that they should be in different trucks from the women and children. I knew that that meant singling them out for aggressive treatment. I decided to speak up as my husband had been interned for four months just before and certainly could not survive any more of the same! The soldier tried to make light of the implications but I was adamant. I told him to go ahead and shoot me point blank, but I was not letting go of my husband or lose sight of him. In hindsight, I am sure my attitude saved the men a lot of aggro later on as they were allowed to stay with their wives and children.

Throughout the long journey to Baghdad, we could not talk together as there was a soldier with a gun in each car. Some, especially the children, started to cry, it was such a very long journey, nevertheless, we were also dreading its ending. Finally we arrived; they took us to a very big mansion in central Baghdad called al Hatheera; this used to be a place of worship for the Baha'ee sect but the Amen requisitioned it as one more of their headquarters! We were led into this very huge hall. Each family found their own *niche* and stood huddled within it surrounded by their suitcases. After taking down everyone's name, the soldiers started calling us individually into a small room where an officer shouted threatening questions at each. We were told not to speak to one another at all. Women who wore gold and diamond rings or bracelets (a sure indication of criminal intent) had to dispose of them somehow before a search of their persons was made, so they chucked them in the toilets. When the blingers refused to go down the pipes because of their weight, they had to hide them behind the bend with a toilet brush; bundles of dinars stashed to pay the smuggler were torn up and flushed as well; never was there so much loathing of material goods. One woman said she hid her diamond ring on top of the very high cistern while I saw another woman throw hers from the window to land clinking under a greyish rotting drainpipe. Unfortunately, I cannot go back to pick it up, no one will let me re-enter Baghdad, not even to visit al Hatheera.

I should not make light of this disaster: we all had to take turns in front of the investigator to be branded criminals; even the four year old with his six year old sister. But the dialogue that took the cake went like this: A cry was heard from the inner chamber to bring in the "criminal Moshe B" to be questioned about his crimes! His Mother had no choice but to pick him up in her arms and present him to the officer: he was all of 6 months old! The men always fared worse than the women and were jeered at and taunted. They wanted somebody to confess that they were trying to leave illegally. They stood shoulder to shoulder on this one and denied the accusation vehemently.

We had not eaten since the night before and now it was evening! As none of our acquaintances had a telephone or an office anymore, there was no one to inform that we were back in Baghdad. Even though we were being charged as guilty, our individual guards had to treat us with respect as our manners and dress were very far from those of prison louts. We gave them money to buy us some very basic food, and then found ourselves getting friendly with them. They allowed us to open the smaller suitcases to brush our teeth; the children quietened down as they saw parents and friends all around. Lucky it was winter and the temperature was cold otherwise hygienic conditions (or lack of them) would have resulted in a multitude of flies and diseases. At night we lay us down to sleep on the ground.

It seems because of the barbaric hangings, the world woke up to our plight and the Iraqi government found itself under pressure to account for the lives of each Jew. The regime could ill afford to have the Human Rights Commission continue treating it as a villain in front of the whole world; we were comforted by the fact that we were still precious even though not so in our country of birth. In the end we were let out without suffering any physical torture. It transpired that the Canadian government, with the help and initiative of some philanthropists, extended warranties to bail us out of prison.

After seventeen days we returned to our houses, relieved, but sad that there was no security left for us in Iraq. This time we did decide that escape was the only way forward, and we should take the first opportunity that presented itself:

A trial run

Said's escape was in a large cavalcade a bit like Noah's Ark

In the North of Iraq, there had been a long standing war between the Iraqis and the Kurdish militiamen; In March 1970, the two sides (Barazini's and the government) signed a truce, welcomed by all Iraqis and especially by us. It was a redeeming truce, as it permitted us to travel to the North under pretext of taking a vacation in the mountains, Baghdad being very hot and sultry in the summer. Northern Iraq has many beautiful resorts to vie with the best in the world, indeed some claim that it used to be the Garden of Eden of yore. Right after the cease-fire, people flocked from round the country to the North again as the war had denied them access to it for years.

Time to test the temperature of the water, I thought: so together with my parents and younger brother, we drove to Salah el Deen to stay in the hotel – incredulously for us, this was achieved normally, just like any ordinary vacationer. We realised we had hit on a golden opportunity to look about us for an escape route through the mountains and into very nearby Iran. We tried to find a likely route or meet an individual with a sympathetic look. For us it was a matter of life and death to get out! Unfortunately, fortune was not forthcoming this time, so after a week we made our way back home.

However, far from sinking into apathy, I told myself it was only one battle lost, and I will have to keepon seeking! So I set a routine of making the ten-hour trip to the North once, even twice a week to reconnoitre, hoping to find a local with a good knowledge of the territory. Without work, there was nothing to stop me staying a few nights at a time in huts in the Kurdish areas! I owed it to my family to find a smuggler that could take us out! The huts, called Kapras, were Kurdish style hotels made of straw and used only in the summer as the inside was cold. They moreover enjoyed all the amenities that a hotel room could offer. Some nights when the mosquitoes prevented me from sleeping, I would go to other huts and watch local Kurdish men playing poker. I enjoyed the company and the card games both; but could not allow myself to forget my mission and kept my eyes peeled in case a potential smuggler happened to materialise. That is how finally I made contact with my man, a local good natured Kurd; of course he would not do it without cash in hand but I was desperate for someone like him! So we came to a deal: he would smuggle four of us into the borders for a very respectable sum (the dinar was worth a lot in those days). I returned home to give him the needed time to arrange transport, food, guides etc. To cement our agreement and friendship further, once I returned to Baghdad, I bought him an expensive swatch of European cloth. He could have it sewn into a smart suit to boast in front of his friends; by the next meeting, we had set the escape date.

So far so good? Not at all! The day before the escape, someone handed my Mother a note received clandestinely from the smuggler to be , while I was out walking to bid adieu to my native country! On it was scribbled a sentence which dashed my hopes at once for the long anticipated morrow: "Said, our meeting is cancelled." This was very disappointing, but maybe something had happened and the smuggler thought the time had ceased to be appropriate. Alas for all my work to pave the way…not only that, but I was left with a real quandary: family members and acquaintance had got wind of what I intended to do (my brother in law and his family as well as the family of his business partner), they begged me to come with, even as I warned them that it might be risky, or that we might get caught on the way.. these people had all set their sights on quitting Baghdad the next day, had arranged for transport, made plans to leave their houses that very night, packed, prepared food for the journey. Postponing it would make everyone sink even further into the gloomy, passive depressive state that was fast becoming worse than death; anyway, I was very loath to give up on my dreams of freedom. Reasoning it out, I thought it best to go ahead with the morrow's agreed departure even though effectively, we no longer had a smuggler to lead the way. "We could always look for another one once in the North", my Mother suggested tentatively. So be it, I thought, any sort of action was better than the inertia that we have been living in Baghdad! Anyway, as it was anticipated that the authorities would give any remaining family members a hard time after their dear ones had bolted, so ours could be the only way to avoid such harassment: to leave in a convoy taking the near and dear along with us.

I then went to alert Odile of the cavalcade: (her husband 'Itzhak' had been a dear friend of the family, but was tragically hanged). With two young children to care for, her situation was dire in all respects! I had given her my word that I would not leave them behind if ever I left Iraq. She embraced the plan instantly, promised to follow us on the morrow whatever the risks.

That evening, while busy with our preparations, we heard a ring at the door: pandemonium broke out in our household; rings at the bell in the evening especially, were ominous - but it was only my friend Eli who was unaware that I was leaving that night; He had stopped by my house for his usual chat and to share his problems with a friendly soul! Under acute stress, he was assiduously searching for a way out of Iraq and was ready to do anything to do so, his days had become that dark …Actually Eli had been living in England and only returned to Baghdad to be near his ailing Father and claim his inheritance! He never anticipated that the authorities would forbid him to leave the country. One day while he was visiting his friend at the office, men from the secret service came and arrested all the Jewish people present. Eli was the only one to be released (much later), escaping by the skin of his teeth. By sheer coincidence or his good fortune, Eli came to me on that day; and view all of the above, I had to make an exception and risk the convoy getting even bigger… so let him into my plans to leave very late that night. The only proviso being that he had to arrange his own transport and join us at a given place in the North by the next morning. It only took him a moment to nod his head and agree. (Much later, with all the adventures behind us, he told me that the minute he left, he went at breakneck speed straight to the taxi station and on to his girlfriend's house where he hurriedly proposed. To her. Together, they then proceeded to the Rabbi's house and picked him up, and then all went collectively to the bedside of his (dangerously ill) Father; there the Rabbi performed the engagement ceremony for the couple, according to the Law of Moses and the customs prevailing at the time.

Earlier that day, I had been much occupied to dispose of sundry personal memento. I did not want my private life to be scrutinized by strangers' eyes after I was gone. I took all the pictures and slides belonging to my family, put them in a large (metallic) laundry basin, poured oil on top, and burned them: I couldn't have taken all of the pictures without arousing suspicion by the soldiers. Imagine how I left: without saying goodbye to friends, or forwarding any of the family's belongings, or selling any assets. It was better thus than risk the Mukhabarat getting a whiff of us trying to escape;

Our driver drove all through the night and did not stop till noon of the next day: he was forced to do so when signalled by an army checkpoint. There, two soldiers stopped our car, and the six cars following were also halted. My parents, brother and I handed over our identification papers. The soldiers went to the other cars as well, to collect their ID's. Of course we did not make any gestures or statements to identify us as belonging together; they asked us where we were heading to: We kept affirming that we were vacationers in the North for the summer only. You can imagine our fear-especially since my brother in law and I were ex-prisoners and out on bail. The soldiers took the ID's back to their cabin and we could see them from the cars, making phone calls in their tiny cabins. They spoke for some time and read all of our names and ID details over the phone.

After a few minutes (which felt like hours) they came back and returned our papers, simply uttering the magic word "Proceed." We breathed a huge sigh of relief, including our Kurdish driver, whose people, at the time, were enemies of the Iraqis. Later, we heard that just forty-eight hours after we passed that checkpoint, another convoy of Jews was stopped, taken back to Baghdad, and imprisoned.

By about 4pm, we reached an area whose inhabitants were all Kurds and allowed ourselves a breather! Their village consisted of huts (kapras); each family rented a hut to stretch out in and relax the nerves after a very fraught 15 hours. At least there were no Iraqi soldiers on the horizon! At least we could not be dragged back to Baghdad. However soon after, Odile came to my hut in a state of absolute panic and insisted that some security men were following her. When I asked her how she identified them, she said she recognised them from her frequent trips to the Ministry of Defence where she used to go to plead for her husband's life. In addition it seems that the very kind man who was accompanying her to be sure she and her children were safe on the trip, developed cold feet from her fears about these men. He instantly decamped back to Baghdad, obviously deciding that the situation was too risky. How I dreaded the mere mention of those men, why, they scared me to death too; so we made a deal that she should stay in her hut and that we would refrain from meeting, instead would communicate through an emissary from now on! And that is how I will let her know once the cavalcade started moving again.

Meanwhile, we began to feel confident enough to go about our business, buying food etc: in the process talking with the villagers, then feeling ever braver, relating our awful experiences in Iraq; finally we started imploring their assistance to take us to Iran. We felt confident in the old adage: namely that the enemy of my enemy is my friend!

Luckily these pleas did not fall on deaf ears, and some young men came forward and volunteered their help; after further consultations between themselves, and calls via the radio and telephone, other armed men introduced themselves as peshmergas and told us everything will be ok, as they knew of a route to Iran and can take us. That was music to our ears even though it was not spoken in Arabic so we only caught the gist of it! Furthermore, they told us to get ready to leave the village very soon. At last things began to look up. We agreed gladly in a mixture of languages, including Arabic, Kurdish and Iranian to accept their help!

Later on that same evening, three land rover jeeps drove into the village. The drivers got out and asked if there were any Jewish families who were ready to leave immediately for Iran. Oh yes, we were! However, as there were only three jeeps, so the drivers asked for the women and children only. I hesitated whether to go along with this development, but decided that the Kurds looked trustworthy .Sure enough; they were back in the camp within fifteen minutes to pick up the men.

When we arrived to the next village, we met more Jewish people and their families, forty-nine people in all spanning different age ranges from infants to elderly. We were treated with incredible hospitality by those Kurdish people. They gave each family huge trays of food that included meat rice and chicken and they made us feel very welcome indeed. How grateful we were and how gratifying in this demoralized state that some people cared about our well being! As a rather cool night set in, we were taken to a place that they called 'the castle.' In reality it was a large mud structure, with several tunnels leading onto long corridors from which rooms branched out and lighting came from lanterns. We were signalled to sleep there. Thankfully there were also rugs on the floor.

As we settled into one of those rooms, four heavily armed freedom fighters entered headed by an extremely well dressed man in a Kurdish uniform. The man sat down on the carpet near us and in a friendly manner, asked us if we required anything to make our stay for the night more comfortable. We thanked him for his hospitality and said we had everything we needed. He then asked us if anyone in our group had encountered a Kurd who was asking for money in exchange for smuggling. Sure, I thought, I have just had first hand experience with them as did others in the group too, but we very politely refrained from divulging it! This important looking Kurd, however, apologized to us on their behalf, and explained that within each community in society there are always those who want to profit from or take advantage of a tragic situation such as ours! He added that we should inform him if we knew any of their names so they would be severely punished. We understood that this leader was trying to raise the status of his countrymen to that of decent and regular army troops obeying international codes of conduct. Then, he asked if we knew of other families in Baghdad who were trying to escape but did not know how. We gave him many names of families, and he wrote them down and promised to make contact with them. Finally he asked in his friendly manner "Might you be going to Israel?" We were all in shock, since even whispering this word would have landed us in hot water in Baghdad! However, I was getting bolder the further Baghdad was receding, so managed to emit a "not sure of the future" in sotto voice!

He looked at his watch and said that he had to leave. He shook each of our hands in a cordial manner, and when he shook my hand, I tried to express my appreciation and gratitude for the risks he and his men were taking on our behalf. But he quickly pulled it away and said, "How will history judge us if we do not help people who deserve help. We must act ethically with you to prove to the world that our society is at one with our morals; we have been oppressed for decades so can understand what you are going through". He added: "Don't worry about owing us any debt, as long as you or anyone from amongst you broadcast our plight even once". Emotively, his hand clutched at his heart: "We will need to struggle very hard to gain our nationhood". Remembering his kindness and sincerity still moves me to tears. I asked him who he was and he said "A commander and close associate of

Mullah Mustafa al Barzani, the leader of the Kurdish people".
He seemed to be a very well educated man, quite high up with
a good command of languages! His turban was at least twice
as big as our Rabbi's and much more colourful.

We were loaded into the land rovers again, armed
Peshmerga taking their place in the front as guards and guides,
and the windows were covered with blankets, making it
impossible to see the criminals inside, namely us; it was night
time. As the jeeps sped along paved roads, our apprehensions
lessened because we could tell that our companions knew the
way well and were very confident. Our happiness (though the
weather became freezing) grew with each mile. When we
peered through the curtains, we saw the deadly serious mien
of our guards, the snowy mountains, the moon and little else!
There were no conversations in the jeeps, each was occupied
with his / hers own worries, while some others prayed! When
we reached the Iranian border, our driver used a flashlight and
gave a signal in the dark to the border patrol on the Iranian
side, who was also Kurdish. This man signalled us to proceed
across to the other side immediately (remember this was
almost a decade before the Iranian Revolution and I am sure
things have changed since then).

And that was it, after months of agitation and planning,
we had made it. We were in a different world now an had
ceased to be third rate citizens. Our driver took us to a small
motel near the border with only four rooms. The women and
children slept in the rooms, while the rest of us anxiously
paced the lobby till the break of dawn, full of plans, hopes and
worries; not only for ourselves but also for the people we left
behind

Next day, two buses especially charted by charity
organisations arrived and drove us to the closest train

terminal, where we boarded the 8 p.m. train to Teheran, the Capital. Each family was put in a small compartment in the train, and as I promised, Odile and her children shared mine and my parents'. The poor woman's nerves were really fraught and she kept insisting that the men from the Ministry were still following her. I assured her that I would stay awake (my third sleepless night) to keep a look out for them, but that she must try and lie down for a few hours. We realised later that she had imagined the entire episode- how anyone can blame her, she must have been very near total breakdown.

Kurds in their traditional outfits

<u>All the family were saved by the sacrifice of a sheep</u>

My brothers who were too restless to stay home for long began to sneak out at night to meet their friends, making their way to the summertime coffee shops on the river bank. One day they came back in an agitated mode; they heard that a big cavalcade from among our friends was leaving early next day to the North to escape; during those last few months people mysteriously disappeared and then we heard they had made their way to the North and through the border; they were cagey about telling their friends in case the authorities got wind of their plans but we could guess that they were asking the Kurds for help. We were feeling pretty depressed about tarrying behind, the climate being every man for himself. But as more houses emptied, so we youngsters grew even more frustrated at my Father's apparent inertia in the face of real danger; we accused him of not seriously trying to find a way out like the others, of caring more about his house and mode of living than he cared for his family. We ended up having one heated row after the other, tempers were that stretched. In the end my Father with much reluctance had to bow to his children's wishes and agree to go to the North. With luck we might bump into a friendly soul or a former business acquaintance who might divulge a secret - or that once in the North, we will hit upon routes, or other means and ways of escape. With hindsight, it could not have been fair to spring this on my Father, who at 55, was not overjoyed at the prospect of risking all to dive into the unknown.

None of us even thought of drawing a detailed map to plan this important journey from amongst the atlases in the house. North was the direction we would take, and getting to the north was all the agenda we needed: the rest must rest"*ala Allah*" on God's shoulders.

The upshot was that the decision was made to leave in 36 hours…my brother rode by bike to a taxi cab company whom we knew (they used to be our neighbours) and they promised to send us a cab at 5 am the next morning to take us to the northern resorts, to escape the heat. That day we carried on as usual so the people watching us would not get any inkling of our plans. In the evening my Mother and I made apple pies which we shared with some visitors alongside some gossip in the *jallallah* under the stars, and it was only when they left the house at ten that could we allow ourselves the luxury to start packing, we were that anxious not to give anything away! My parents said each person was allowed one suitcase, I remember putting in the tennis racket as a most prized possession along with a few picture albums: how can anyone pack a lifetime in one little suitcase? Duty done, we the youngsters went upstairs to sleep blissfully on the rooftop, all our troubles seemingly over – maybe we had no imagination - In our mind we were already in the free utopia - as usual we left the parents to do the work! They didn't sleep the whole of that night valiantly trying to clear up in the flickering light of the candles.

Only items that justified a summer trip to the mountains could be taken; so we left a whole room full of books and dictionaries that reached almost to the ceiling: French to French, English to Arabic, Arabic to English, English to English, atlases and text books. Did the people who inherited our house make any use of such wisdom I wonder still? More treasures in that house. My Father used to love spending hours with a magnifying glass looking at his stamp collection; fascinated with their scope which covered the era of the Ottomans and the three Kings both! He laid them out in three very neat (red) books, and wanted very much to take them with. Unfortunately for him he forgot them on the kitchen table. They are now worth a lot of money to whosoever found them. What about sharing the commission?

It also transpired that my Father had a whole load of worries on his mind! These manifested themselves at 4 a.m. when he took a suitcase which my fashion conscious Mother had crammed with her best clothes, and turning it upside down in a fit of anger, pronounced that it was downright silly to think of fine dresses, the journey ahead being fraught with danger. Why, we might have to spend the whole winter in the mountains. What if somebody got ill? What about the threat of freezing? Accordingly, he replaced the suitcase with warm blankets, pills and medical potions, plasters, etc

The next day the taxi turned up at 5.a.m., and in the deathly quiet street, we crept in. We hazarded a look behind us and the watchers had not installed themselves yet, although we could just distinguish a shadow trying to light a lamp. My Father cautioned us that as we were pretending to go on holiday so we must be full of good spirits. And that was exactly the case as we approached the soldiers' first checkpoint on the outskirts of Baghdad. We turned up the radio, it was playing pop songs and we all joined in. We were going to Sarsank for the summer and the outlook was glorious. The taxi driver must have started to get an inkling of the purpose of this trip, but he was a good man and kept schtum.

By now we had made good progress and were out of Baqouba' but then a bit of a catastrophe struck: The taxi came across a herd of sheep meandering in the middle of the road, as they do in Iraq, and swerving to avoid one of them, the driver inadvertently hit another. Worse still, the horns of this big sheep penetrated the engine of the car and so we halted. The farmer was mad because of the loss of his animal. To calm him the driver gave him the equivalent price of the sheep, and then the men managed to pull the car to a coffee shop at the side of the high road, where our driver fell to to remove the damage!

Here I will make a little aside to talk about the significance of the killing of this sheep. In Iraqi tradition and superstition, when this happens it is automatically assumed that it was a "sacrifice" to God and as such gives a lot of luck and good cheer to the people concerned. In fact this is exactly what happened to us afterwards as our smuggling efforts progressed smoothly just like in a story book!

The coffee shop was big, empty in an oasis of shady trees and the exhausted driver begged a relaxation! It suited us also to have some breakfast and the owner proved to be very generous; he brought us tea, large brown khubuz and double cream keimer. He made a fuss of us, offered his best wooden chairs to sit on while very near, a tiny stream kept gurgling at our feet. It was heaven. For one hour, we acquired our namesake of real holidaymakers; not having left Baghdad to visit the countryside or anywhere else for years because of the "situation" it was incredible how much a bit of outdoor scenery could relax our nerves!

We took our positions in the car again and made our way to Mosul, then Sulaimaniyah where we had a laffa kebab lunch in a takeaway on the high road, and on to Arbil. At each of these stops, my Father left the car to try to find someone who looked remotely like an acquaintance he could trust! Failing which - because of bad luck, we booked ourselves into a hotel one night in Arbil, with the idea of pushing onto nearby Salah el Deen the morrow. It was advisable to rest and recharge our batteries and our sad selves in the famous resort.

Big anxiety though as we entered the lobby of the hotel: Lo and behold, the friends and relatives that we assumed had already escaped were all sitting there looking extremely glum. How come they were turning around again, doing nothing, just like in Baghdad? We were eager to know.

The explanation that they came up with was that their smuggler has not turned up because of unfortunate circumstances or maybe had decided to disappoint them. Meanwhile, they could not show their frustration but had to put a "touristy" face on it, and "enjoy" the amenities and the welcome that was reserved for the normal holidaymaker. So we joined the crowd.

A recipe for a quasi murderous existence followed: pretending to be happy, putting on the finer clothes from the bits and pieces in the suitcase, sitting in the elegant dining room to digest three full meals a day. It was sickening, the meals stuck in our throats and the whole time was spent worrying. The waiters seeing us wandering around aimlessly (maybe we looked pitiable) started to remind us of the fun we were missing including the various tours to be booked. The resort was beautiful especially at night, where crowds of normal people sat outside in the many hotel gardens enjoying the atmosphere. But for us it was as sight unseen, we were that nervous.

One lunch time meal gives an example of the opposing factors that we were up against there. Some of us girls were sitting in the dining room bemoaning the fact that if no way out was found very soon, the suspicions of the collective hotel staff will bring the Amen on our tracks. In marched a troupe of Iraqi soldiers followed closely by Kurdish Peshmergas both armed to the hilt; they headed towards a very large table behind us. It seems because of the armistice between Kurds and Iraqis, the higher ranks among them were being honoured with a big lunch. There were representatives from two armies sitting behind us making merry while we shook in our chairs. Soon enough the waiters brought a very big Kuzzi on an enormous silver tray, surrounded by rice and other delicacies. As they mucked in with their hands appreciatively amidst lots of expressions of good will, we stole out of the room as fast as our legs could carry us.

My Father was starting to take outings outside the hotel by taxi or walking in the lanes, in the hope of finding a way out of the deadlock. After 10 days he met his just reward in the form of a boy in his early twenties walking along a lane; he recognised him as being a second cousin of my Mother's who lived in Baghdad He stepped down to speak to him. "What are you doing here on your own Nessim, hundreds of miles away from your family, are you out of your mind?" Nessim replied that as it happened he did know what he was doing! He was trying to find someone he had chatted with in Baghdad, who promised to meet up with him in the North, wi th a vague pledge of assisting him to escape. So my Father told Nessim to jump in the taxi with him, as two lost souls were better than one and together they sped further north towards the Kurdish areas. Very luckily (I never asked how it happened) they managed to locate that person. He in turn took them to some strong Kurdish enclaves belonging to Mullah Mustafa Barzani's army, and the leader, after listening to the usual tales of misery, offered to help. He told my Father to bring his family near these caves the very next day, and finalize arrangements again with him, as there was a huge transport that was all ready to leave on the morrow. Back at the hotel we were worried sick for my Father's whereabouts; At last he turned up at 11 pm. He was very excited though, even over the moon at what he had achieved and sat for another hour on the tiny bed in the tiny room to explain what he said to the Kurds and what they said to him and how the outcome was that we must leave at 6 am the very next day! At midnight, when we knew everyone had retired to sleep, my Father asked Abdullah to come to our room. He explained the plan and how to make contact with the same people after our exit. Too many risks were involved if a lot of people left the hotel at once, and the Kurds had made it clear that the capacity of the lorries was full for that run

Up very early the next day, we settled the bill with a sleepy receptionist. Why so early she asked? Well we were going a very long way. The taxi was waiting and took us North along the unpaved roads, till it stopped at a clearing with a waterfall. Here my Mother, my younger brother and I were dropped off. Only two men, Nessim and my Father went forwards to finalise the deal -it seems they were not allowed to take us with them to the secret caves.

Much to our annoyance and fear, we ended up staying the whole day in that clearing. As it was shaded with big trees and the sun could not filter in, it became freezing cold in the afternoon. The suitcases with the warm clothes had stayed in the taxi and we only had summer clothes on. We had had nothing to eat since the evening before, and there was no food or drink here at all. There were some Kurdish men nearby, armed and in their traditional attire, but they showed us much ill will and rudeness; As we spoke Arabic, they got the wrong impression about us of being enemies, snapped at us and told us in sign language that we were not welcome in their territories, and to go back to Baghdad.

The Kurds in the north wanted autonomy and cessation from Baghdad, and the authorities fought with them at every turn. These Kurds we encountered have never heard of the term Jewish! I still cannot imagine how my meticulous Father dumped us with strangers who might have disposed of us and our corpses; no one would have known, the land was not ruled by any law, only warring factions! They could have been deserters, bandits, anything.

Unbelievable as this may sound, I never did ask my Father why he had left us for the whole day in that no man's land. After we left Iraq, circumstances were presenting with fresh problems and dilemmas almost daily; solving those required exclusive attention to the present; It almost brings to mind the injunction given to Lot's wife in the Bible when she left Sodom, not to indulge in any degree of longing

Thus it only occurred very lately to my neighbour in Iraq, to tell me that our house was requisitioned the same evening that we left it! She saw the new occupants, an important looking man and his family move in the very same day. Ever since I have had visions of us going back to Baghdad after failing to find a way out, trying to resurrect a life, and not finding anywhere to stay. What would have become of us? What a nightmare about something that did not happen all those years ago? Our house was taken over while we were still in the North, what if my Father did not chance upon Nessim walking? It looks like a scenario from "Zorba the Greek" when all the neighbours started sharing the booty of the old woman; why, she hadn't even died yet.

It seemed this cavalcade had been arranged long beforehand with all the names recorded at HO; similarly when my Father was interviewed (investigated), he was afraid to say that his family was still in Salah el Deen, as this would have been deemed too far for comfort! All the rest of the escapees were residing very near on a local farm so he claimed that we were in the locality too. Probably this is why he picked us from the hotel, to be nearer the action whenever the zero hour was declared.

At long last, the taxi with the men returned. They looked triumphant though exhausted, my Father proffering his V sign signifying everything was shipshape; it seemed like a dream come true! My Father has always been self reliant, moving quickly without wasting time. For him this was the ultimate in business deals.

I often wonder though what would have happened if they hadn't found us waiting for them, pale and stone-faced from the cold, the thirst and the hunger?

On and on we sped northwards through a magic vista of snow-capped mountains, chillingly beautiful and near. The North of Iraq is absolutely breathtaking, some of the roads very straight and wide. We arrived to a tiny Kurdish village in the mountains. Its way of life was decidedly primitive: its inhabitants lived in tiny huts made of cheap metal and were drastically poor. It was night and they were cooking their supper on very primitive utensils outside. Neither electricity, toilets nor kitchens existed. Nevertheless, these good people tried to share with us some of their bread and vegetables.

Among the many shadows, we started to distinguish silhouettes of friends we had not seen for months, it seems for want of an alternative, they were camping here awaiting *alfaraj* (deliverance)! People who had boasted an immaculate living style in Baghdad were now sharing a mud building in a farm containing all sorts of domestic animals! Others had paid rogue agents a lot of money. In the dimness, I recognized Umm Sabah and Sitt Eliass, Abu Farid and Umm Farid, the whole *Joqua* and crowd no less and felt instantly at home. As we met, we talked in whispers still in fear of the dreaded

Mukhabarrat. They could spring in on us last minute and foil all of our plans just as we were nearing that Utopian destiny! We forced down the packet biscuits for supper but the taste buds had capitulated from the anticipation. No one volunteered any clues as to our destiny.

At long last near midnight three rather dilapidated coaches came and picked us up (we must have been 100 at least, spanning quite a few generations, including a two month old baby), it was imperative that we made no noise. The coaches drove away very fast for some 3 hours with all lights switched off. I stuck my head outside, away from the sardine like conditions inside the lorry. The Kurdish soldiers looked so grim, they had guns at the ready too, while their colourful headgear trailing behind them from the fresh wind hid everything save for the eyes. It was critical that no one detected the lorries, otherwise there would most certainly be a lot of fireworks. Talking was rare. On the roof of the lorry there was a miniscule rack where were crammed all the suitcases in the world, and for want of better protection, some boys who had found no place inside the lorries, were told to hang on to them…they clung for dear life, they said later, as the lorries went into vertiginous moves around the more mountainous areas; a Harry Karry kind of dance no doubt. The climax came when a transistor in one of the suitcases decided to go off unexpectedly when the lorry hit a bump on a mountain lane: pandemonium struck; but the guards made short shrift of the suitcase with their razor sharp daggers; they opened it and smashed the radio to pieces; no room for hesitation here with one hundred lives in the balance! The crossing was being accomplished on a moonless night and without realizing it all of a sudden there were shouts from the Kurds as they hailed their friends from both sides of the border; triumphantly they confirmed to us that we had just crossed and were effectively in Persia. We were too tired having been up since dawn to dance or to open a bottle even had there been one. So we hugged each other and any smuggler who would let us, on the other hand the culture did not allow for such expressions of gratitude by females. Just like the finale of a marathon, there was exhaustion and exhilaration accompanied by a flood of relief. These Samaritans have not asked us for any money as payment for their services, nor for a reward either. We wished them well!

They deposited us at a house in Khaneh where we slept ten to a room on basic mattresses. The valiant work of other emigrants before us had "opened" the way. We stayed in a good hotel in the centre of Teheran where we joined up with many more escapees

We were much too traumatised though to enjoy the good life that existed in Teheran in those days. That is why all the *émigrés* gravitated to the hotel basement for a *ga'da* "gathering" most evenings. We sang songs and talked late into the night about where and what we were aiming for. Which country, what career, what university or further studies to undertake? The future stretched rosy, like the beginning of time.

This generation had been throttled by people and circumstances, therefore shared a strong feeling of cohesiveness; it did not diminish, no, not even when we waved our comrades goodbye from Teheran Airport. Their destiny beckoned, the luck was getting better all the way!

For a while, Iraq and smuggling dominated our thoughts, especially as we thought of friends still intent on finding the way out, or those in the hotel of Salaheldinn: Had they acted on our tip? Were they heading for the same route?

Imagine our consternation when we heard later that the Mukhabarrat raided the hotel in the early hours, taking everyone under heavy security back to Baghdad.

The Iranians gave us a *Parwanat Ebour* (a document of transit) to facilitate matters, which served us well for many years. Of course it being in Persian, we never deciphered it but still proferred it blindly everywhere, having to explain to complete strangers the story behind it each time. We needed it to be allowed entry into an aeroplane or a country (buying clothes in a department store with a cheque, I had to show it once as the only proof of identity I had). We were kept late in queues and at airports, while people consulted their superiors and scratched their heads. However, it being written on a mere A4 paper, it turned shabby very quickly, with the writing undistinguishable in places. But since a passport proved so difficult to acquire, we relied on that blessed Perwaneh for years

Following is a very important official document signed by the Ministry of Interior (Nazem Kezar), dated 17/10/1970, less than a month after our departure. In contains a list of 25 Jewish families charged with illegally escaping across the border (We are number 13), along with their addresses and type of residences. Their houses and all material wealth are confiscated because of their dire crime. That is the tip of the iceberg I expect! Other formalities included sealing the doors with red wax.

بسم الله الرحمن الرحيم

الجمهورية العراقيــــة
مديرية الأمن العامـــة
استخبارات العامة

العدد ز م / ١٩٧٤٤
التاريخ ١٩٧٠/١٠/١٧

وزارة الداخليــــة
م / معلومات

وردتنا معلومات موثوق بصحتها هؤلاء الموسويين المدرجة اسمائهم محل اقامتهم أدناه
قد هربوا الى ايران بصورة غير مشروعة عن طريق المصالية اشعالتهم تاركين اموالهم وأملاكهم ...

٣ ٥ مك
٢٤/١/٢٨ مك

334

CONCLUSION

All these adventures must put paid to the media's erstwhile lie when they painted this community as cowards hiding under the bed at the least *taqqa* (bump). Multiple risks have been taken on board since then, definitely not for the fainthearted. In the mammoth hardships we encountered and surmounted to adapt and be adopted, others have sunk! We went on to study for new certificates and careers in a world that did not recognise third world ones, while still battling against prejudice from all sides. And when the going became hard, we tried even harder.

In the good old scheme of things no one should be forced to flee a country; it is a horrendous undertaking. While it is true that vast amounts of people do migrate and are very happy to do so, choosing to leave a country is different; it is seen as a happier alternative made with full awareness of future challenges and a *Ahlan Wasahlan* right back into the fold whenever you visit back home, your friends have kept the welcome fires brewing. As you reidentify with all the familiar landmarks you reclaim them back, along with the comforts of that past life.

On the other hand being forced to leave a country carries with it a definite aura of rejection. The Mother has abandoned her progeny to wolves and wrung her hands in total denial. With no future visits and no welcome back where a community has vanished, the past and the present are separated by vast schisms! Ah, but what if the cultures of the two countries are totally opposed as well? Here nothing less than a new birth and a new identity will do.

Iraq used to be a cocoon from materialistic values. The kudos of an individual arose from an aura of inherited standing in the community and from the respectful status associated with a good family name. All this had to change. Complete new values needed to be taken on board in the West where the individual's achievement is the only criterion. The émigrés can try hard or not so hard to merchandise their way into a culture where television is the most frequent point of contact with the natives; for most adult émigrés though, the pattern of thinking has already been set in the brain and this option is impractical.

Still, far better to try and chip away at this "foreign" status than not to try at all and continue underneath a cloud of inferiority. Hope springs eternal and the accessibility is there. After all how difficult is it to drink cappuccino every day instead of Turkish coffee, eat meat and two vegs instead of *kubbas*, watch Coronation Street instead of Fareed Attrash's old movies? For the woman to get out of boring household chores by working and bringing a takeaway on her way home- becoming a shopping icon in a shoppers' paradise; total integration must have been achieved by now, whatever more can one do?

Not so fast: what about getting hooked on Mozart and Beethoven and abandoning *Qahwat Azzawi* style gatherings? Going to painting exhibitions and museums? A guilty silence greets those attempts still. And then what about that tell tale foreign accent that the next generation accuse their parents of having without fail? Tragically this revealing accent will always be the émigré's eternal downfall, the real Achilles' heel.

People will point us out wondering that we still look amazingly normal after a lifetime consorting with a totally foreign culture. We have even come to anticipate the next question that they might be too polite to ask to our face: "How inconceivable that they are not extinct yet? And shouldn't they have been exhibits in a museum by now?" We nod our head with the sagacity of the years: *Kan wa makann wa alAllah el Tiklan (*once upon a time an awesome tale existed).

It all puts me in mind of a famous but blind Syrian poet: Abu Ala' al Maarri. He describes himself as *Muttakhathram* meaning a person who has lived in many cultures and countries, a bit like a wandering Jew. This description must suit us to a tee, so we can allow ourselves to be identified with this same verb in the plural. However, we must not miss out on the plight of the many Iraqis who have also left their native country and have been let out in the big wide world because of the "situation". The title of *Mukhathrameen* can describe them too. Their presence lends a very Mediterranean feel to the area around the Edgware Road - while between them Marroush, Fattoush, Tarboush and Mazgouf (not forgetting Alloush) do a whopping trade providing everyone with the welcome that is sadly missing in our own country! Thus Baghdad's dishes and spices have been translated into the West actively helped by the Turkish, Kurdish and Lebanese cuisines. On the other hand seasoned travellers continue to swear that the real flavour is still missing, that the Baghdadi chicken and the Baghdadi shish kebab are incredibly more appetizing. No matter, those émigrés will pounce on anything to cherish an era long past!

And that is how very unexpectedly after forty years away from those shores, we find ourselves looking on and identifying readily with our ex countrymen's miscellaneous inroads into memory lane.

BIBLIOGRAPHY

Al Khammasi, Abd al-Hadi: *al-Amir Abd al-Illah dirassah tarikhiya (1939-1958)* Al-Mu'assasa al-Arabiyya, Beirut. 2001

Al Sheick, Faeq, *Wareethat al Arroush*, Dar al Hikma 2002

Barak, Fadil: *Al Madaris al Yahudiya* 1985

Baum, Phil: the *Jews of Iraq*, American Jewish Congress 1969

Bekhor, Gourji, z"l: *Fascinating Life and Sensational Death*, Peli Printing 1990

Benjamin, Marina, *Last Jews of Iraq*, 2004

Darwish,Salman:*Kull shay'hadi' fi al-'iyadah,* 1981

Elliott, Matthew *Independent Iraq* Tauris Academic Studies 1996

Erskine, Beatrice: King *Faisal of Iraq,* Hutchinson *1933*

FO Papers:FO371/91702,91703,97880/98781,104673,104726

Gat, Moshe: *The Jewish Exodus* 1948-1951 Frank Cass (1997)

Hanzal, Falih: *Asrar Maqtal Al Alllah Almalikah Fil Iraq,* Lubnan s.n., 197-]

Jawahiri, Sabiha: *Baghdad I remember*, Makor Australia 2001

Khaṭṭa   b, Raja   Ḥusayn Ḥusnī.: Al-Masu l iy ah al tarikhiyah fi maqtal al Malik Ghazi, Maktabat Āfāq Arabīyah, 1985.

Morrison, Elizabeth, *Governess of King Faisal II*, West Meadow Books, 1995

Najdat Fathi Safwat Restoring *Constitutional Monarchy in Iraq,* Al-Hayat, 2003

Rejwan, Nissim: the *Jews of Iraq*, 1998

Sasson, Shaoul Khedoorie, *In the Hell of Saddam Hussein (*2000)

Salman, Muhammad Hassan, *Tabib al Malik faysal al thani wamudhakkaratuh al siyasiyya 1940-1958*, Dar al Arabiyah,Beirut 2001

Sasson, Shaoul, Khedoorie *Ra'ee wa ra'ya*, Assoc of jewish academics from Iraq (1999)

Satloff,Robert B: *From Abdullah to Hussein,* Oxford University Press US, 1994

Saudayee, Max: *All waiting to be hanged,*Levanda Press, 1974

Shiblaq, Abbas *the lure of Zion*, Al Saqi, 1986

Shlomo al Kuwaity: Internet blogs, 2008

Sinderson, Harry Pasha, *One Thousand Days and* Nights, Hodder & Stoughton 1973

Zubaydi, Muhammad Husayn: *al Malik Ghazi wa murafiquhu*, Dar alHuriya, 1989

ACKNOWLEDGEMENTS

This is very much a home grown book; personal reminiscences from faraway shores prompted most of its input, while my friends' tales of a still ongoing sweet and sour existence make it all seem still so near! Through them Baghdad's *alef layla wa layla* (thousand and one nights) and its anecdotes will live on in our spirits until the end of time.

My immediate family must be thanked for unravelling the mysteries of the computer, which kept crashing and committing various other unmentionable deeds. Thanks also to my Mother for hosting an incredible launching party. To Eileen Kalastchi for her ready help and encouragement, Joyce Sopher and Dia Kashi who between them set me right in remembering and editing various aspects of community life. To Lily for always being there with concrete e-mailable advice, as well as writing a resplendent review on the web; thanks also to Eli Timan for sharing his transcripts about Sitt Semha's and Selman's adventures, H. Kojaman and Shuaiib Elrajab for some insight into Iraqi singers, Emily Theodore for drawing the cheeky cartoons, Sharone Theodore for her even cheekier pictures, Eli Sawdayee for permission to raid his evocative paintings, Esperance for her fascinating escape story, Aziza for her brother Shaoul's story, Shula Paneery for relating her adventures and Souham for the hanging of the lamb. While Raina Chaby kindly filled me in on later episodes

Last and not least my very sincere appreciation go to the many more of my friends from the Mother country who read bits and pieces of the story, criticized it while giving me their moral support and suggestions.(Elsie Shlomo,LisetteAdes, Niran Timan, LindaMenuhin and Sabah Rashti). While both

Hamed and Lydia envisage a translation of the book in other lands; I also give homage to Yasmina for embracing it as almost identical to her idyllic Bahraini childhood.

While many other members, namely Maurice K and Ian S, Rav Amroussi and Menashe C gave me no end of satisfaction by voicing their enjoyment in reading it.

I am sincerely indebted to Lyn Julius for reading extracts from the book at the Launch – as well as writing a complimentary review in the Sephardi Bulletin. I am equally thankful to Emile Cohen for analysing the book thoroughly while not forgetting to give its writer a few "bon mots" in the Exiled Ink magazine.

In the context of surviving in the gallut (the exile) I must tip my hat off to Mr Naim Dangoor for his excellent contributions to our Iraqi culture in editing and publishing the Scribe magazine. Both he and Iraqijews.com provided a struggling community with that much needed meeting space /forum. Without them, we would have felt much more acutely the scattering of the tribes.

ILLUSTRATIONS

Author's own: 22, 57, 59,65,75,86, 99, 101, 123, 135,136,144, 151,,230,240

Gourgi Bekhor: 4, 17, 35, 93,132, 191,198,200.201,207,209, 243, 269

Eli Sawdayee: his own painting "Kapparot" p:205 and "Shakarjee"p:179

Tore Kjeilen,University of the Orient,Looklex: 15,225

The Scribe:31, 33, 35,38,59,125,142,143,151,159,164,172,174,254,269,270

Imperial War Museum:221,222

Giselle Toledo: 161

James Gordon,282

Golda Gareh:78

Edwin Shuker: 303

Elsie Solomon: 78,82

Sharon Theodore: 162,310

Burda: 192

Every effort has been made to contact all copyright holders and mention their contribution! The publishers will be glad to make good in future editions any inadvertent errors or omissions brought to their attention

Lexicology of Arabee Meqassar (jewish dialect)

a faux pas: an awkward step

Entente cordiale: friendly agreement (French)

Backsheesh: money tips, can be underhand

Eib: embarrassing therefore forbidden

Kubba: a concoction made up of a rice shell, stuffed with meat or chicken

Timman: rice

Khalass: no more

Einny: dear one

Umm al jahal: mother of the kids, housewife

Bassturma: garlicky sausages, strung up to dry to acquire a flavour

Agoule: clump of dry hay

Dashdasha: nightgown

Addel: right

Ashlon: What are you saying? How come?

Baad el tawba: I confess I sinned

Jahesh: donkey in Lebanese speak

Kanza wanza: flu bout

Nabeq:a very small soft fruit with a pith

Yabahdellah: embarrass her

Ammi: Sir

Matroudeen: expelled (students)

Enthibaat: legislative comittee

*Licence: D*iploma

Fi Adaab allugga alarabiyya: B.A. in Arabic Literature

Lijan: committees
Wissam: medal
Ma yessem-khon: fidgety, not capable of staying put
Areetha: a formal letter of application
Wasstatt: acquaintance who can waylay the system
Chellaqa: a kick on the backside
Channa wa Martel amm: mother and daughter in laws
Tassa: bump
Battal: a hero
Mu buttel: not a bottle (a funny play on words)
Qubbat el khettar: parlour
Jellallah: a huge metalic swing
Massa'e el Khair : good evening
Machbouz: a homemade pastry
Da-he-bbek,abdallak: endearing terms from an older generation
Balamat: a large serving dish
Istikannat el chay: transparent mini tea cups
Frakh: baby chickens
Farah: a glad occasion (marriage)
Tawli: a table in Arabic, or a backgammon game
Do jahar: Turkish for double four
Walak: come on (not very respectful term)
Aya jahesh: what an ass
Gam el dass ya abbass: everything is lost (idiom)
IL faut souffrir pour etre belle: we have to suffer to be beautiful (French)
Misenplis: a hairdo involving rollers (French)

Mash'houf: a tiny, narrow river boat
Dishdashah: a floaty garment worn by men (or nightgown)
Sha'er kallabdoun: blonde hair
Kashkha: high class
*Dunbuk:*drum (music instrument)
Kanader: shoes
Bargash: flies
Kullush eib: very embarrassing
a la sacheen: Sacheen is the knife that the seller uses to cut a corner in the melon to show it is dark red and oozing with flavour
kaleb ibn sitteen kaleb: Son of 60 dogs (a common swearing term)
Bonnefete: Wishing you a happy feast (French.)
Sallats: Moslem prayers
Haram shareef: Sacred Moslem site
ala Allah: let's rely on God
Allah wiyyahum: May God protect them
Niche: enclave
Mitzvah: a good deed
Rabbak may tallu'hah: Even God cannot unravel (too complicated)